RIVERBOAT
THE EVOLUTION OF A
TELEVISION SERIES
∽ 1959-1961 ∾

by S.L. KOTAR
and J.E. GESSLER

Pre-publicity shots of Darren McGavin, posing in a set used as the interior of the Enterprise. *He is wearing more traditional Western garb than the costume later sported by Grey Holden.*

Publicity shot of Darren McGavin taken in the pilothouse set of the riverboat Enterprise. *His character wore the dark shirt and trousers in the first half of Season* One.

ACKNOWLEDGEMENTS

As with any worthwhile endeavor, it takes a team of dedicated friends to bring any project to fruition. Our appreciation goes out to Keith Simpson, probably the greatest Riverboat fan ever, and to Howard Peretti, who gave us unflagging encouragement and helped with the research on Revue and the *Enterprise,* herself.

We would also like to thank those who visited our web page at *www.darrenmcgavin.net* and asked all those questions about *Riverboat,* for you were truly the inspiration for this book.

On the cover: Darren McGavin as Captain Grey Holden on the bridge set of the Enterprise. *The dark shirt and pants indicate the publicity still was taken for early First Season. At mid-season the costume changed to a light shirt and dark trousers with a watch fob hanging from his belt. He also had a sheathed knife worn at the back. McGavin was not fond of the costume and after the series was canceled, the only item he kept was the captain's cap.*

Riverboat: *The Evolution of a Television Series, 1959-1961*
© 2010 S.L. Kotar and J.E. Gessler. All Rights Reserved.
No part of this book may be reproduced in any form or by any means, electronic, mechanical, digital, photocopying or recording, except for the inclusion in a review, without permission in writing from the publisher.

Published in the USA by:
BearManor Media
P O Box 71426
Albany, Georgia 31708
www.bearmanormedia.com

ISBN 978-1-59393-505-4

Printed in the United States of America.
Book design by Brian Pearce.

TABLE OF CONTENTS

DEDICATION

Riverboat: The Evolution of A Television Series can only be dedicated to one unique individual: Darren McGavin. He brought countless joys into our lives, and so often seemed to be an integral part of our family. He inspired us from Joe Bascome, David Ross, the cherished and indomitable Carl Kolchak, the perennial father figure in *A Christmas Story,* and finally through the sad and yet ultimately triumphant Van Conway in "Distant Signals." While it is not in our power to bring Darren back to finish filming the ending to a mythic TV series as did the alien, Mr. Smith, he lives forever in our hearts. The world is a better place because of Darren McGavin.

SLK
JEG

RIVERBOAT
THE EVOLUTION OF A
TELEVISION SERIES
⚬ 1959-1961 ⚬

PART I.
INTRODUCTION

Our interest in *Riverboat* was twofold: like nearly everyone else of our generation, our formative years were nurtured on Saturday morning Westerns, most notably *The Lone Ranger*. Add some near-Westerns into the mix: *Fury, My Friend Flicka* and reruns of *Hopalong Cassidy*, along with visitations from Gene Autry and Roy Rogers thrown in for good measure, and you have our childhood.

Advancing to more adult Westerns, we were sustained by such classics as the Ward Bond/Robert Horton years of *Wagon Train*, and, of course, Jack Kelly and James Garner as the iconoclastic riverboat gamblers of *Maverick*.

It was only a step beyond that to *Gunsmoke*, which inspired our souls and gave us both a second family with whom to grow.

Set in the time before Bart and Bret Maverick and Marshal Dillon was Grey Holden. The time period of the mid- to late-1840's intrigued us, but here our memories were more elusive. *Riverboat* ran only once and was never repeated, nor has it ever been officially released on video or DVD. *Riverboat* might have been left to the recesses of youthful memory were it not for our enduring affection for Darren McGavin. It's hard to remember now when Darren first came into our lives, for he has TV credits as long as your arm, but certainly by the time he guest starred on an episode of *Gunsmoke* called "Gunfighter R.I.P." (arguably the best guest-star-driven episode in that series' history), our attachment was sealed.

Years later, it became our privilege to create and serve as webmasters for Darren and Kathie Browne's (Mrs. Darren McGavin) authorized web site (www.darrenmcgavin.net). This precipitated a nearly fanatical desire to obtain copies of all their film and television work. The one area where we hit a brick wall was *Riverboat*. Resting untouched in the vaults of Universal Studios, all conventional ways of retrieving episodes failed. Over the course of a dozen years we eventually uncovered all 44 episodes, most on 16mm film. These were affiliate copies never returned to the network, now floating around obscure Internet sites. (All TV series were shot in 35mm; when sent out for broadcast, the process was a physical one: copies were transferred to a less expensive 16mm format and delivered to individual stations.) The quality was variable, but generally the old films we retrieved were in pristine condition, occasionally with previews.

With the episodes in hand, we set about creating what we originally contemplated as an episode guide. However, it soon became apparent there were many stories to tell on many levels, and the book expanded as we searched for buried treasure. There were several mysteries: the McGavin-Burt Reynolds feud: what really happened? What prompted the acrimonious relationship between the two actors? Why did Darren McGavin miss two episodes; why did the series have such a horrific turnaround in regulars and production staff?

Anyone who watched television in the Golden Age can recite the names of favorite actors and identify the faces of hundreds more. Here, before our eyes, was a lifetime of cherished memories: not only Darren McGavin and the crew of

First Season publicity shot of Darren McGavin on the exterior set of the riverboat Enterprise.

the *Enterprise,* but all the character actors who belonged to our extended family. Writing a book, then, assumed another purpose: to preserve the talent of those who made the medium what it was.

Adding to the urgency was the possession of over one hundred negatives from *Riverboat.* Obtained by the trade of a half dozen original *Night Stalker* scripts, most of these photos have never been published, and stand as a unique glimpse through the curtain of time. While some were merely head-and-shoulder shots, many more were of the "staged action" variety, bearing no relation to the script: Grey Holden knife-fighting a character with whom he is on the same side in the story; Darren kissing one of the guest stars for a publicity shot. You see actors shyly smiling for the camera, actors showing off elaborate costumes, actors posed, actors relaxing on the set. The photos are a slice of history that will live as long as anyone remembers black and white TV.

As webmasters, we were constantly asked questions about *Riverboat.* People wanted to know more about the series, often reciting the plot behind favorite scenes, asking the titles of episodes and requesting any and all information on the background, the characters, the story lines.

When the inquiries became too numerous and too detailed for email replies, we set about making a permanent and as complete a record as possible. Almost 50 years have passed and most of the principals involved have died. We tried, but were unable to reach Burt Reynolds for his side of the twice-told feud, but enough information remains in the realm of hearsay and fact to piece together a fairly substantial recounting of the tumultuous 1959-60 years.

Better yet, for those of us who loved the series, we were able to contact little Mike McGreevey (who is now all grown up). Listening to him share his memories and his fondness for *Riverboat* and the actors with whom he worked made it all worthwhile. As fans of the show, people really want to know the actors cared about one another and what they did. Through Mike's eyes, we found that and more.

(In a follow-up call from Mike on August 22, 2008, he specifically mentioned that one of the things Darren strove for on *Riverboat* was characterization. Mike said Darren was very interested in the background and relationship between the characters on the *Enterprise,* and was extremely disappointed more was not done to develop this. For *Night Stalker* fans, Darren's interest should not come as a surprise, for one of Darren and Kathie Browne's main goals when developing Kolchak was to establish a family atmosphere in the newsroom. That they succeeded as well as they did, against opposition from, or ignorance by, the various producers who drifted through the series, is a wonder.)

As this book expanded, we realized this was not just the story of a long-ago television series, but a glimpse into the early days of the new and exciting medium that came into our homes and subtly — at times not so subtly — affected our lives.

On the celluloid-transferred-to-tape, all the old, familiar faces jumped out at us: actors we had grown up with across the three networks, CBS, NBC and ABC. There were Charles Aidman and Gene Evans; R.G. Armstrong, Tommy Nolan, Kevin Hagen, George Macready, James Nusser, Denver Pyle, John Milford,

Sandy Kenyon, William Fawcett and, of course, DeForest Kelley. Add to them the actors who were, or went on to stardom: Elizabeth Montgomery, Vera Miles, Robert Vaughn, Vincent Price, Ricardo Montalban, Beverly Garland, Suzanne Pleshette, Richard Chamberlain and Charles Bronson. They all had a story to tell and putting it all together became a labor of love.

No story of a TV series is complete without including the people behind the camera. The search into their histories provided new revelations. No one who

First Season publicity shot of Darren McGavin standing on the pilothouse set of the riverboat Enterprise.

ever watched a Universal series in the 1960's can fail to recognize the names of Bud Thackery, Florence Bush, Vincent Dee, Elmer Bernstein, Alexander Courage, Tom Seller, Hollingsworth Morse, Douglas Heyes or even Darren McGavin (who directed an episode of *Riverboat*).

While it is impractical to list all a person's credits in such a book, we offer first and last credits and those from such popular series as *Gunsmoke, Thriller, The Twilight Zone,* and *Star Trek* in hopes of eliciting a face or a familiarity with the name. (Credits were assembled from personal records and the Internet Movie Database.)

Nor can any book be complete without also taking a look at the studio where *Riverboat* was filmed, so we include a brief history of Revue, along with some background on the mighty *Enterprise,* herself. She had a long life before coming under the guiding hand of Grey Holden, and survived for years after. But surely she was never treasured so much as for the brief period of 1959-61.

With all that in place, we hoped to present the series with as many fresh impressions, speculations and comments as anyone might have had in 1959. It is impossible to entirely eliminate hindsight, but we hoped to translate this curiosity and rekindle some of the questions viewers have been harboring over the ensuing years.

As historians of the mid-19th-Century, we have made historical comments as appropriate on such varied topics as spelling ("Pittsburgh" was spelled without the "h"), to the actual traditions and code of law used on the Mississippi during the great decades when steam-powered vessels held sway.

Occasionally, our criticisms are harsh and sometimes we nitpicked, but that's the fun of going through each episode with a fine-toothed comb. We took advantage to add humor when we thought the situation required, and occasionally poked fun at the sometimes dismal scripts.

As an important aside, we know better than anyone the changes a script goes through once it falls into the hands of producer and director, and if we were unfairly harsh to the writers for plot convenience or dialogue beyond their control, we apologize. All that is left to us are the names and the finished product and that, unfortunately or fortunately, is how they must be judged.

On an additional note, the end credits did not list character names, so the spelling was left up to us. In all cases we opted for the most conventional spelling and in instances where the names were not clearly enunciated (even Jack Lambert persisted in calling Pickalong "Piccolo"), we made the most logical determinations.

Riverboat came and went in a season and a half. For one, Darren McGavin never looked back. But the series and his legacy endure, and we hope you are able to relive some old memories or create new ones with this book. Certainly, we enjoyed the trip.

PART II.
EVOLUTION

Not ostensibly a Western in the classic cowboys-outlaws sense, or farmers-cattle barons story line, *Riverboat* promised to be a new take on the familiar (and by TV standards) lucrative time period. Like many series in the 1950's, the studio took the concept and immediately attached a name star to it, in this case, Darren McGavin. McGavin was well known at Revue and had a proven track record. In 1958, he was already starring in *Mike Hammer*, a popular detective show with a steady audience and respectable-ratings. Despite reservations (for he had little interest in period pieces), McGavin commented in 1960, "I'm trying to stay away from this Western nonsense. I'm just not a Western actor. The whole area of fast draw and gun-toting doesn't interest me in the least." The allure of a substantial raise drew him to the project. Having already found his acting ability unchallenged by *Mike Hammer*, McGavin expected more of the same from the character of Grey Holden, describing him as a man who "chases after 'Back to Methuselah' Indians." The added workload did not bother him, and for several months he went back and forth between sets, merely donning a longer-locked hairpiece to bring his appearance more in line with mid 19th-Century fashion.

Jules Bricken was brought in to produce. Born in 1919, he had successfully produced several episodes of *The 20th Century Fox Hour, Suspicion* and *Schlitz Playhouse of Stars.* Notably, these were anthology series and he adopted this format for *Riverboat*, instead of following the early advertising that suggested a more character-driven format.

A relatively unknown actor named Burt Reynolds was given second billing as pilot Ben Frazer. Having only three credits to his resume, two proved significant, for one was *M Squad*, shot at Revue, and the other was *Schlitz Playhouse of Stars*, Bricken's former series. Dick Wessel was cast as Carney, the engineer. A back-lot stalwart, Dick began his career in 1935, and by this time had countless Western credits. William Gordon, who began his acting career in 1958 on an episode of *Maverick*, played Travis, the more-often-than-not riverboat pilot during Season One.

Once principal casting was complete, Bricken hired Douglas Heyes to write and direct the premiere episode. Heyes was a familiar face at Revue, already having worked on *Circus Boy* and *Tales of the 77th Bengal Lancers* as writer/producer and as writer on such series as *Cheyenne, Naked City* and *Maverick*.

In the late 1950's, *Maverick* was the quintessential series featuring two gamblers known for plying the riverboat trade. While *Maverick* often took Bart and Bret away from the Mississippi, the show thrived because the characters were cleverly written and were portrayed as loveable rogues. *Maverick* also employed an evenhanded mix of humor and drama, never taking itself too seriously. It was felt that if Bricken could bring this charm to *Riverboat*, the Revue venue would have a substantial opportunity of garnering a loyal viewership.

St. Louis, New Orleans, Natchez, Memphis and Cincinnati were fascinating places in the mid-1840's, teeming with unsavory characters, strange flavors and tastes, and a new blending of cultures. In the time between Robert Fulton's invention (of the steamboat) and the beginning of the Civil War, a great transition took place in America: steam-powered vessels had developed into floating palaces, transporting penniless immigrants in the hold, while luxurious parties took place in the gambling halls and opulent dining rooms above.

More importantly, vast amounts of freight were shipped along the mighty rivers as the invisible borders of the United States stretched. Steamboats (never actually referred to as "riverboats" in contemporary accounts), made this possible, providing a means of rapid transit and creating an entire economy unto itself. Livestock, fresh produce and bales of cotton headed to the open-air markets of the East, while manufactured goods, heavy machinery and luxuries traveled west. Tales of romance abounded, rugged individualism became the order of the day, and the economy of the developing nation thrived.

Men who had previously made their living on rafts were challenged by this new technology and many became lawless outcasts, lurking in the seedy towns or hiding beyond the next bend to hijack the unwary captain. There was also the excitement of riverboat races, where shipping lines established their reliability and consequently their reputations on the outcome. It was a "winner-take-all" world where financial and occasionally corporeal life hung in the balance.

Little of this appeared in Heyes' script. "Payment in Full" (1.1) showed some hopeful signs: the direction touched briefly on riverboat gambling, showed some of the passengers dining in style, had Grey haggle for cargo, and offered exciting views of the boiler room and the crew working the engines. However, as happened too often, the story began ashore, and the action merely carried over onto the *Enterprise*. This set the tone for future episodes where the setting could as easily have been Dodge City, and the boat was used as an adjunct or an afterthought, rather than a controlling factor.

Worse, the premiere offered nothing in the way of introduction to the characters. Grey Holden appeared as the captain, but his position merely directed the action rather than being part of it. Ben Frazer had few lines, and none of a contributory nature. At this point, it was unclear what effect either would have in subsequent weeks.

The second episode, "The Barrier" (1.2), seemed as though it had been designed as the premiere. Captain Holden took the *Enterprise* up the Missouri River, stating he had never before navigated those waters. The Missouri was a dangerous waterway, and the story developed around the concept of the crew being forced to burn green wood and the subsequent use of lard to make the fire hotter. The plot was also more pertinent, detailing the assignment of a government agent to a river outpost. As protector of the Indians, he stood between them and unscrupulous traders seeking a fast profit by smuggling liquor in barrels of flour. More scenes of the boiler room were used, but already by the second episode, they looked suspiciously similar to those used in the pilot.

Darren McGavin and Burt Reynolds posing in the pilothouse set.

By episode three, "About Roger Mowbray," the *Enterprise* had already become little more than a backdrop for a love story gone awry. More significantly, after three episodes, no attempt had been made to develop the series' regulars. Aside from a casual comment that Ben was Grey's "partner," and the implication the captain was running the boat with little profit margin, the viewer knew nothing of their history or relationships. The audience was expected to accept them on face value. Few series could survive such treatment and this seemed to underscore the fact that *Riverboat* had been thrown together without any serious discussion between producer, writers and directors.

More inexplicably, Ben Frazer's minimal role was augmented by an antagonism with Grey Holden. See, for example, the confrontational scene between the two in "The Barrier." Although co-starring, Reynolds already seemed unnecessary and the ill-feeling between characters created a sense of discord, only heightened by subsequent episodes when McGavin and Reynolds' personal dislike increased.

In hindsight, it is easy to see why trouble would develop between the two actors. McGavin insisted, and rightly so, to be the unqualified star, and Reynolds had every expectation that his role would give him the opportunity to make a name for himself. Two "stud" actors is a bad mix, and without clear guidelines, the writers only accentuated the problem by making the captain and pilot at odds with one another.

The bulk of the dialogue and screen time actually went to William Gordon, who played Joe Travis. This character eventually assumed the unofficial position of pilot (Frazer's job) and more often than not, when the script required a regular to convey information or carry the action, Travis was called upon to do so.

It was not until the fifth episode, "The Unwilling," when two new producers (Richard H. Bartlett and Norman Jolley) were brought in, that Reynolds had a chance to act. Setting the tone for future "Ben" episodes, McGavin barely made a cameo. While this episode, too, was guest-star driven, Reynolds had the opportunity to interact with the characters. Whether or not he succeeded is a matter of personal taste, but it is noteworthy that even at this early juncture the two stars were not going to share screen time together. Reynolds would not have another chance until the ninth episode, "A Night at Trapper's Landing," where Bricken (already being eased out) continued to separate the actors, as McGavin again had little more than a few lines at the end.

Bartlett and Jolley worked on the following episode, "The Faithless" (1.10), another "Ben" episode before John Larkin returned as producer, having previously worked on "Escape to Memphis" (1.7).

By 1959, John Larkin had a score of films to his credit and had recently done an episode of *M Squad* at Revue. He assumed the bulk of the producing chores but little changed. The scripts did not noticeably improve and the atmosphere on the set continued to deteriorate.

Much blame has been assigned to either McGavin or Reynolds, but in fairness, little compromise was made by either actor. From the outset, the chemistry between them was often contentious. Persistent discord over screen time and the ultimate clashing of egos made filming awkward. Larkin was unable to broker a peace. They continued to be separated on the series, with few shared scenes.

By the fifteenth script, "The Face of Courage," John Larkin apparently felt a radical change was necessary, so the character of Travis was unceremoniously killed. Although writing him out was better than just giving William Gordon the boot and pretending Travis never existed, the brief scene of carrying the body back to the boat, then forgetting about him, was almost worse. Elimi-

Darren McGavin and Burt Reynolds, at an early and more hopeful time, posing in the interior set used as Captain Holden's quarters.

nating the second-most-used regular might have seemed the opportune time to feature Burt Reynolds, but such was not the case. Instead, two new regulars were introduced.

Joshua McGregor (Jack Lambert) stepped in as a crewman, and soon took over the pilot's chores. More attempts were made to give him a background, and nearly every subsequent episode referred to some experience (real or imagined) in which he participated. Although Dick Wessel was still given billing over McGregor, that, too, would change, and Lambert became, in essence, to the co-star of the series.

Finally, realizing that after half a season they had created too little good will among the characters, Larkin also introduced eleven-year-old Mike McGreevey to play Chip, the cabin boy (along with his dog, Andy Jackson). Not insensitive to the fact McGavin related to children (as shown to best advantage in "The Boy from Pittsburgh" [1.11]), having a boy aboard the *Enterprise* radically altered the dynamics of the series. He permitted Grey Holden to show off his more tender side and the scenes between McGavin and McGreevey marked the highlights of subsequent episodes. Chip appeared in every show until the end of Season One, including two where he played major roles: "The Treasure of Hawk Hill" (1.22) and "Night of the Faceless Men" (1.28).

Chip became the one uniting factor around whom the adults could relate. This feeling was not shared with Burt Reynolds, however, for he had no major scenes with McGreevey, further alienating him and predicating Ben Frazer's ultimate departure.

By episode 16, "Tampico Raid," nothing had been resolved between McGavin and Reynolds, and Richard H. Bartlett was summoned to produce the introduction of yet another series regular in the character of Pickalong. He popped up without any more explanation than that he had been recruited along the way when the boat's (unseen) cook jumped ship. Played by John Mitchum (Robert Mitchum's brother), he, like Jack Lambert, presented no challenge to McGavin's claim of being the heartthrob aboard the *Enterprise,* although what positive influence Pickalong was meant to serve (besides utilizing Mitchum's singing ability) is questionable. His character was the least likable of the crew. Usually bloodthirsty, Pickalong was often employed to present the opposing, more violent side to any argument, and in some scenes he was downright bloodthirsty. He never caught on, and after episode 1.26 he disappeared, apparently joining the other hapless cook.

Not surprisingly, in the episode McGavin directed ("The Blowup," 1.18), Reynolds' character had no more to do than stay on the *Enterprise,* while engineer Carney (Dick Wessel) was given an unusually large role. The following episode set the stage for Ben's ultimate departure when the character stated his father recently died and his mother wished him to return home. While nothing more was said, it raised the possibility of another rework in the making.

Reynolds did not appear in "The Salvage Pirates" (1.20) when Bartlett oversaw the introduction of yet another regular character, Terry Blake. Younger than Reynolds, actor Bart Patton provided the handsome face of youth, standing in age between Chip and Grey. This was a common ploy used throughout time, to put the older, more established and expensive series star on notice. A similar trick was employed on *Gunsmoke* in 1965 when James Arness started making what CBS considered too many demands. The character of Clayton Thaddeus Greenwood (portrayed by Roger Ewing) was brought in to serve as Matt's deputy. Like Arness, Ewing was very tall and blond (although Jim's hair was dyed "manly" brown for the role). The implication was not meant to be subtle: get fancy with us, said CBS in so many words, and we'll replace you.

Much like Burt Reynolds, Ewing had little acting experience, and it showed. But unlike the writers of *Riverboat*, those working the venerable *Gunsmoke* took every effort to ease his transition. They guarded his appearances, yet offered several substantial scenes, making Thad likable and taking (too many) pains to have Doc, Kitty, Festus and even Matt appreciate his company.

One of several publicity shots of Darren McGavin taken to promote the day and time change of Riverboat. *He is wearing the new costume presumably adopted to give the character of Grey Holden a different look and a softer image promoted in the second half of Season One.*

Probably too young to take over the role of captain, Bart Patton was meant to assume Reynolds soon-to-be-vacated position. He was actually given more screen time in his introduction than Reynolds received in "Payment in Full," and was later worked into other episodes as the co-star in waiting.

Burt Reynolds only appeared in one more episode, "Path of the Eagle" (1.21) and that was shown out of order. It should actually have been the nineteenth episode, but the producer held it back because *Riverboat* was being moved from Sunday to Monday nights. Had it been aired in proper order, Reynolds' last appearance would have been January 24, 1960, before the introduction of Terry Blake the following week. The thinking was likely that the radical transition of dropping a co-star would be too jarring for viewers, already having to make the transition to a new evening. The explanation of Ben going to New Orleans served as his good-bye, and no mention was made of him again.

Not all things were well behind the scenes of *Riverboat*, however. With Reynolds effectively dispatched and McGavin now the sole star, the bulk of the work (including the responsibility for a positive ratings change), fell on his shoulders. He demanded his contract be renegotiated to reflect this, but the studio had no interest in reworking their deal. Darren threatened to walk out, and those pulling the strings at Revue/Universal countered by threatening to replace him. McGavin called their bluff and sat home while John Larkin hired Dan Duryea to temporarily take over the helm. Duryea seemed a logical choice. He had the same physical characteristics as McGavin, a solid reputation and credible acting skills. On the face, it appeared he could step into the captain's role with little disruption.

To augment their stance, McGavin's name was removed from the opening credits of "The Wichita Arrows" (1.24), replaced with the title "Tonight Starring Dan Duryea." While the script remained virtually unchanged, a narration by Duryea explained that Captain Holden had gone ahead to scrounge for cargo and that they would pick him up "in fifty miles." Negotiations dragged on, and Richard Bartlett again stepped up to produce what could have been a transitional episode. He dropped the "Tonight," leaving "Starring Dan Duryea" over the beginning theme, adding Turner's narration, "I thought I was on the *Enterprise* for one trip, but my friend Captain Holden asked me to make one more trip for him."

Reportedly, when McGavin remained obstinate, the studio asked Duryea to permanently keep the part of Captain Turner. Whether this was just another shot in the ongoing contract fight or a sincere offer, Duryea turned it down, unwilling to get between McGavin and the studio.

There would have been serious issues had Duryea's decision been otherwise. Dan was fifteen years older than Darren and looked it. He also lacked McGavin's vivacious personality. Darren could walk onto a set and brighten it, while his edgy, controlled kinetic energy transformed mediocre scripts into entertainment. McGavin also brought with him high viewer identification. In 1960, he possessed one of the most recognizable and respected names in television. Viewers would watch *Riverboat* for him, but it remained an open question whether they would stay tuned for any prolonged absence.

Terms were eventually hammered out and production resumed with Grey Holden back in his accustomed place. McGavin's name was restored to the opening and closing titles, and thereafter only his name appeared over the theme, using the same stock footage as previously, but without Burt Reynolds.

His return also signaled the end of Terry Blake. He appeared once with McGavin in "Three Graves" (1.26), then quietly disappeared, leaving Darren in sole command of *Riverboat* and the *Enterprise*.

Publicity shot of Dan Duryea, wearing the costume of his character Captain Turner. He is standing outside the exterior set of the Enterprise. *Duryea worked two episodes before McGavin returned from his "auto accident."*

Other changes were coming. Jack Lambert, as Joshua, saw his role expanded, immediately assuming the bulk of the screen time previously taken by Reynolds, Gordon and Patton, for which he received credit over Dick Wessel. Mike McGreevey, too, earned his keep, often having long scenes with Grey and actually having significant roles, including two episodes where his character was pivotal to the plot.

By the conclusion of Season One, it seemed *Riverboat* had finally found its formula. It was no longer a disjointed series that could not decide whether it wanted to feature guest stars, the theme of a riverboat in the 1840's, or follow a more tried-and-true Western approach. While the six episodes after McGavin's return were hardly any different than those preceding them, the tone had altered. More emphasis was put on the series regulars and some attempt was made to give them characterization and positive relationships.

Faded from memory were the tense, often outright antagonistic Burt Reynolds episodes. Gone was the threat of a younger crewman stealing McGavin's thunder. Disappeared, as well, was the sometimes-pilot Travis, who had played such a pivotal role until his untimely "death," and the singing crewman, whose brief stint remained a puzzle.

This was heavy attrition for a series that had filmed only 31 episodes. Replacing Ben, Travis, Pickalong (and monkey, Petie), Terry, Captain Turner and the maybes, Tom Henshaw and Captain Nick Logan (see episode commentary for "Fort Epitaph" [1.25] and "The Sellout" [1.31]), were Joshua and Chip, supported by Carney, who remained as engineer.

Over the course of one season, *Riverboat* also saw a change in guest star casting. Long gone were the ilk of Anne Baxter, Vincent Price, Elizabeth Montgomery, John Kerr and Vera Miles, replaced by lesser knowns Charles Aidman and Hank Patterson. After episode 1.12, "Jessie Quinn," only a handful of name actors appeared, and the bulk of the episodes listed no guest stars after the title. This was both an economy move and a warning. If the show were to succeed, it would have to do so with the Backbone of the Industry and McGavin's presence, rather than draw viewers with star attractions.

Riverboat was put together by stalwarts, assembled to provide solid entertainment on a level no greater or lesser than that which aired on 1950's television. Primarily Western producers, writers and directors, their backgrounds came through loud and clear. But even they were not immune from conflict, as the staggering turnover suggests. The series used an astounding six producers over the course of 31 episodes, with the original producer, Jules Bricken, phased out after only eight episodes (one inexplicably as late as episode 21). John Larkin emerged as the "safe" producer and Richard H. Bartlett became something of the hatchet man, producing the episodes where Pickalong, Terry Blake, Tom Henshaw and Captain Nick Logan were introduced. He also produced "Fort Epitaph" (1.25), which could have stood as Captain Tucker's baptism into the ownership of the *Enterprise*.

The open door policy of producers underscored the flux of Season One. Each had his own ideas of which direction to take *Riverboat*, and none of them assumed predominance. Adding to the confusion, the staff (14 directors, 24 writers, 12 men who were given credit for the musical score, 7 directors of photography, 5 art directors, 10 film editors, 11 sound editors and 14 assistant directors) created a stunning turnover that left the series without a sound foundation.

The writing, too, was a mixed bag of (over) experience and novice writers. Most of the episodes were little more than standard *Wagon Train* plots transported to a riverboat setting. Few particularly stood out as rising above the rest, and as a whole, they failed miserably to create any significant characterization for Grey Holden or the crew. Other than being called a "Yankee," and one reference to having grown up in Boston, we learned nothing of Grey. Occasionally well off and more often than not broke, he made staggering sums of money in one show and came back broke in the next.

There were too many "love affairs," and not enough genuine drama for Darren McGavin to get his teeth into. Not until the introduction of Chip did he have any chance to emote, and by this time, it may have been too little, too late. None of the other regulars (except Joshua) had any better characterization, and they pretty much marched through their scenes without making an impression. Child actor Mike McGreevey stood out as a scene stealer and if the rest had disappeared, leaving Grey and Chip alone on the *Enterprise*, few would have noticed.

There were some better episodes ("The Barrier," "Race to Cincinnati," "The Faithless" and "Night of the Faceless Men") and some terrible episodes ("Guns for Empire," "Forbidden Island" and "The Long Trail" among them), but nothing that rose head-and-shoulders over routine TV fare. Considering the premise and Darren McGavin, this was disappointing, to say the least.

The same could be said of the direction. While most episodes were acceptable, many of the fight scenes (supposedly a strong point of the experienced directors) were only fair, and too often the substitute of stunt doubles was obvious and painful. The sole shining example of creativity, ironically enough, was "The Blowup" (1.12) which McGavin directed. Not surprisingly, it also represented his best acting performance.

Having survived Season One, *Riverboat* was renewed — not an inconsequential accomplishment in the era of the one-season series. However, whatever tone the series managed to establish by episode 31, it was quickly and definitively destroyed by major changes coming to Season Two.

Over the hiatus, a new producer, Boris D. Kaplan, was hired to alter the dynamics of *Riverboat*. Kaplan was new to the West Coast, having recently arrived from New York, where he served as film supervisor for the landmark *Omnibus* series. Although this was his first job as producer, he was not shy about instituting changes. Mike McGreevey's contract was not renewed and while Jack Lambert returned as Joshua, his appearances were reduced to mere cameos, in which he played no significant role, appearing in only 5 of the 13 episodes. Dick Wessel's character of Carney retained approximately the same screen time, but he was alternately overused or lost his accent.

Noah Beery, Jr., was hired to play Bill Blake, a "master pilot" who, by the second episode, "That Taylor Affair" (clearly meant to be the premier, but as in Season One, ran second) bought a 50% share in the *Enterprise*. This time, the co-star's presence was purposely antagonistic, and during the half-season *Riverboat* ran, was constantly at odds with Grey Holden. As opposed to the original premise, where Captain Holden was supposed to be the one who suffered over making a living, this character trait fell to Blake in Season Two, and served as a constant irritant between them.

Beery certainly didn't challenge McGavin's stardom and he brought a recognizable name to the show, but as in first season with the Ben Frazer character,

Darren McGavin and his new co-star, Noah Beery, Jr. pose in front of the Enterprise *exterior, in a pre-publicity shot for Season Two. The chemistry was better between the two men, but the new character of Captain Bill Blake still maintained the antagonistic attitude toward Captain Holden first displayed with the departed Ben Frazer.*

he was basically relegated to being Grey's foil. Occasionally an authority figure (being nine years older than McGavin), little attempt was made to endear him to the audience. While antagonism occasionally has its place between recurring characters, in this case it merely served as plot convenience and did nothing to promote camaraderie or viewer loyalty. Considering the results of the previous foray into a tense bridge set, this decision seemed ill-advised.

Worse, the likeable Holden was completely reworked into a hardnosed, do-anything-and-damn-the-consequences womanizer. Gone were his soft edges and morality, replaced by schemes, tricks, fists and superiority. Anyone following the series from one year to the next would hardly have recognized him, nor would they have appreciated the reincarnation of Mike Hammer on the Mississippi.

McGavin had the lion's share of screen time, but this new Grey Holden did not suit him nearly as well, and the plots often placed him in dire, albeit embarrassing situations. While several scripts actually used the 1840's setting along the river as their inspiration, achieving good effect, too many fell back on guest star episodes involving ludicrous and/or tepid situations. Contrasting "The Two Faces of Grey Holden" (2.3), possibly the worst episode in either year, to "No Bridge on the River" (2.5), one of the best, was enough to drive anyone away.

Adding to this dichotomy, too many scripts seemed reworks of past episodes. There was also an apparent quota of names permitted to writers, as "Blake" was used for two series regulars (Terry Blake and Bill Blake), Muldoon ("The Barrier," 1.2 and "River Champion," 2.4), Wingate ("The Quick Noose," 1.30 and "Duel on the River," 2.11), Jennings ("About Roger Mowbray," 1.3, "The Water of Gorgeous Springs," 2.7 and "Devil in Skirts," 2.8), Murrell ("The Unwilling," 1.5 and "The Treasure of Hawk Hill," 1.22), Crane ("The Faithless," 1.10 and ""The Blowup," 1.18) and Fowler (""The Fight Back," 1.6 and "Hang the Men High," 1.27). A Los Angeles phone book might have helped, for the repetitions were careless and dog-eared by series end.

Kaplan produced 12 of the 13 episodes with John Larkin producing "River Champion" (2.4), ironically one of the better shows and so similar to the feel of Season One, it might have been a leftover script. Continuing another trend, 9 directors were used, as well as 14 writers, 5 directors of photography, 4 film editors, 6 sound men and 7 assistant directors. Unfortunately, Elmer Bernstein's memorable theme was altered by Gerald Fried (given credit for the "Riverboat song"), and he proved a poor substitute. Too often the "song" was used in place of original music and in nearly every episode, Fried's choice of background music was inappropriate, usually giving a lilting air to dramatic scenes — it appeared he never bothered to watch the episodes he scored.

Even the set direction suffered. James M. Walters worked solo for the first five episodes and his effort on these was fine. However, by episode 2.6, he was joined by John McCarthy (who received billing over him) and the quality immediately diminished. Exteriors were lifeless, swamps were dry and too often the interiors were identifiable as the redresses they were.

Riverboat could have been successful (artistically and financially) and a more entertaining series if more care had been taken. As it was, a vague series concept, no single strong hand to oversee the development, tension on the set, too many cast changes and ultimately the lack of likeable, identifiable regulars doomed the series.

In a small blurb dated "1/23/61 – Hollywood," the end was spelled out in brutal fashion. "'Don't do me no favors,' the captain shouted as the crew abandoned ship. Those were the sentiments of Darren McGavin, skipper of the *Riverboat* TV series which sank recently without a trace on the Revue Studio

Darren McGavin poses with Suzanne Pleshette in a publicity shot from the Season Two episode, "The Two Faces of Grey Holden." Not even good acting could save this script from being a huge embarrassment.

lot." The weekly episodic series which didn't pay off, died after a two-year run. Said McGavin, "It was the kindest thing the network could do."

Darren wasn't finished yet. He still had swords to cross with the studio, this time over the way residuals were paid. Darren owned a percentage of the show, and the last title of the credits, along with the Revue logo, included the words, "Meladare Co. Productions." The word "Meladare" represented "Melanie," Darren's first wife, and "Darren." He wanted his money up front, and those

Another pre-publicity shot for Season One, taken before a costume had been settled on for Grey Holden.

in charge wanted to dole it out. This led to an unpleasant parting of the ways, with McGavin giving up the West Coast and returning to New York, where he had a family farm. He subsequently devoted his time to performing in summer stock. Ultimately, of course, he did return to Los Angeles and Universal Studios, where he saw his most enduring success as Carl Kolchak in the cherished *Night Stalker*. Sadly, that and his previous series *The Outsider* (also filmed at Universal), lasted no more than one season, making *Mike Hammer* and *Riverboat* his most successful (in terms of longevity) television work.

PART III.
REVUE STUDIO

Revue Productions, Inc., 1952 through the end of 1957
Revue Studios, 1958 - December 1964

Universal Pictures, known today as a major production company responsible for numerous film and television successes with big name actors, was not always associated with stars, quality or financial stability. Created by Carl Laemmle in 1912 as the Universal Film Manufacturing Company (later shortened to Universal Pictures, Inc.), the production facility was built on 230 acres of converted farmland not far from Hollywood.

Earning a reputation as a major studio with minor audiences, Universal became known for melodramas, Westerns, serial films and one other major notoriety: tourists. From its earliest days, Universal bucked the trend of isolation and secrecy harbored by other studios by opening its doors (and thus supplementing its pocketbook) to the Great Unwashed.

In 1928, Carl Laemmle, Jr., became head of the studio. He immediately began a revamp of Universal, attempting to modernize production facilities. Expanding films into more lavish productions, his early works included the 1929 film *Show Boat*, and the musical *Broadway* (1929). He also was at the reins for the production of *All Quiet on the Western Front*, which won an Academy Award in 1930 for Best Picture. Beginning the same year, the horror genre, often explored to good effect in the silent era, came to full fruition with Bela Lugosi's brilliant performance in *Dracula* (1931). Responding to that success, Boris Karloff's tortured *Frankenstein* (1931) followed. Subsequent years saw a proliferation of sequels, including Lon Chaney, Jr.'s, *Wolfman* series. Together, they formed what has become known as "Universal Horror."

An attempt to take Universal into the upper echelon of filmmaking led it into temporary receivership. The Laemmles abandoned their recent attempt to create a massive, national theatre chain dedicated to promoting their product, but managed to retain the studio, production and distribution business.

After the expensive failure of *Sutter's Gold* early in 1935, Depression-era investors were uncomfortable with the proposed idea of using Broadway actors from the stage version of *Show Boat* to film a remake. They preferred more familiar and marketable film stars and demanded the Laemmles obtain a loan to finance the project. This they did, eventually receiving money from the Standard Capital Company by using their controlling interest in Universal as collateral. This represented the first time in the history of the studio that it borrowed money for a film.

Cost overruns on *Show Boat* ran up an unexpected $300,000 tab, and when Standard called the loan, the studio could not meet its obligation. Standard foreclosed, taking control of Universal on April 2, 1936. Ironically, when it was released in 1936, *Show Boat* was acclaimed as being one of the greatest musicals ever filmed, yet success had come too little and too late to save the creators of Universal Studios.

Charles Rogers of Standard Capital assumed control of the studio and Universal fell back into the production of "safe," low-budget films, which had been their mainstay in the past: Westerns, melodramas, serials and horror sequels. Losing many of their big name stars, producers attempted to extract the last dime out of their coveted mastery of horror by turning the legendary Frankenstein monster into a caricature, inexplicably all but abandoning Dracula, and stringing out the Wolfman and the Mummy into a plethora of uninspired and depressing sequels.

Prospects improved when Abbott and Costello began working for Universal. The success of their work opened the door for other ventures during the World War II years, and such stars as Mae West, Marlene Dietrich and W.C. Fields were brought into the fold. These actors created some memorable work for the studio in low- to medium-budget films.

In 1945, British speculator Arthur J. Rank bought a quarter interest in Universal. In 1946, he arranged for the merger with an independent film production company called International Pictures. Under the control of William Goetz and Leo Spitz, the new association renamed itself Universal-International (UI).

Success eluded Goetz and by the late 1940's, films had reverted once again to safe (and occasionally inspired) low-budget productions. Rank bailed out of the business, selling his shares to Milton R. Rackmil of Decca Records. By 1952, Decca controlled Universal and production went along pretty much as usual, but never bringing in enough revenue to make the business self-sufficient.

By the mid-1950's, television had succeeded to the point where TV series were becoming more and more dominant on film studio lots. With the industry in flux, talent agency MCA (featuring agent Lew Wasserman) became a major force in the entertainment business, acting as producer for a number of TV series that featured the stars represented by the agency.

MCA initially rented space at Republic Studios for its "Revue Studios" subsidiary, but in 1958, a failing Universal Studios sold its 360-acre studio lot to MCA for $11 million. MCA immediately brought its television work there, thus Revue took up a new residence.

MCA did not own Universal Pictures, but became involved in its artistic creations. By mid-1962, MCA officially took over Universal, keeping the name of the studio intact while MCA/Universal Pictures, Inc. became the name of the parent company. Universal-International Pictures, Inc., served only as the export-international release arm for Universal films. Closer to home, Revue Studios officially became known as Universal Television.

Many venerable TV Westerns were shot for Revue during its short life. Besides *Riverboat*, they included *Wagon Train* (Ward Bond, Robert Horton, John McIntire and Robert Fuller, 1957-62), *Laramie* (John Smith and Robert Fuller, 1959-63), *The Virginian* (James Drury, Doug McClure, Lee J. Cobb and John McIntire, 1962-71), *Tales of Wells Fargo* (Dale Robertson, 1957-62), *Laredo* (Neville Brand, Peter Brown, William Smith and Philip Carey, 1965-67), *The Adventures of Kit Carson* (Bill Williams, 1952-54), *Restless Gun* (John Payne, 1957-59), *Buckskin* (Tommy Nolan and Sally Brophy, 1958), *The Deputy* (Henry Fonda, 1959-61), *Shotgun Slade* (Scott Brady, 1959-61), *The Tall Man* (Barry Sullivan, 1960-62), *Cimarron City* (George Montgomery, 1958-59), *Overland Trail* (William Bendix and Doug McClure, 1960), *Whispering Smith* (Audie Murphy, 1959-60; aired 1961), *Frontier Circus* (Chill Wills and Richard Jaeckel, 1961-62), *The Wide Country* (Earl Holliman, Andrew Prine and Slim Pickens, 1962-63), and *Destry* (John Gavin, 1964).

Crime/drama series, anthologies and the occasional comedy also found their home sets at Revue, including *Thriller* (Boris Karloff, 1960-62), *M Squad* (Lee Marvin, 1957-60), *Coronado 9* (Rod Cameron, 1960-61), *Checkmate* (Anthony George, Doug McClure and Sebastian Cabot, 1960-62), *Going My Way* (Gene Kelly, 1961-63) *Love That Bob* (Bob Cummings, 1955-59), *Bachelor Father* (John Forsythe, 1957-62), *Arrest and Trial* (Ben Gazzara and Chuck Connors, 1963-64), *Biff Baker, U.S.A.* (Alan Hale, Jr., 1952-53), *City Detective* (Rod Cameron, 1953-56), *Soldier of Fortune* (John Russell and Chick Chandler, 1955-57), *State Trooper* (Rod Cameron, 1957-59), *Special Agent 7* (Lloyd Nolan, 1958-59), *Markham* (Ray Milland, 1959-60), *Staccato* (John Cassavetes, 1959-60), *Johnny Midnight* (Edmond O'Brien, 1960), and *Alcoa Premiere* (hosted by Fred Astaire, 1961-63).

Any fan following the new so-called "TV actors" in the late 1950's and early 1960's will readily identify any number of guest actors appearing back-to-back-to-back on credit lists. Kathie Browne, for example, had starring roles in *Wagon Train* (twice), *Tales of Wells Fargo*, *Laramie* (twice), *The Virginian* and *Laredo* from 1960-66. A casual reading will also prove that the average life of a TV series was under three years and that stars went from one to the other, often as soon as one was cancelled.

Aside from actors, sets and props (which reappeared with regularity and actually became recognizable), another factor Revue series had in common was the catalog of incidental and transitional music.

The set of *Mike Hammer* (1956-59), a detective series also shot on Universal's back lot, was only a hop, skip and jump away from Park Lake, the manmade "Mississippi River." That proved fortuitous, because for one season, Darren McGavin worked both series simultaneously.

PART IV.
THE MISSISSIPPI AND THE *RIVERBOAT*

Constructed on the back lot of Universal Studios, "Park Lake," as it became known, was a recreation of the Mississippi riverfront. A wave-making machine created authentic movement for background shots and possessed the capacity to create a fountain of spray and any number of storm conditions ranging from gales to hurricanes.

To go along with the river, Universal crafted a full-scale stern-wheel steamboat (riverboats were either stern-[rear]wheeled or side-wheeled). The chimneys created an authentic cloud of smoke and portions of the boat could be made to move, duplicating the swaying sensation of a watercraft.

None of this substituted for actually steaming along the Mississippi or Ohio rivers, however. To add authenticity and local flavor, stock footage was shot and used in the background.

Nearly every film scene shot at Revue/Universal requiring a river or running water used this locale, and stock images can be identified in hundreds of celluloid adventures. Park Lake and the steamer appeared in *Show Boat* (both the 1936 *and* 1951 versions), and equally notable in the Tyrone Power riverboat adventure, *The Mississippi Gambler* (1953). Additionally, the boat was used in Audie Murphy's color remake of *Destry, Winners of the West* (1940) and *Bend of the River* (1952).

Riverboat fans quickly grew accustomed to seeing the major exteriors — the *Enterprise* on the river with lush foliage along shore; the boat in a scene with a darker and slightly larger craft going in opposite direction; the boat coming in to dock and another where it rams into the shoreline.

In 1973, the recreation of the Mississippi River on Park Lake was transformed into the "Parting of the Seas" after the opening of the film *The Red Sea* the same year. The 1970's also marked the end of any significant television Western production with the cancellation of *Gunsmoke* after its record-shattering 20th season (1955-75). With little need for frontier sets or Mississippi Rivers, many long-standing and cherished studio landscapes were taken down and replaced with other sets or office space. CBS's Studio City, for example, filled in the pond used in countless Westerns (most recognizable from *Gunsmoke* and *The Wild Wild West*) and turned it into a parking lot.

Darren McGavin posing with a model of the riverboat Enterprise. *During a typical season, series regulars would pose for hundreds of publicity stills, with less than one percent ever making it into print. Fortunately, the photos in this collection were saved out of the trash bin after the series was cancelled.*

PART V.
THE ORIGINAL PREMISE AND CHARACTERS

Created in what might be considered the heyday of television Westerns, early advertising styled *Riverboat* as a series where stories revolved around the 100-foot-long stern-wheeler named *Enterprise,* steaming up and down the Mississippi and Ohio rivers. The format was one hour in length, shot in black and white and aired over the NBC Television Network on Sundays from 7:00-8:00 P.M.

The series featured Darren McGavin, a Universal star concurrently playing the title role in *Mike Hammer,* also shot at Revue. He played Grey Holden, who oddly used the English spelling of his first name. Captain and owner of the boat, Holden was described as a former fighter, rumrunner, swordsman, dock foreman and soldier. Always on the verge of poverty, heavy emphasis was to be placed on Holden's attempts to make a profit from his unusual and occasionally dangerous business venture.

Winning the boat in a card game, this "fun-loving romantic" anchored the series and early episodes were promised to feature Holden in a variety of escapades.

Newcomer Burt Reynolds played the pilot, Ben Fraser. This character was described as an orphan who had spent his life as a "river rat."

Additional regulars were Travis (William D. Gordon), crewman and occasional pilot, and Carney, the engineer portrayed by Dick Wessel.

Guest stars, including many who had made their careers at Universal, appeared in early episodes, adding to the attraction. Louis Hayward guested in the premiere, while John Kerr, Anne Baxter and William Bendix appeared in the opening weeks.

Early promos included these less than helpful descriptions:

Adventure: Background: Areas along the Mississippi and Missouri rivers during the 1840's. The experiences of Grey Holden, the captain of the riverboat Enterprise.

Slightly more informative was... *RIVERBOAT (NBC, Sunday) Darren McGavin, familiar as Mike Hammer, is debonair Grey Holden, but he's still in there slugging. This time, Darren owns a riverboat (piloted by Burt Reynolds) plying the Mississippi in the 1840's. Each hour stars McGavin and Reynolds, but otherwise is a drama — with guest stars like Barbara Bel Geddes, William Bendix and Aldo Rey. In essence, it's* Wagon Train *on water. Begins September 13, 1959.*

An action still of Grey Holden, displaying his rough and tumble side. Unfortunately, the producers of Riverboat *could never decide on the type of character they envisioned for the series' star, and the show suffered as a result.*

PART VI.

HISTORICAL CONSIDERATIONS

The original *Riverboat* set was built for Universal's major theatrical releases as an exciting backdrop to capture the flavor and times of the historical steamboat era, traditionally considered the 1850's. It is logical to presume, therefore, that the data released in *Riverboat's* early press represented information derived from the studio's research department. Unfortunately, it was either incorrect to begin with, or skewed to fit the circumstances of an 1840's river tramp.

The *Eclipse*, the belle of her day in 1852, reached 350 feet. The *Enterprise* could hardly be expected to match the speed, cargo capacity or luxury of this "floating palace," describing Holden's boat as being a mere 100 feet in length, making it an extremely small vessel. In the earliest years of Western navigation, steam-powered boats averaged 120 feet. By 1850, the largest class ran from 240-270 feet.

The closest we can come to matching the *Enterprise's* description comes from 1823. The steamboat *Virginia* became very famous as the first boat to start at St. Louis and navigate the entire length of the Upper Mississippi. The *Virginia* was built in Wheeling, Virginia, in 1819. She was a small, stern-wheeler of 109.32 tons, 118 feet long, eighteen foot, ten-inch beam and drew a depth of five feet, two inches. The *Virginia* had a small cabin on deck, but no pilot house, being guided by a tiller at the stern.

Using mathematical calculations, a boat of 100 feet equated to 100 – 115 tons (tonnage representing the amount of freight capable of being hauled). The average length by 1841 was 130 feet, with an average tonnage of 133. Although various episodes implied (but never actually stated) the *Enterprise* was an older vessel (which corresponded with the state of Grey Holden's finances), there is no way those original figures make sense in light of the passengers and freight carried on the *Enterprise*.

Additionally, the original construction of the set is a bit curious. Very early on in the development of steamboats, stern-wheelers were considered inferior to side-wheelers. Probably developed to get around early patents owned by Robert Fulton and his partner, Robert Livingston, stern-wheelers were viewed with scorn; most were considered "dull" boats, used only for the most menial work. For speed, beauty of construction and performance, side-wheelers dominated the public's imagination from the beginning to the end of the steamboat era.

While there were some navigational advantages to stern-wheeled boats, they had basically disappeared by the 1830's, making only brief comebacks in cities like Pittsburg where hauling freight was a primary concern.

In the parlance of the 1800's, the *Enterprise* would have been classified as a river transient, or "tramp" of the river, acting as a freelance vessel, following the trade wherever it took her. Transients had no fixed field of operation, no set schedule and lacked any regularity. Through the 1820's and beyond, tramps were the most numerous of the riverboats. Usually owned by three or fewer men, these small enterprises could never hope to vie for the better passenger trade. Although all steamboats carried passengers, the primary source of income derived from freight. While history has colored the era by glorifying the magnificent boats decked out with gleaming smoke stacks, white-painted sides, fluttering banners and luxury accommodations, there was little romance associated with tramps. They survived from season to season on a hand-to-mouth basis, depending on the season, the reputation of the captain, and luck to make a profit.

Competition played a key role in balancing the ledger and owners spent a great deal of time underbidding one another for cargo. With the advantage of lighter draft (how deeply the boat sat in the water), tramps were able to work in all seasons. Heavier draft vessels, including all luxury boats, were always put up at ports during the summer and winter seasons when water levels were low.

While large tonnage boats employed as many as 200 crew, including clerks, second and third mates, cooks, waiters, cabin boys, chambermaids, firemen, pilot "cubs" and a huge contingent of deck hands, transients usually got by with 4-5 men: the captain (who acted as his own clerk), the pilot, engineer, the mate and the jack-of-all-trades rousters. The mate had responsibility for the deck crew, overseeing the wooding (taking on of wood), and the loading and unloading of cargo. By the late 1840's, deck crews were drawn primarily from the rapidly swelling emigrant class. On boats trading in the lower Mississippi, it was also common for owners to employ slaves to serve in this capacity. Not surprisingly, however, owners often preferred free whites. If a slave were injured or killed while in service, the captain was required by law to make good the loss to the owner. On the other hand, if an Irish or German immigrant were maimed in an explosion or other hazard, he had no protection under the law. As the job was considered dangerous, employees were expected to accept responsibility for their own life and limb.

A pilot's authority held supreme in the operation of the boat, pilots being considered the elite of steamboat society. Most were hired by the trip and changed boats often, particularly when the transient steamed into a new trade. Since pilots tended to have a working familiarity with only small sections of the river (for example, the Pittsburg to Cincinnati trade), when the boat owner opted to seek cargo on a new route, he hired a pilot more familiar with those waters.

Deck hands were also hired by the voyage and were usually completely changed before the boat started a return trip. Due to the physical demands on deck hands, it was not unusual for a man to work two or three trips in a row, and then take "refreshment" ashore before hiring out again. Hands could be fired at will and troublesome ones were often left on the side of a riverbank when they did not obey orders.

Engineers, usually native-born Americans, also occupied elite status. Since they were usually among the first causalities of a boiler explosion, it is hard to imagine why anyone would want such a job.

Many small riverboat owners also served as captains. The captain's prime responsibility was to oversee landings and departures and the procurement of freight and passenger comfort. While desirable, it was not necessary for the captain to possess river skills.

Steamboating carved out a niche in American lore, but little if any of it was reflected in the day-to-day realities of the life. Cutthroat competition, river hazards, boiler explosions, tariffs, taxes, crew discontent and weather all had a far more tangible effect on the occupation than the more heralded races, floating palaces and shipboard romances. That said, steamboats were integral to opening the West and advancing commerce, making the names of such cities as New Orleans, St. Louis and Pittsburg familiar to such faraway metropolises as New York and Philadelphia.

Steamboats brought emigrants to a new land, steamed the produce of the Ohio Valley to New Orleans, and sent cotton upward to the river cities, and in its heyday, employed thousands of men. The era of greatness was small but enduring, and before the coming of the railroads, riverboats dominated both the Western economy and the American imagination.

PART VII.

INTERVIEW WITH MIKE MCGREEVEY

Conducted March 10, 2008

Mike McGreevey, who played Chip on 17 episodes of *Riverboat's* first season, was good enough to talk with us about the series and his experiences on the set. Although only eleven years old at the time, his memories are warm and appreciative of the actors with whom he worked.

When asked about Darren, Mike's reaction was immediate.

Oh, God, yes, he was like a father figure to me. Although as a child actor I was only on the set when required, my relationship with Darren was very warm and friendly. There was a lot of fun on the set and I learned a lot about acting from Darren. Darren taught me how to let a scene play, how to let it breathe. I remember one episode ["The Sellout"], *where he said, 'Slow it down, let's listen to one another.'*

There was a lot of emotion in one scene (where Chip goes in to tell Grey he is setting out on his own because none of the crew was going to take him ashore with them). *We did that scene in one take; it was like reality meeting fantasy for me. I really liked Darren a lot.*

Darren had a lot of energy, he was a tornado in the room. Perhaps that's what got Burt (Reynolds) *bent out of shape. He had little experience and as you explained it — dueling egos — that's what got in the way between them.*

I knew there was tension on the set, I was aware of it, but not to the extent it reached. Burt was a jock — he bought me a football that we tossed around the set. In fact, Burt's stand-in was an old friend of his from Florida State, and the fact I was with football players impressed me.

I went to Darren's home in Beverly Hills a number of times and played with York (Darren's son). *My memories are all really positive. If there was one downside, it was being the only child on the set. We did an episode* ["The Treasure of Hawk Hill"] *with another boy* (Steve Wooten). *I was so thrilled to have a playmate close to my own age. I knew some of the other kids on the lot* — Jerry Mathers (Leave it to Beaver) *and* Michael Burns (Wagon Train) — *that I also played with.*

My life was wonderful, a fantasy. I only lived five minutes away from the studio. Sometimes I only worked an hour and then had a tutor teach me. I had a great tutor — Mrs. Lowins — where it was one-on-one. I went to school for three hours and then got the rest of the day off. She was a wonderful teacher and really turned me into a student.

My memories were all really positive. I adored Jack Lambert. The year before, I had worked with him on "Day of the Outlaw" [1959]. He was so thrilled that on Riverboat *he had the chance to play a character more like his own personality* (rather than being cast as a heavy because of the sharp features of his face). *He was a big sweetheart, as was Dick Wessel. Then there was John Mitchum, who became a lifelong*

Darren McGavin poses with little Mike McGreevey in this Season One publicity still. The character of Chip was added to the crew of the Enterprise *in episode 1.15, "The Face of Courage." The scenes between Darren and Mike were some of the most memorable in the year and a half* Riverboat *ran.*

friend. I had a chance to work with him again later in The Way West [1967]. *I never worked with Darren again, although I remember going to the set while he was film-ing the second season of* Riverboat, *and saw him with Noah Beery.*

I remember Dan Duryea as being a distant guy. He was a great actor, but quiet on Riverboat. *The energy level on the set diminished. Being a child, I wasn't privy to* (the contract negotiations) *going on during that time. The studio put out a release saying Darren had some physical problems, a neck injury, as I remember. During that season, there was a writer's strike, as well, so it was a pretty tumultuous time.*

I especially remember Bill Witney (one of the directors). *He was a terrific guy. We shot episodes in five days, then. Bill was a man's man; very strong and forthright and kind. Hollingsworth Morse* (another director) *was also a very nice man.*

Many years later, my youngest son wanted a dog. We had just put down our Cocker Spaniel and my son wanted a puppy. He picked out the runt of the litter. He was a Jack Russell terrier, just like Andy Jackson [Chip's dog on *Riverboat*]. *When I played an episode of* Riverboat, *Max barked at Andy. I was always carrying Andy around and after awhile, that became a pain in the butt. Frank Weatherwax was Andy Jackson's trainer, and I always thought he was a better trainer than his brother, who I saw work when I did three episodes of* Lassie.

Working through the 1970's as an actor, Mike then went behind the camera to work as a highly successful writer, director and producer. He lives in Los Angeles with his wife and children and is currently working on a series of documentaries.

EPISODE GUIDE

PART VIII.

SEASON ONE
1959-1960

The premier episode begins in St. Louis, Missouri. A horse race is in progress. Several men bet on the winner, but when they go to collect their prize money from Johnny, a senator's son, they discover he had gone against their advice and wagered the collective sum on another horse. In fury, Monte Lowman strikes the youth, inadvertently killing him. To avoid the retribution that is surely to come, Monte's best friend, Hunk, hides him in a crypt which mysteriously happens to have a lock on the inside.

Captain Grey Holden is introduced while haggling for cargo. In an amusing scene, the merchant accuses Grey's "Yankee hide" of having some trick up his sleeve, but eventually agrees to ship his "mechanical apple peelers" to Natchez. Securing himself a profitable trip, Grey returns to the *Enterprise*, where he oversees deck space to those passengers traveling at reduced rates.

Hunk has a falling out with his girl, Missy, who has thrown him over for a gambler with better chances of earning money. The new couple has booked passage on the *Enterprise* and is planning to leave within the day. Desperate to win back her affection, Hunk turns Monte in for the $1,000 reward, and is then horrified to see him killed by the sheriff. Desperate to get out of town, he follows his girlfriend and the gambler, Ash, onto the *Enterprise*. The boat departs and despite being racked by guilt over his betrayal, Hunk spends money like water in an attempt to impress his lady love.

Another passenger aboard the boat is a nun, who speaks to Grey about her plans. Although grievously short of funds, she is determined to go west and establish a school for Indians.

Grey works through the puzzle of how Hunk suddenly has money to burn and is very angry over the circumstances. Everyone was fond of Monte, and he warns there will be trouble. Hunk is remorseful over his act, trying to convince the captain he only meant for Monte to be jailed, not shot. Holden cannot find it in his heart to offer solace, however, and turns him away. He suggests Hunk talk to the nun, who might be able to offer spiritual guidance.

The nun speaks of redemption and advises Hunk to make good from evil. He promises to try and attempts to make up with Missy. After learning what he did, however, she wants nothing more to do with him.

At a card game going on in the main parlor, Ash cheats Hunk of his blood money. Grey figures out what has happened and determines to put the gambler

Early publicity still of Darren McGavin posing on the waterfront exterior.

off at the next wood stop. Going to the pilothouse, he relays these new orders to his partner, Ben Frazer.

A group of men out to avenge Monte's murder board the steamer. Realizing they have come for him and that he probably deserves whatever they have in store, Hunk turns his reward money over to the nun "to do good things." Finally at peace with himself, he faces his accusers. They gang up on him and he is killed by being thrown into the paddlewheel.

Douglas Heyes, a veteran writer/director well established at Revue, was hired to handle both jobs for the pilot episode. As such, he brought a steady, tried-and-true hand to the work, but presented an episode hardly worthy of note. He took pains to display the riverboat by having shots of the engine room, the decks, passenger quarters and gambling parlor/dining room (called the saloon), and they served to good effect. The script, however, differed little from standard television fare of the late 1950's, and the plot might have taken place in Dodge City rather than on the Mississippi.

Little was done to introduce Riverboat's *series regulars. Aside from the comment about Holden's "Yankee" background (an odd fact in itself, considering few Northerners became riverboat captains), Darren McGavin was left on his own to shape Holden's character. Perhaps more tellingly, the throw-away scene in the pilot house between Grey and Ben Frazer (meant to establish the fact the pilot was a partner in the* Enterprise*), was awkward, almost antagonistic. It (mistakenly) created the impression of tension that actually came from the actors, not the characters, but one which was hardly dispelled by dialogue in this or subsequent episodes. Adding to the confusion in the viewer's mind, Burt Reynolds had little screen time in the premiere. While credited as being a co-star, his position was initially left as small and ambiguous.*

"Payment in Full" challenged no one's acting talent, created little tension (none for the series' regulars), and contained no memorable scenes with which to draw an audience back the following week. If this were an example, then Riverboat *was not going to be a character-driven series, but more of an anthology, where the plots centered around outside guest stars. Considering* Riverboat *had only two distinguishing features (the presence of the highly popular Darren McGavin and the exotic locale of the Western waters), the first episode created an unpromising precedent.*

Unfortunately, the amorphous tone would carry over into subsequent episodes. Without identifiable, well-drawn regulars, a meaningful camaraderie and shifting locales, the Enterprise *was already in deep waters without the proverbial paddle(wheel).*

GUEST CAST

Nancy Gates *(b. 2/1/1926, Dallas, TX)*. Under contract to RKO by age 15, her first film was *Hitler's Children* (1943), followed by *The Great Gildersleeve* (1943) and *The Magnificent Ambersons*. (1943.) Most of her TV work was done in the 1950's and 60's. Her last credit was an episode of *The Mod Squad*, 1969.

Aldo Ray *(b. 9/25/1926, Pen Argyl, PA; d. 3/27/1991, Martinez, CA, from throat cancer.)* Character actor usually playing Spanish or Latin roles; made the rounds in the mid-60's on such episodes as *The Outsider, Run For Your Life* and *Love American Style*. His first role was on *My True Story* (where he was billed as Aldo DaRe). His last role was in the film *Shock 'Em Dead* (1991).

Louis Hayward *(b. 3/19/1909, Johannesburg, South Africa; d. 2/21/1985, Palm Springs, CA, of lung cancer and renal failure.)* Romantic leading man originally patronized by playwright Noel Coward, he was the first of many actors to portray Simon Templar in a series of films, beginning with *The Saint in New York* (1938). A distinguished actor, usually cast as a suave hero or rogue, he appeared in *Son of Monte Cristo* (1940) as Edmond Dantes, and *Son of Dr. Jekyll* (1951) as Jekyll/ Hyde. He had his own production company, producing and starring in the 1954 TV series *The Lone Wolf.* He also produced the British series *The Pursuers* (1966) and the American *The Survivors* (1969). One of his more memorable TV guest star appearances was on the episode of *Night Gallery*, "Certain Shadows on the Wall" (1970). He retired in the mid 1970's.

Barbara Bel Geddes *(b. 10/31/1922, New York, NY; d. 8/8/2005, Northeast Harbor, ME, of lung cancer.)* While appearing in *I Remember Mama* (1948) and *Vertigo* (1958), she will always be remembered as Eleanor Southworth Ewing Farlow on the TV series *Dallas* (1978-1984 and 1985-1990).

William Bishop *(b. 7/16/1918, Oak Park, IL; d. 10/3/1959, Malibu, CA, of cancer.)* After gaining experience on the Broadway stage and a brief career with the Mercury Theatre, he left for the army. On his return, he went to Hollywood. He Played Steve Connors on the syndicated TV series, *It's a Great Life* (1954).

John Larch *(b. 10/4/1914, Salem, MA; d. 10/16/2005, Woodland Hills, CA.)* He played Father Nuncio in *The Amityville Horror* (1979) and had several series, including *Arrest and Trial* (playing Dept. District Attorney Jerry Miller – 1963- 64), as well as recurring characters in *Dynasty* (as Gerald Wilson) and *Dallas* (as Arlen/Atticut Ward). He appeared in three *Twilight Zone* episodes – "It's a Good Life" (1961), "Dust" (1961) and "Perchance to Dream" (1959).

1.2   "The Barrier" . . . . *September 20, 1959*
Directed by Richard H. Bartlett
Written by Tom Seller
Produced by Jules Bricken

The episode begins in Cairo, Illinois. Captain Holden has decided to take the *Enterprise* up the Missouri River, a trip he has never before made. While he is away from the boat, Ben Frazer accepts a load of flour being shipped by a shady merchant, named Muldoon, who is accompanying his cargo. Also going upriver is a young couple having marital problems. Three years ago in Washington, Jeff Carruthers had an affair, and his wife, Abby, cannot forgive him. Embittered by the fact Abby holds her pride above their vows to love, cherish and overlook indiscretions, Jeff loses his lucrative government position. After a year of traveling from post to post, he is finally assigned as territorial administrator in charge of Indian affairs in the distant, isolated state of Illinois.

When Grey returns to the boat, he is skeptical of the commission Frazer accepted, and complains that he is also bringing aboard wood too green to burn. In an interesting aside, Holden is then forced to spend extra money to buy lard, used to make the wood burn hotter. This emphasized the extra expenses of operating a steam-powered boat, gave an excuse to show the boiler room and the workings of the engines and later, was cleverly woven into the finale of the script.

Carruthers soon discovers the barrels of flour are actually filled with whisky and that Muldoon intends to cheat the Indians. The scurrilous merchant offers to bribe Jeff, reminding him that a government agent does not make much money. If Jeff ever hopes to regain his wife's affection he will need a better job and ready cash to spend. Jeff reluctantly buys into this argument.

Accused of being too unemotional and without flaw, Abby reexamines herself. She decides that if she, too, had an affair, then she and her husband would both have been disloyal to one another. Leveling the playing field would finally make them equal and open the way for reconciliation. Abby vies for Grey's affection, and after rousing his interest by kissing him, feels herself significantly compromised.

When the *Enterprise* reaches the river outpost, a representative from the native tribe introduces himself to Jeff. He explains how the Indians appreciate his help in keeping alcohol away from them because unscrupulous traders get them drunk and then negotiate unfair deals for their furs. This, however, does not stop Jeff from standing against Grey when the captain discovers the true nature of the cargo he has carried up the river and refuses to unload it.

Abby is dismayed by her husband's action, compelling him to confess the deal he has made and the reason why. She hurriedly explains she is no longer "without sin" and that her attraction to Captain Holden was solely to alter her character. He readily forgives her, and when she finally finds it in her heart to put the past behind them, he no longer has any reason to betray the Indians.

Confronting Muldoon on the dock, the new territorial agent stands firm, rescinding his bargain with the whisky-runner. A fight ensues between the crew of the *Enterprise* and Muldoon's men. Jeff is wounded and Abby grabs his gun, blowing Muldoon away. This represents a unique scene for a television series of the time which traditionally reserved rescue scenes for men — a tradition, unfortunately carried over for many more years on many great and small screen dramas.

While this is transpiring, Grey and Ben dive into the river and swim to the barrels of whisky. Using lard-covered logs to ignite a fire, they destroy the alcohol, which goes up in a grand explosion.

The acting in "The Barrier" was particularly good and the three guest stars were headliners in their own right. The plot was better developed without overshadowing the regulars, and writer Tom Seller put an interesting twist to the story by having Jeff Carruthers admit to infidelity — a nearly taboo subject for 1959. Even his wife's attempt to equalize herself by having "an affair" was scandalous and Grey's attraction to a married woman was a bold character development. As mentioned above, the final scenes, where Abby was permitted to take charge and save her husband, were stunning. As we can attest, as late as 1973, Gunsmoke's *Kitty Russell was not allowed to defend herself from an irate mob and protect the man she loved.* Gunsmoke's *producer, John Mantley, chose to have her knocked on her face and brought Marshal Dillon in to save the day, so kudos to Jules Bricken.*

The historical facts in "The Barrier" were pertinent and represented very real problems for settlers and Indians, alike. Territorial agents were often all that stood between men like Muldoon and the safety of the inhabitants, and bribery was a sad reality. Although Grey despised him for his action, Jeff Carruthers was no worse, and ultimately better than his contemporaries.

Incidentally, although Grey Holden was not transporting government supplies to the Indians, many riverboat captains secured contracts to steam up the Missouri and Mississippi to deliver annuities to the various tribes. This was an extremely lucrative trade that usually departed from St. Louis. By 1844, four tribes were being supplied with goods valued at $218,910: the Sioux received $40,510; the Sauk and Fox $85,540 and the Winnebago received $92,860.

Director Richard H. Bartlett took exceptional care to show off the riverboat and develop a better feel for life in the 1840's. It inspired hope that Riverboat *might use the setting to distinguish itself from other series.*

GUEST CAST

Elizabeth Montgomery *(b. 4/15/1933, Hollywood, CA; d. 5/18/1995, Los Angeles, CA, colorectal cancer.)* Married three times (to Fred Gallatin Cammann, Gig Young and William Asher) before settling down with Robert Foxworth for over 20 years until her death, she was the daughter of Elizabeth Allen and Robert Montgomery. Not surprisingly, nearly her first three-dozen television credits were from *Robert Montgomery Presents* (1951-56). Primarily a television actress, she possessed stunning beauty and talent, and ultimately became synonymous with Samantha Stephens on *Bewitched*, but truly displayed her awesome command of the medium by portraying the title character in the 1975 TV film *The Legend of Lizzie Borden*. She also had an early but memorable role opposite Tom Poston on an episode of *Thriller*, entitled "Masquerade" (1961).

John Kerr *(b. 11/15/1931, New York, NY.)* The son of Broadway actors, he graduated from Harvard before trying his acting luck. John created the role of Tom Lee on Broadway before having the unusual good fortune to play it in the film adaptation of *Tea and Sympathy* (1956). He repeated the same luck by creating the character of Lt. Joseph Cable in the stage version of "South Pacific" and then went on the do the film (1958). His career as a film actor never propelled him into stardom, but he has a credible list of TV parts, including the recurring role of D.A. John Fowler on *Peyton Place* (1965-66) and Assistant Deputy Barry Pine on *Arrest and Trial* (1963-64). Horror fans will remember him for his role as Francis Barnard in the Roger Corman film *The Pit and the Pendulum* (1961). After receiving a law degree from UCLA in 1969, he wound down his acting career to practice in Encino, CA.

William Bendix *(b. 1/14/1906, Manhattan, NY; d. 12/14/1964, Los Angeles, CA, pneumonia.)* Famous for his growly voice, Bronx dialect and bulky frame, he became a household word from the radio series *The Life of Riley*, which he subsequently starred in on television. As a youth, he worked as a batboy for the NY Giants and Yankees. After going from Broadway to film, he garnered an Oscar nomination for his role in *Wake Island* (1942).

Read Morgan *(b. 1931, Chicago, IL.)* Primarily a Western actor, his career spanned the 1950's through the 1990's. He made numerous episodes of *Gunsmoke*, including playing Dan Slade in the episode "Sam McTavish, M.D." He also starred in an episode of *The Outsider* with McGavin entitled "Tell It Like It Is and You're Dead" (1968). He played Sgt. Hapgood Tasker on *The Deputy* (1960-61) and also appeared in an episode of *How the West Was Won* (1978).

1.3 **"About Roger Mowbray"** . . . . *September 27, 1959*
Directed by Felix Feist
Teleplay by Hagar Wilde
Story by Gene Coon
Produced by Jules Bricken

The story begins in Vicksburg. Roger Mowbray is established as a young and up-and-coming partner in a lucrative business, newly married to the overly protected daughter of a wealthy merchant. Jeanette (Mowbray's bride), is seen discussing her wonderful luck in one scene and in the next, we are confronted by Roger's former fiancée, Cassie, a waitress who takes it extremely hard when informed Roger is breaking their engagement.

It soon plays out that Roger is not what he seems. Instead of being a rich businessman, he has been fronted by his father, Jonathan Reed, to make him appear successful. The old man has spent his life's earnings on his son and seems to have achieved his ends: Roger is allied with a powerful firm, he has married an heiress and soon the father-son team will sell cargo being brought aboard the *Enterprise* in Natchez for a staggering profit. Reed intends to mark up the price on the merchandise without telling Roger's partner and predicts that soon the pair will have legitimate wealth.

Cassie books passage aboard the *Enterprise* to follow Roger and try to win him back. In what develops into a standard "dueling females" episode, the remainder of the hour centers around Roger's wife and Cassie, who is only too glad to tell Jeanette she had Roger first and intends to regain him.

Roger defies his father's wish to cheat his new partner and spends much time going back and forth between the two women in his life, telling his wife he loves her and asking his former girlfriend to leave him alone. This, of course, does not stop Cassie, and she continues to hang onto him while taunting Jeanette for being spoiled and buying everything she wanted, including a husband.

Stretching credulity to the bone, Reed suddenly turns addle-headed and moans how he sacrificed his life so Roger could make good and he could become rich. This seems to contradict the fact he spent considerable money setting his son up in Vicksburg with a mansion and wardrobe and also paid off his gambling debts, to say nothing of the fact he spent a small fortune buying Roger into the firm, a detail much made of in the episode.

In a delusional state, Reed shoots Roger in the back. Afraid to have his father blamed for the crime, Roger staggers on deck, where Cassie is found near his severely wounded body. Suspicion falls on her, but when she pleads her case before Grey, he believes her. He discovers Reed, still babbling to himself about profits and how much he sacrificed for Roger, his son, and Grey puts the pieces of the shooting together.

Grey manages to reconcile Roger with his wife, then orders Ben to steam down the river to get Roger to a doctor. In another short scene between the two characters, Ben refuses, saying there is too much fog on the water. Grey makes his command an order, but then apologizes for his blunt tone.

By the final credits, Cassie reluctantly realizes Roger loves his wife and she decides to get off the boat. Grey cheerfully reminds her she is an attractive woman and can make a new life for herself, but she is hardly convinced.

The tense scene in the pilot house between Grey and Ben implied there was no love lost between the characters. For the third episode of a new series, this was perhaps ill advised, as it established an unexplained and likely unappreciated edge to their relationship. Pre-production advertising for Riverboat *gave no hint of an intended conflict, indicating the writers had no clear direction and few guidelines under which to craft dialogue.*

Like "Payment in Full," this episode resorted to the format of featuring guest stars. Little was done to feature McGavin and less for Reynolds. The plot was already old by 1959, and entirely too predictable. Robert Vaughn played his part with perhaps more sincerity than required, making it all the more difficult to swallow, while the embattled women were rendered trite and unsympathetic. Gene Coon (later of Star Trek fame) could and did write better for other series, and his name on this episode was a disappointment.

GUEST CAST

Robert Vaughn *(b. 11/22/1932, New York, NY.)* Born Robert Francis Vaughn, he is of Welsh and Irish descent, and both his parents were in show business. He earned a Master's degree from L.A. State College and later earned a Ph.D. in communications from the University of Southern California. A friend of Robert

F. Kennedy and a liberal Democrat, he was encouraged to run against Ronald Reagan for governor of California, but opted to support Jerry Brown, instead. One of the most recognizable of all the TV actors of the 1960's, he is forever immortalized for his role of Napoleon Solo in *The Man from U.N.C.L.E.* He earned an Oscar nomination for *The Young Philadelphians* (1959) and an Emmy award in 1978 for the mini-series *Washington Behind Closed Doors*.

Vera Miles *(b. 8/23/1929, Boise City, OK.)* Anyone who watched television in the 1960's cherishes Vera Miles for her incredible talent in any number of favorite series, including *The Fugitive, Judd for the Defense* and most wonderfully, for playing Dr. Sam McTavish, Doc Adams' love interest in a 1970 episode of *Gunsmoke*. Vera came to Hollywood after winning a beauty contest and achieved fame in *The Searchers* (1956), *The Man Who Shot Liberty Valance* (1962) and Hitchcock's *Psycho* (1960) after losing out on the lead role in *Vertigo* because of pregnancy. She went on to work for Disney in *A Tiger Walks* (1964) and *Those Calloways* (1965).

Cameron Prud'homm *(b. 12/16/1892, Auburn, NY; d. 11/27/1967, Pompton Plains, NJ, cancer.)* Beginning his career in the 1930 film *Abraham Lincoln*, where he played John Hay, he made several films and a handful of guest star appearances, including an episode of *Tales of Tomorrow* (1952) called "The Duplicates" with McGavin. His last role was a 1963 film called *The Cardinal*.

Madlyn Rhue *(b. 10/3/35, Washington, D.C.; d. 12/16/2003, Woodland Hills, CA, pneumonia and multiple sclerosis.)* A beautiful, prolific actress, most familiar to TV audiences in the late 50's, 60's and 70's, she usually guest starred as the hero's "flame for an episode." Later audiences remember her for her recurring role in *Murder, She Wrote*, as the librarian, but at the height of her fame, she guest starred on TV series such as *Star Trek, The Night Stalker, Mission: Impossible* and *Route 66*. When Madlyn was diagnosed with MS in 1977, her best friends Suzanne Pleshette and Faye Mayo became her main emotional support. She continued to work through the debilitating disease, starring on the soap opera *Days of Our Lives*, and on the series *Executive Suite* and *Fame*. She eventually donated time and energy to the MS fight, going public with her disease and even posing in a wheelchair. She spent her last years in a retirement center in Woodland Hills, CA.

John Hoyt *(b. 10/5/1905, Bronxville, NY; d. 9/15/1991, Santa Cruz, CA, lung cancer.)* He played Martin Peyton on *Return to Peyton Place* from 1972-74, but will be best identified from playing Dr. Phillip Boyce on the unsold pilot "The Cage" from *Star Trek*. Seemingly never without work, his credits span the gamut from playing Cassius in the film *Cleopatra* (1963), to the principal in the ground-breaking film *Blackboard Jungle* (1955). He also appeared in an episode of *Twilight Zone* called "Will the Real Martian Please Stand Up?" as Ross, the Martian (1961). His first credit was a film called *O.S.S.* (1946).

Hank Patterson *(b. 10/9/1888, Springville, AL; d. 8/23/1975, Woodland Hills, CA, bronchial pneumonia.)* Born Elmer Calvin Patterson, he wanted to earn a living as a musician, but spent the early part of his career performing in vaudeville shows. One of those character actors who never seemed to be young, any *Gunsmoke* fan immediately recognizes him as having played Hank, the beloved stableman of Dodge City, for many, many years. He also played a recurring role on *Green Acres* and was part of the original cast of *Petticoat Junction* (1963-66).

Sandy Kenyon (see episode 2.5, "No Bridge on the River," page 242).

1.4   "Race to Cincinnati". . . . . *October 4, 1959*
Directed by Jules Bricken
Teleplay by William Raynor
Story by Richard N. Morgan
Produced by Jules Bricken

Contrary to expectations in the title, the "race" did not involve steamboats but rather fruit. The episode begins when Ellen Jenkins arrives with a cargo to ship aboard the *Enterprise.* The horse pulling her wagon spooks, however, and with a deadline of 72-hours to get downriver, Captain Holden reluctantly refuses to retrieve the wagon. Flaunting Southern charm and femininity, Ellen gains the sympathy of the crew, "blackmailing" Grey to hold departure until her cargo is aboard.

What he finds does not please him: it seems to be a shipment of logs. She explains that inside are hives of European black bees, being transported to Natchez for her father's fruit farm. The pair intend to cross-breed the bees with the domestic variety and thus increase pollination.

Annoyed at being forced to take aboard the cargo, Grey orders the logs stored in the boiler room. Warning him this is not a good idea, Ellen pleads that they be stored in her stateroom. He refuses and remains unswayed as Ellen practices a "scientific experiment" on him in the form of a kiss. In order to fill the empty space in her cabin, however, he does assign a deck passenger by the name of Miss McCabe to room with her.

In order to reach their destination in time, the *Enterprise* opens the safety valve and steams full speed ahead. Although Ellen warns him this is too dangerous, the captain persists. As luck would have it, the river is full of floating debris and as steam from the engines awakens the bees, they escape from their hives and attack the stokers. Eventually, the drive shaft is broken and although temporary repairs are made, Grey is forced to pay a towing charge, consign the rest of his shipment to other boats and go to the expense of making major renovations to the machinery.

Stuck in Natchez with a $2,000 bill he can't pay, Holden attempts to win the money by gambling. He loses his $200 stake and tries to borrow more off the locals. Unfortunately, they, too, are penniless. No one in Natchez has any money because the crops have been poor.

This forces Grey to apply to Mr. Jennings, Ellen's father. They strike a deal whereby Grey will transport the farmer's peaches to Cincinnati for the $2,000 he needs. This is an unusual gamble for both parties in that no one has ever managed to transport out-of-season fruit to a Northern market without having it spoil. But Captain Holden has a plan: cover tons of ice with peat to preserve it, then lay the crop on top in a makeshift form of refrigeration.

Mr. Jennings (unaffected by the financial turndown), is so excited about the possibility of success, he takes his remaining savings and puts down-payments on many of the cotton planters' land in anticipation of vastly increasing his fruit farm. The men cannot refuse the offer because they are nearly bankrupt, but they also determine to prevent the peaches from being successfully sold. If Jennings cannot finish making payments, they retain their plantations and also keep the earnest money.

The *Enterprise* departs in a race against the clock. It takes four weeks to reach Cincinnati. If Holden's plan works, it will be a tremendously profitable achievement.

Adding spice to the adventure, Mr. Jennings observes that Ellen has fallen in love with Grey and that the captain certainly has the "brains and backbone to make her tow the mark." He decides they ought to get married.

The cotton growers hurry to a wood stop called Jethro's Landing and destroy the stockpiles, hoping the *Enterprise* will run out of fuel and be unable to complete her mission. Grey thwarts this plan by having his crew cut trees. With the lard they already have, this will enable the green wood to serve as adequate fuel.

While the crew chops, the planters take over the *Enterprise*. In a room full of peaches hung from the ceiling by their stems (ostensibly to protect the fruit from spoilage), a fight breaks out. Grey, Ben and the crew beat back the takeover and Ellen goes to the pilot house, where she steers the boat. Grey later relieves her and they kiss again, this time with less science and more intent.

The boat successfully runs the river route to Cincinnati and the peaches sell like hotcakes in the open-air market. Mr. Jennings predicts Natchez will become the peach capital of the South and begins planning a wedding. Grey, however, decides a riverboat captain will not make a good husband and predicts Ellen will be happier with her European bumblebees.

This episode attempted to strike a balance between drama and comedy and succeeded in capturing the nuances Riverboat *needed. There were a few miscues: the peculiar lilting score during the fight scene; the overly broad characterization of Mr. Jennings and the compressed plot, but overall this episode touched on the best the series had to offer. Grey was much more likeable, the story line offered an interesting glimpse into the times and the production balanced a serious situation with a lighthearted touch.*

Anne Baxter was a perfect foil to Darren McGavin and the chemistry between them worked on every level. All together, this episode came closest to capturing the formula McGavin would later immortalize in The Night Stalker, *sans the romance.*

Of note, this is the first episode to bear the credit "Meladare Co. Productions" above the Revue and MCA logos on the end credits.

GUEST CAST

Anne Baxter *(b. 5/7/1923, Michigan City, IN; d. 12/12/1985, NYC, NY, brain aneurysm.)* The granddaughter of Frank Lloyd Wright, Anne began her career early and never looked back. She played Joseph Cotton's daughter in *The Magnificent Ambersons* (1942), and received an Academy Award for best Supporting Actress for the film *The Razor's Edge* (1946). She also received an Oscar nomination for *All About Eve* (1950). While her film work was much more significant than her TV guest star appearances, later in her career she became a regular on *East of Eden* and *Hotel*.

Monica Lewis *(b. 5/5/1925, Chicago, Il.)* The wife of Jennings Lang, she appeared in numerous films he produced, including *The Sting II* (1983), *Concorde: Airport '79* and *Airport '77*. She also appeared as Aunt Clara in *Zero to Sixty* (1978), a film starring and co-written by Darren and produced by Kathie Browne McGavin.

Robert Lowery *(b. 10/17/1913, Kansas City, MO; d. 12/26/1971, Hollywood, CA, heart attack.)* Born Robert Larkin Hanks, he was related on his father's side to Nancy Hanks, Abraham Lincoln's mother. An early Batman (*Batman and Robin*, 1949), he made many science fiction/horror films, including *The Mummy's Ghost* (1944, as Tom Hervey) and *Revenge of the Zombies* (1943, as Larry Adams). He co-starred in *Circus Boy* (with Mickey Dolenz and Noah Beery, Jr.) in the 1956-57 series (also at Revue), playing Big Tim Champion and later played Buss Courtney on *Pistols 'n' Petticoats* (1966). Married to actress Jean Parker from 1951-57, he operated a celebrity travel cruise business with Jackie Coogan in the 1960's.

Lloyd Corrigan *(b. 10/16/1900, San Francisco, CA; d. 11/5/1969, Woodland Hills, CA.)* A regular actor in TV, he also wrote a number of films in the 20's and 30's, among them *The Mysterious Dr. Fu Manchu* (1929) and *Return of Dr. Fu Manchu* (1930). As a director, he worked with Boris Karloff on a very underrated film, *Night Key* (1937).

Don Haggerty (see episode 1.24, "The Wichita Arrows," page 148).

1.5   "The Unwilling". . . . . *October 11, 1959*
Directed by Richard H. Bartlett
Written by Norman Jolley
Produced by Richard H. Bartlett and Norman Jolley

This is the first "Ben episode." Captain Holden warns Ben that as a pilot, he knows little about people and warns him to be careful. That said, he remains behind in St. Louis on business while Ben captains the *Enterprise*.

In Natchez, Ben takes aboard a saloon girl named Lill and strikes a deal with Dan Simpson to transport 300 bales of cotton to St. Louis. Dan is unusually afraid of river pirates and cannot buy marine insurance because he is not really transporting cotton but mercantile goods disguised as cotton. He explains that bales are too cumbersome for pirates to steal. He learned his lesson three years before when a similar cargo was stolen. His dream is to take what amounts to a general store and go from St. Louis, west, where he hopes to become a shopkeeper.

Unfortunately, his plans become known to John Murrell, the same pirate who earlier stole his cargo. Murrell sends Leila Russell, a woman who has worked for him in the past, aboard the *Enterprise* to gain the details and set the stage for their eventual robbery. Leila does not want to go because on the previous trip Dan fell in love with her and she has never forgiven herself for the deception.

Murrell forces her to go, so she gives Ben a song-and-dance story about being wanted by the law. He feels sorry for her and permits her to book passage. She is also a dancer of considerable talent and after a long choreographed scene on the dock, Ben invites her to entertain the passengers on their voyage to St. Louis.

Leila and Dan meet aboard ship and she makes him believe she still loves him. Stating she had not actually run out three years ago, but merely went to the wrong hotel to meet him, they reconcile.

Murrell's gang pretends to be shipwrecked and Ben allows them aboard although he takes the added precaution of having them searched for weapons. He does not have a woman with the rescued party searched, however, which is unfortunate because she is the one carrying the guns.

Leila tells Murrell she does not want to betray Simpson but the pirate threatens Dan's life, so she is forced to go along. Dan confesses to her his mercantile cargo is disguised in the cotton bales and she relays this to Murrell. While the *Enterprise* is docked, he and his men steal the "cotton" and escape.

Dan is very angry that the pirates have seen through his scheme and blames Ben for telling them. Ben accuses Leila and she confesses, trying to explain that she did so only to save Dan's life. A man who has never hurt anyone in his life, Simpson decides he has reached the point where he wants to inflict pain on someone and strikes her across the face in a rather brutal scene.

Discovering she is truly in love with Dan, Leila attempts to make amends by leading Ben, Dan and the crew to Murrell's hideout. Despite the high water table around the river, the goods are stashed in a cave. When the good guys arrive there is a gunfight and Leila is shot. The "cotton" is retrieved intact and the voyage resumes to St. Louis.

Grey appears on the dock for his second cameo. Ben gives him a rapid summary of the trip, concluding with the information that Leila survived, she and Dan were to be married and both were soon to set out for the West.

Setting the standard for "Ben" episodes, the story featured a girl and a love affair. The plot was standard fare and a bit odd. Considering the value of cotton, the excuse it was too bulky to steal doesn't wash — and was certainly made moot when the pirates stole the cumbersome bales without any trouble.

Writer Norman Jolley did not give Reynolds any scenes in which to sink his teeth and offered no endearing characteristics that would make the character of Ben Frazer stand out from any number of like characters around the dial. It also stretches belief that Dan would be unable to buy maritime insurance. For a price, anything, as they say, could be bought along the riverfront. (And if the excuse was he had been robbed on his first voyage, why didn't he have insurance then?)

The character of "John Murrell" was based on a real-life individual reputed to have been a "land pirate." His history was highly fictionalized and his exploits chronicled in a very popular book in the mid-1800's. Murrell was also immortalized in a long chapter of Mark Twain's "Life on the Mississippi," which seems to have been the inspiration for a number of Riverboat *stories.*

McGavin's absence stood out like a sore thumb and began a precedent that would carry over to all subsequent Ben episodes. Of note, this is the first episode Jules Bricken did not produce. Writers Richard H. Bartlett ("The Barrier") and Norman Jolley were brought in to produce and Bartlett also directed, giving him complete control over the episode. While Jolley disappeared after this attempt, Bartlett went on to produce other Riverboat *shows where significant changes were implemented. Not only did he mean to separate his star and co-star (seeing whether Reynolds could stand on his own), he was later involved in major decisions concerning the cast and tone of* Riverboat, *none of which could be said to favor McGavin.*

Interestingly, the end credit "Meladare and Co." is absent from the end titles.

GUEST CAST

Eddie Albert *(b. 4/22/1906, Rock Island, Il; d. 5/26/2005, Pacific Palisades, CA, pneumonia.)* A circus trapeze artist before becoming an actor, he was forever typecast as Oliver Wendell Douglas in the popular TV series *Green Acres* (1965-71). Because of his work for environmental causes, the date chosen for "Earth Day" was April 22 in honor of his birthday. He was awarded the Bronze Star with combat "V" for rescuing 70 Marines at the Battle of Tarawa, 1943.

Debra Paget *(b. 8/19/1933, Denver, CO.)* Coming from an acting family, her sisters Teala Loring and Lisa Gaye were film stars in the 50's and 60's, while her brother, acting under the name Ruell Shayne, had some work in the industry. Real name Debralee Griffin (she took her stage name from Lady Paget of England), she received a 20th Century-Fox contract at age 14 and went on to work for many years. Among her notable credits are *Broken Arrow* (1950), *Les Misérables* (1952) and *The Ten Commandments* (as Lilia; 1956). She appeared in the episode "The Facts in the Case of M. Valdemar" as Helene Valdemar in the film *Tales of Terror* (1962). She retired in 1962 after marrying a Chinese millionaire.

Russell Johnson *(b. 11/10/1924, Ashley, PA.)* Long before this actor became identified as the Professor on *Gilligan's Island* (1964-67), he had a long list of impressive credits. His first appearance was on *For Men Only* (1952), and he worked steadily through the 1950's on such series as *The Adventures of Superman* and *The Lone Ranger*. He played Marshal Gib Scott in the series *Black Saddle* (1959-60), appeared in the classic *Thriller* episode, "The Hungry Glass" (1961) and two episodes of *The Twilight Zone* ("Back There" and "Execution."). He continued to work steadily, with his last listed credit *Meego*, 1997.

1.6 "The Fight Back". . . . . *October 18, 1959*
Directed by Jules Bricken
Teleplay by Robert E. Thompson and Mel Goldberg
Story by Robert E. Thompson
Produced by Jules Bricken

This episode differs from those that have gone before in that it is told in flashback. It opens with Captain Holden standing in front of a burning town. He narrates that Hampton is a monument to "greed and rottenness" and he has the explanation of what happened.

The scene then shifts to the *Enterprise,* where the crew is angry because Grey does not have the money to pay them. After more narration, Grey and Ben discuss how the captain's money has been spent; then Holden sweet-talks the crew into staying by promising the next voyage to New Orleans will be a profitable one. Ben is impressed with the captain's skills in handling an unpromising situation, but doubts Holden's ability to make good.

They steam for a hitherto unknown town called Hampton, where Holden hopes to pick up produce. The fields are filled with ripe crops but when he lands, a farmer states the vegetables will rot on the vine because Mr. Fowler, the man who controls the town, has forbidden them to harvest.

Surprised by this turn of events, Holden goes to the local saloon, which is a very successful den of sin and gambling. After a confrontation with Fowler's thugs, Grey is taken to see Mr. Fowler. In a script which appears to have either been written on the fly or over-edited (a sad fact which plagued McGavin's series' career), Fowler offers some explanation that having been driven out of New Orleans, he intends to exact punishment on the locals by ruining them. In a small, utterly wasted role, Henry Danielle plays one of Fowler's henchmen. He has a series of inexplicable lines which reek of too many script rewrites.

When it appears Grey will not have any produce to transport to New Orleans, a farmer with money to burn (unlike the others, who are all starving), offers to rent the *Enterprise* for the marriage of his daughter because, he explains, there are no churches in Hampton. Having inexplicably turned down the proposal once, Grey now readily accepts and puts up a magnificent shindig for the festivities.

After the wedding (fortunately, a minister lived in Hampton), a fight breaks out between Fowler's drunken kid brother and the bridegroom. Chris Slade kills Tom Fowler with a knife and Grey recognizes Slade's prowess with such a deadly weapon. It turns out that seven years earlier, three prisoners had been transported aboard the *Enterprise*. One of them was Slade. He and his companions managed to escape, but in the process, Slade injured Grey with a knife. Gray now intends to turn Slade in for the considerable reward.

It seems he may not get the opportunity to pick up such easy money, however, because Fowler wants to hang the murderer of his brother. The townspeople are all afraid of what Fowler will do if thwarted and decide to turn Slade over. Holden refuses to go along and in a long, dramatic, talky scene with Ben that ultimately made no sense, explains his reasons.

The bulk of the script concerns Holden's attempts to convince the townspeople to stand up to Fowler and regain their town. Finally determining to take matters into his own hands, he sets out on a rowboat with a keg of priming powder to blow up a dam Fowler threw up across the river when no one was looking! When he is wounded, Chris swims to him, saves his life and blows up the obstruction.

After such heroics, Grey determines not to turn Slade into the authorities and the townspeople burn Hampton.

The scene reverts to that of the opening, where McGavin's closing narration announces that it is well such a place was destroyed.

By the sixth episode, the change in format indicates the series still had not found its voice. Nor had the producer found any writer capable of delivering a cogent, entertaining script. While Hampton must have been inhabited for years, no one knew of it, although Holden apparently garnered knowledge by second sight that there was produce waiting to be shipped that no other riverboat captain knew of.

Steaming on divine inspiration, he discovers his prophecy has a catch: a madman with a grudge against the citizens of New Orleans has decided to turn his ire on the people of Hampton. Although they cower at his every whim (including populating his saloon, although what they spent there remains questionable), Fowler is determined to destroy the town — something the farmers had a better grasp of, as they succeeded handsomely in the end.

The stars were certainly on Grey's side when one of the locals — clearly not a farmer with crops rotting in the field — desires to throw the Party of the Century. Although there is no church (where did it go?), there is a minister, ready, willing and able to perform the ceremony. Holden & Company break out the party supplies and decorate the Enterprise to the hilt.

In a lengthy scene, boldly delivered by McGavin as though he were Henry V addressing the troops, Grey explains to Ben why he must do the right thing, or something of the sort. While he may have rallied Ben, he fails to have a similar effect on the deadbeats of Hampton and ultimately determines to save the day. A wiser Grey Holden might simply have taken his fee from the bride's father and steamed away, but unfortunately, there were loose ends to tie.

Not surprisingly, the wayward bridegroom saves the day, as well as his marriage, and wiggles out from under the prison sentence hanging over his head.

"The Fight Back" was a dismal, disjointed, clearly rehashed script that producer Jules Bricken hoped to salvage or at least mitigate the damage by casting a premiere guest star in the lead. With a nod toward the acting, that only made it worse.

GUEST CAST

John Ireland *(b. 1/30/1914, Vancouver, BC, Canada; d. 3/21/1992, Santa Barbara, CA.)* Raised in New York, he earned his first money as a swimmer in a water carnival before moving into acting. He was nominated for an Academy Award for his role in *All the King's Men* (1949). More often than not a heavy, he appeared in many low budget Italian films and also appeared in TV series as a recurring character in *The Cheaters* (1961) and the 1965-66 season of *Rawhide*, as well as the brief series *Cassie & Co.* (1982). In 1988, he had been cast to replace Lorne Greene in the sorry TV movie *Bonanza: The Next Generation*, but the series never came to fruition. His name frequently appeared in tabloids of the time, stemming from his romantic interests in young actresses, including 16-year-old Tuesday Weld, Natalie Wood and Sue Lyon.

Karl Swenson *(b. 7/23/1908, Brooklyn, NY; d. 10/8/1978, Torrington, CT, heart attack.)* An easily recognizable character actor, he usually played foreigners, particularly those with a European accent; typically Swedish or German. He played Lars Henson on the series *Little House on the Prairie* (1974-78) and a lawyer in *Judgment at Nuremberg* (1961). He made several episodes of "Cimarron Strip" and several *Gunsmoke* episodes, most notably as Lars Karlgren in the episode "The Newcomers" opposite a very young Jon Voight.

Joan O'Brien *(b. 2/14/1936, Cambridge, MA.)* Her show business break came when she got a part on a local California TV show with Tennessee Ernie Ford. As a singer, she had considerable success before going into action drama. Her most famous role was probably as Lt. Dolores Crandall, RN, in *Operation Petticoat* (1959). Her last role was the film, *Get Yourself a College Girl* (1964). Afterwards, she went back to singing, touring with the Harry James Orchestra. She also had a successful career with the Hilton Hotel chain.

Henry Danielle *(b. 3/5/1894; d. 10/31/1963, Santa Monica, CA, of a heart attack while filming My Fair Lady.)* Born in London, he began his career on stage and continued theatrical work on Broadway after immigrating to the US. Usually cast as the suave British gentleman, he was equally adept at portraying the fiend lurking in the background. Innumerable films include *The Private Lives of Elizabeth and Essex* (1939), *Sherlock Holmes and the Voice of Terror* (1943) and *Witness for the Prosecution* (1957). Perhaps his greatest role, especially for horror fans, came as the concurrently arrogant and tortured physician in Val Lewton's brilliant film, *The Body Snatcher* (1945). His later worked focused on TV anthologies, with his most memorable work coming on *Thriller*, where he appeared in five of the most outstanding episodes ("God Grante that She Lye Stille," "The Grim Reaper," "The Prisoner in the Mirror," "Well of Doom," and "The Cheaters").

Tom Laughlin *(b. 8/10/1931, Milwaukee, WI.)* His first credit (as writer/director/producer) was *The Proper Time* in 1960, while his first solo acting credit was

Climax! in 1955. He had a role in *Tea and Sympathy* (1956) and made the usual Revue rounds before making his *Riverboat* episode. He is best known for the 1971 film, *Billy Jack.*

Ken Lynch *(b. 7/15/1910, Cleveland, OH; d. 2/13/1990, Burbank, CA, virus.)* Ken started in radio, went into films and TV production and never looked back. With a tough Irish face, he was often cast as a cop. His first credit was *Suspense,* in 1949. He appeared in everything from *The Honeymooners* (1956) to *Zorro* (1958). He was the sheriff in *Whirlybirds* (1959), was in three episodes of *Thriller,* played Lt. Barney on *Honey West* (1965-66), Big Jim Todd on *The Virginian* (1963-69) and was seen in 12 episodes of *Gunsmoke,* including "Lynott" with Richard Kiley. He played a tough cop on "The Ripper," an episode of *The Night Stalker,* and played Sgt. Grover on *McCloud* (1972-77). His last credit was *The Winds of War,* 1983.

1.7 **"Escape to Memphis"** . . . . *October 25, 1959*
Directed by John Rich
Teleplay by Bob and Wanda Duncan
Story by Richard B. Larkin
Produced by John Larkin

The teaser opens with Laura Winters being abused by her husband while his brother Sutton looks on with bemused interest. In order to preserve her life, Laura shoots and kills her attacker. This might have been the end of it, but Jarrod Sutton announces that as her only witness, the price for his testimony of self-defense is her new-found inheritance and all her affection. Recoiling in horror, she flees the house.

Running all the way to the river, she is rescued by Captain Holden. Laura tells him she is being pursued by a killer and must get to Memphis. He takes her aboard the *Enterprise* and asks Ellen Rollie, a doctor's wife, to nurse her.

A subplot quickly develops. Mrs. Rollie's husband is a drunk and a philanderer, taking every opportunity to play the field. He flirts with women aboard the boat and quickly notes the new arrival's beauty. This alienates Laura from Ellen and the two rapidly separate.

When Grey comes in to get her story, Laura is reluctant to confess. He notes the recent removal of a wedding ring and questions why she was carrying a pistol — one recently fired. She makes up a story about running from the drunken friend of her brother. Grey disbelieves her, but leaves it at that for the time being.

Jarrod Sutton catches up to the *Enterprise* when she stops again for wood and books passage on the boat. He wastes no time blackmailing Laura and threatens that if she doesn't become one of his possessions, he will lie to the authorities by saying she willfully murdered her husband. To make matters more interesting, he also holds a warrant for her arrest.

Laura confesses her story to Grey, who wants to put Sutton off at the next stop. She pleads with him not to antagonize the man, reiterating the fact only his truthful testimony can save her from a murder charge.

Mr. Rollie astutely discerns Laura is a hunted woman and makes her a proposition. Considering the fact he has just stolen money from his wife's cash box and Laura is a fugitive, they could make good their escape together. No one would be looking for a couple, and thus they could travel far away without fear

Captain Holden spent too much time off the riverboat, giving the series the feel of an "oater," rather than one designed to capture the feeling and flavor of the Mississippi and Missouri rivers.

of detection. She accepts, but at another stop for wood, she disembarks and tries to hide in the swamp.

Grey and Sutton both go after her. There is the inevitable confrontation, this time in the water, as the two men duke it out. Grey wins and succeeds in making Sutton confess the truth: the killing was self defense and he only wanted to have everything his brother had so men would envy him.

Sutton writes a confession and at Memphis, Laura is put aboard to stand trial. Mrs. Rollie, who has come to the realization her husband is no good, throws him over. Finding it in her heart to forgive the "other woman," she opens her home to Laura while the latter awaits judgment.

In a completely unanticipated ending, Grey has apparently fallen in love with Laura and suggests she write to him when her legal troubles are dismissed. They can meet again and steam off into the sunset together. The parting shot as she departs the boat makes this seem problematic.

"Escape to Memphis" had several problems and underscored others. While the ending was well played by McGavin and Crain, it came out of nowhere. Nothing in the script made you believe this was coming. The writers had also played the "green wood and lard" card too often and this was only the seventh episode. They also displayed consistent trouble with time. It is hard to imagine Sutton getting an arrest warrant and catching up to the Enterprise *at her second fuel stop, even if his brother "had the fastest horses in the county." (The precedent of compressing time was established in the premiere when the avengers easily caught up to Hunk aboard the* Enterprise, *and would be used numerous times again.)*

Nor did anyone mention the fact that Laura could just as easily have turned the tables on Sutton by claiming he shot his brother out of envy. Since no one else witnessed the killing, that might have been a plausible alternative. Men in the 1840's were much more likely to believe a man killed another man, than think the epitome of womanhood had the wherewithal to fire a gun.

The directors also persisted in using the same riverboat suite (front, right) for every guest star. Since the corridor set was a front with no actual cabin behind it, they apparently did not want to be bothered with setting up different camera angles to have the characters go through doors on the left. Clearly, fast and easy was the order of the day.

More troubling for the health of the show was the fact that the second-billed star, Burt Reynolds, had little to do in any episode not specifically written for him. Not counting "The Unwilling," Travis (William D. Gordon) had far more screen time and lines than Ben. If Reynolds' name had not been featured in the opening, it would have been easy to imagine Gordon as the co-star. To date, the series had also used four different producers (Bricken, Bartlett & Jolley and Larkin) — a serious indication that all was not well.

GUEST CAST

Jeanne Crain *(b. 5/25/1925, Barstow, CA; d. 12/14/2003, Santa Barbara, CA, heart attack.)* Frequently cast in musicals, a contract employee, Louanne Hogan, dubbed in her singing voice. She appeared in the original *Cheaper by the Dozen* (1950) playing Ann Gilbreath.

Claude Akins *(b. 5/25/1918, Nelson, GA; d. 1/27/1994, Altadena, CA, cancer.)* After serving in the US Signal Corps in WWII, he began a career in acting and once started, never seemed to be without a role. While he did film work, his TV characters stand out, primarily as Marshal Clint Tucker in the 1966 season premiere of *Gunsmoke*, and the *Twilight Zone* episode, "The Monsters Are Due on Maple Street," in 1959. He also played the sheriff in *The Night Stalker*, in 1972.

Philip Reed *(b. 3/25/1908, New York, NY; d. 12/21/1996, Los Angeles, CA.)* A familiar face in the mid-1930's and 40's films, his credits from that decade include *Klondike Annie* (1936) playing Insp. Jack Forrest alongside Mae West, and *Song of the Thin Man* (1947). He made episodes of the TV series *Alfred Hitchcock Presents, Burke's Law* and *Hawaiian Eye*. His first role was in *College Coach* (1933), billed as Phillip Reed. His last role was in the film *Harum Scarum* (1965), although he basically stopped working in the late 1950's.

June Dayton *(b. 8/24/1923, Dayton, OH; d. 6/13/1994, Sherman Oaks, CA, cancer.)* Her real name was Mary June Wetzel. Her first credit is an episode of *Lux Video Theatre*, in 1950. She made numerous anthology series of the time, including the 1948 *Studio One* episode "They Came to Baghdad," with Richard Kiley, and two episodes of *Mike Hammer* with McGavin before her *Riverboat* appearance. She made a *Twilight Zone* ("A Penny for your Thoughts," 1961) and continued to play girl friends through the 1960's. Her last credit was *Quincy, M.E.* in 1983.

1.8 **"Witness No Evil"** . . . .*November 1, 1959*
(No credits available)

Otto Justin, dealer in wild animals, is escorting a shipment of his captured beasts to St. Louis aboard the *Enterprise*. Widow Aby Saunders and her young son Paddy are both impressed with Justin's manner. (Review taken from *Television Westerns: Episode Guide*, by Harris M. Lentz, III.)

GUEST CAST

Vincent Price *(b. 5/27/1911, St. Louis, MO; d. 10/25/1993, Los Angeles, CA, lung cancer.)* Vincent Price did everything in his life from establishing himself as a premiere horror star to collecting art and writing cookbooks. By 1959, when he guest starred on *Riverboat*, he had already earned a reputation as a wonderful character actor as well as a character, starring in such films as *The Fly* (1958), *The Tingler* (1959) and *House on Haunted Hill* (1959). He had "monster parts" behind and ahead of him, from portraying Simon Templar of *The Saint* on radio (1947-48) to the kindly inventor on *Edward Scissorhands* with Johnny Depp (1990). He said one of his favorite roles was that of Professor Ratigan on Disney's *The Great Mouse Detective* (1986).

Barbara Lawrence *(b. 2/24/1928, Carnegie, OK.)* Never achieving the stardom everyone held out for her, she had a good career until retiring in the 1960's to sell real estate in Beverly Hills. She played the role of Gertie Cummings on stage, then reprised it for the film version of *Oklahoma* (1955). Before that, she won the title "Little Miss Hollywood" in 1942.

1.9 "A Night at Trapper's Landing" . . . . *November 8, 1959*
Directed by Felix Feist
Written by Halsey Melone
Produced by Jules Bricken

This is the second "Ben episode," as well as the second *Riverboat* script to be presented in flashback.

The story opens with Ben, arm in a sling, refusing to transport more soldiers upriver to Trapper's Landing. The army wishes to wipe out the Indians because of a recent massacre, but Ben insists they have the facts all wrong. He demands to be taken to the general and explain the true events.

On Frazer's request, a civilian named Rothgate is brought in for interrogation. It was on his original report of an Indian uprising at the fort that soldiers were sent to quiet them. Ben wants Rothgate charged with lying and complicity. The general doesn't want to hear Ben out, but similar to "The Unwilling," Captain Holden breezes in and requests they listen. Thus begins the flashback.

Lieutenant Andre Devereaux commands the platoon assigned to put down the Indian uprising. His first appearance is not a promising one when he arrives on a buggy accompanied by four lovelies. Announcing that he is in no danger, they fawn over their favorite and make him promise to return as quickly as possible.

It is soon made apparent that although a brave man, Devereaux is not battle tested. He has taught his men about honor, camaraderie and swordsmanship, but he is also lenient, and his company has earned the reputation of being soft. Aboard the *Enterprise,* a group of laborers being transported to the Landing jeer the soldiers, accusing them of being little more than cardboard cutouts. Devereaux takes exception and gets in a fight to defend their honor.

Ben does not think it appropriate behavior for an officer and later, when the two are alone, Andre tells his story. While Ben has "spent his entire life on the river" (the closest the writers have yet come to a modicum of characterization), Devereaux is the son of wealthy parents (Spanish and French), raised to a life of meaningless luxury. He once considered being a priest because he felt that religious orders would give him purpose, but eventually abandoned the attempt. Buying the uniform of an officer, he was recruited into the United States service at that rank and given a company.

He states his intention that none under his command will die, and concerns himself with rationale: why did the Indians attack? What was their motivation? To date, they have been surviving peacefully on government payments. He feels if he can find the answers, bloodshed will be avoided.

When the boat reaches Trapper's Landing, the crew discover it has been burned to the ground. There are only two survivors: a man named Woodley, who is Rothgate's trapping partner, and Thompson, the Indian agent. Ben takes them aboard and they tell a tale of horror. The braves attacked without notice and killed everyone. They were able to survive because Thompson was wounded early in the battle and Woodley dragged him into the woods to hide.

The crew infer the Indians are still lurking about and state it is too dangerous to go ashore. Ben needs wood for the boat, however, as they do not have enough to make the return trip. He requests the soldiers guard his men as they chop green wood. The lieutenant feels this is too dangerous and when Ben remains obstinate, the officer attempts to steer the *Enterprise* away. He wastes what little fuel they have left and inadvertently rams the boat into shore. No harm was done, but his rash act makes it imperative they get more fuel.

A publicity still of Darren and Carol Daniels from "A Night at Trapper's Landing." Typically, publicity stills were used to show off the actors, rather than represent a scene from the episode. In this case, Carol Daniel's appearance went uncredited. The photo was credited to Elmer Holloway and is dated "Nov 1959," with a hand-written date, "11-8-59" which was the air date.

While the soldiers are guarding the choppers, a delegation of Indians appears. Woodley translates their message, doesn't like what he hears and scares them off. The Indians attack and kill several troopers and crewmembers, sending the party back to the relative safety of the boat.

It is then Thompson makes a confession: Woodley and his partner Rothgate have been stealing the Indians' money. As Indian agent, he went along with their scheme, getting his cut of the profit. Realizing they could not continue their thieving ways, Rothgate determined to concoct a story about the renegades and have the army kill them all. That way, he and Woodley would have both sides of the river to trap animals for their fur.

Lieutenant Devereaux thus has his rationale. If the Indians had not been cheated, they never would have rebelled. They only burned the landing because they were starving and had no money to pay for food.

Before Thompson dies, he says he has proof of his claim. Woodley has the latest shipment of government money in his leather pouch. Before Ben can catch him, however, he escapes to a nearby fort.

Without wood, the *Enterprise* cannot return downriver. Ben must therefore take the chance of tracking Woodley on foot and returning the money to the Indians or risk a full-scale attack. He and Andre's troops go after the trapper and find him outside the fort. Already having defeated the soldiers, the Indians are inside. Firing from a position of advantage, they cut down the troops. Devereaux might have gotten them away in good order, but he foolishly risks his life to save Woodley, who is pinned down between the combatants.

Woodley is killed, but Devereaux refuses to leave his body. He heroically goes after it, with Ben close behind. They recover the proof of Woodley and Rothgate's complicity but before they can escape, Devereaux is killed. His dying wish is that Ben explain the situation to the authorities so a new peace treaty can be brokered and the money returned to its rightful owners.

As the flashback ends, the general calls off the campaign and clears Devereaux's name of being a poor soldier. His men are commended for bravery and innocent Indian lives are saved. Satisfied with the result, Grey hauls Ben away.

As in the first "Ben episode," the end credits lacked the "Meladare Co. Productions" credit.

Superbly played by Ricardo Montalban, the Devereaux character was likeable and the plot based on historical precedent. There were rather poor backscreen projections of the riverboat moving in the water and as in previous episodes, shots of an actual steamer were spliced in to add realism, if not actual continuity.

The main flaw of this episode was the total lack of chemistry between McGavin and Reynolds. Although a consummate professional, Darren fairly shouted his lines and conveyed the air of someone totally annoyed by the situation, making it obvious things were not going well on the set.

Three credits were given for the music, which seemed out of place, since most of it was canned.

Music by: Elmer Bernstein
Arranged and adapted by: Leo Shuken and Jack Hayes
Musical supervision: Stanley Wilson

In subsequent episodes and throughout Season One, numerous individuals would be given credit for the score. Continuing an alarming trend, other production personnel were also scrambled, with a new film editor (Edward Haire), sound (William Lynch) and assistant director (George Bisk). Jack Lambert, who would later be cast as series regular Joshua McGregor, played a Polish workman in this episode.

GUEST CAST

Ricardo Montalban *(b. 11/25/1920, Mexico City, Mexico; d. 1/14/2009, Los Angeles, CA.)* Immortalized for his role in *Star Trek* as Khan in "Space Seed" (and later reprising his role for the film version, *Star Trek II: The Wrath of Khan*), he became an everyday face for his role as Mr. Rourke on *Fantasy Island* (1978-84). He won an Emmy for his portrayal of a Native American Sioux in the TV miniseries *How the West Was Won* (1976). In 1951, he was severely injured while filming *Across the Wide Missouri* and underwent extensive spine surgery. This caused him constant pain and eventually reduced him to a wheelchair (1993). Early in his career, he vied with Fernando Lamas as a leading Latin lover in U.S. films.

Peter Whitney *(b. 5/24/1916, Long Branch, NJ; d. 3/30/1972, heart attack.)* An actor resigned to small roles, he frequented TV lots throughout the 1950's and 60's, making many Westerns. In 1964, he played Lafayette 'Lafe' Crick on *The Beverly Hillbillies*.

Judson Pratt *(b. 12/6/1916, Hingham, MA; d. 2/9/2002, Northridge, CA.)* His first credit was an episode of *Armstrong Circle Theatre* called "Blaze of Glory," from 1950, and his last was a TV movie, *The Ordeal of Patty Hearst* (1979). In between, he worked on everything from *The Wonderful World of Disney* ("The Flight of the Grey Wolf," 1976), to *Gunsmoke* and *Thriller* ("The Mark of the Hand," 1960).

R.G. Armstrong *(b. 4/7/1917, Birmingham, AL.)* Full name Robert Golden Armstrong. He attended the famed Actors' Studio in New York and had success in the theatre before going to Hollywood. His first credit was *Garden of Eden* (1954) and he went on to work on every series imaginable. He was a series regular on *T.H.E. Cat* (1966), made five episodes of *Gunsmoke*, three episodes of *Dynasty* (1982) and six episodes of *Friday the 13th* (1987-89), playing Lewis Vendredi. His last credit was *The Waking*, 2001.

1.10 "The Faithless"............................*November 22, 1959*
Directed by Richard H. Bartlett
Teleplay by Richard N. Morgan
Story by Richard N. Morgan and Kate and Howard Phillips
Produced by Richard H. Bartlett and Norman Jolley

For the seventh time in ten episodes, the story begins off the *Enterprise*. It opens in a swamp where Marshal Kester chases and finally captures an escaped criminal by the name of Paul Drake. The lawman angrily snaps the wrist cuffs on him with obvious hatred and Drake remarks that despite their relative situations, he is the better of the two men.

In the second consecutive "Ben episode," Frazer (called "captain" three times in the course of the hour) checks passengers aboard at Natchez. Mr. and Mrs. Abner Crane and their small daughter, Lucy, come aboard, followed by Miss Catherine Norris, a young woman traveling to Sioux Country as a member of the Indian Missionary Society. Lastly come Marshal Kester and his prisoner, whom he chains to the flagpole for safekeeping.

Baby Lucy gives Drake an apple to eat, but her kindness is misinterpreted and the passengers think Drake has stolen it. This sets the stage for the future animosity that develops between him and the rest of the travelers.

Miss Norris also takes pity on the convict and later brings him something to eat. He is surly and embittered toward her generosity, which she explains by saying she wishes to help the unfortunate. He calls her a "do-gooder," and relates his history, stating he escaped from Meckendridge Prison, where he was serving a term for murder.

A storm comes up. Travis again acts as pilot while Ben performs the duties of captain. When it begins to rain, Miss Norris returns to the deck, placing a makeshift tent over Drake. Getting beneath the overhang with him, they enter into a long discussion. He remains bitter and cynical, establishing himself as a loveless man. She declares she would die without love and tries to make him understand her commitment to the unfortunate.

In a very intense scene of implied sexuality, Drake accuses Cathy of smoldering with passion. Why else, he says, would she huddle under the tent with him, knowing he hasn't been with a woman in seven years? She runs away, but there is clearly truth to what he says.

In the morning, the river is full of debris and a floating log smashes through the side of the boat near the boiler room. It nearly floods before Carney shoves a log through the hole, temporarily keeping the *Enterprise* afloat.

To complicate matters, little Lucy has gotten gravely ill with "choking fever." Ben saw a lot of this disease on the river last year and knows it can be fatal. It is also highly "catching," for when they stop to refuel, the townspeople will not let any of the passengers depart, nor will they allow any of their men to bring aboard wood.

Ben strikes an agreement that the townspeople will toss the logs into the water and he will then fish them out. They salvage what they can, noting they will have to use lard to make the wet wood burn.

Once back on the river, Kester appeals to Drake. He tells him Lucy is dying and begs him to help. Drake diagnoses the disease as diphtheria and although he was a doctor before his conviction, he has no intention of serving as one, now.

Apprised of the situation, Miss Norris asks to see Drake in her cabin — alone. Paul explains that the man he was "died in a courtroom at the hands of his friends." He tells his story: a rich man fractured his skull and was brought to Dr. Drake for treatment. This man was an enemy to all, and those who brought him to the doctor imposed on him not to operate. Drake let them persuade him and the patient died. Because of this, charges of criminal intent were brought.

Because Drake also hated the man, he is convicted and sentenced to eight years. He does not disagree with the term. What has made him bitter is the fact those who influenced him "got the town."

Miss Norris decides Paul "murdered his own honor as a doctor" for not treating the patient and he accuses her of being less holy than appearances would indicate, and of hiding behind Biblical platitudes. He asks if she has faith in him and they embrace and kiss. Her convictions re-instill his own lost belief and he is inspired to once again be a doctor.

Upon cleaning up, she takes him to the sick room. After an examination, Dr. Drake decides he could perform a tracheotomy to aid Lucy's breathing. The odds are not good, however, only 50-1. The stricken parents have faith in him and give permission. Cathy also gives her approval and he attempts the surgery. In a well-played scene involving the principals, it is never said but only implied that the child dies.

Outside the cabin, the passengers rebel, feeling it was wrong for a prisoner to operate on an innocent child. "Captain" Frazer holds them back and Cathy defends Drake, finally shaming the mob into standing down.

Drake has made a believer of Marshal Kester and he will not put the wrist cuffs back on his prisoner. He also says he will fix it so Drake has no more than a few months to serve on his jail term.

The *Enterprise* pulls into port and Grey Holden shows up, having recently returned "from a wedding in Connecticut." Ben explains why the boat was late and states he is in a hurry to go to a wedding. Travis, too, is invited and he is wearing Grey's best shirt that is "too big in the collar." Grey suggests he "better lose some weight," and the script ends.

This was an interesting episode on several levels. It played far darker than any episode that had gone before, and was especially intense. The implied sexuality was way beyond the typical television fare of the late 1950's and the fact the authors had the child die, another unwritten taboo, was as surprising as it was effective. The discussions of faith transcended the established norms of what TV usually tackled, and Richard Carlson's performance was undoubtedly one of the best, if not the best, he ever gave.

Beyond that, this entirely guest-star driven episode had the uncomfortable feel that Ben's role had originally been written for Grey, and Travis' lines scripted for Ben. The fact the producers let stand Ben's position as captain without explanation served to underscore that in later episodes he might very well be the captain and that the char-acter of Holden was becoming extraneous to Riverboat.

GUEST CAST

Richard Carlson *(b. 4/29/1912, Albert Lea, MN; d. 11/24/1977, Encino, CA, cere-bral hemorrhage.)* He played the title role in the TV series *Mackenzie's Raiders* (1958), but is probably better known for his role as David Reed in *The Creature From the Black Lagoon* (1954) and as John Putnam in *It Came From Outer Space* (1953). He also had a notable role in the episode "Kill My Love" on the series *Thriller* (1962).

Bethel Leslie *(b. 8/3/1929, New York, NY; d. 11/28/1999, New York, NY, cancer.)* She began her career at age 15 on the Broadway stage and later earned a Tony nomination for *Long Day's Journey Into Night* (1986). She appeared in numerous films and TV roles and appeared very frequently in soap operas, including *All My Children* (1991) as Claudia Conner, *One Life to Live* (1994) as Ethel Crawford and *The Doctors* (1965-68) as Dr. Maggie Powers. She was also the head writer for the soap *The Secret Storm* (1954). Her other series were *The Richard Boone Show* (1963) and *The Girls* (1950).

Bert Freed *(b. 11/3/1919, Bronx, NY; d. 8/2/1994, in Sechelt, British Columbia, Canada, from a heart attack while on a fishing trip.)* He was the first actor to play Lt. Columbo in a 1960 episode of *The Chevy Mystery Show*. He played the heavy Rufe Ryker, on the TV series *Shane* (1966) and had the small role of Ben Golden in *Whatever Happened to Baby Jane* (1962). He played Captain Akins in the epi-sode "Mr. R.I.N.G." on *The Night Stalker*.

William Phipps *(b. 2/4/1922, Vincennes, Indiana.)* Hitchhiking to Hollywood in 1941, his first film was RKO's "Crossfire" (1947). Known as much for his voice-over work as his acting, he supplied the voice of Prince Charming in Disney's *Cinderella* (1950). He had small roles in *The War of the Worlds* (1953) and *Invad-ers from Mars* (1953) and appeared in an episode of *Twilight Zone*, playing the sergeant in "The Purple Testament" (1960).

Jeanne Bates *(b. 5/21/1918, Berkeley, CA.)* She played the lead role in the radio mystery series *Whodunit* in the early 1940's and her scream became the show's audio identification. She was married to the program's producer Lex X. Lans-worth from 1943 until his death in 1981. For horror fans, she played the first victim (uncredited) in Bela Lugosi's 1944 film, *The Return of the Vampire.*

Katie Sweet *(b. 8/31/1957, Hollywood, CA.)* A child actor her entire career, her first credit was *The Adventures of Ozzie & Harriet* (1959). Altogether, she had nearly two dozen credits, appearing on such series as *Ben Casey, Wagon Train, The Fugitive,* and *My Favorite Martian.* She played Peggy Dayton in four episodes of

Bonanza as the daughter of Adam Cartwright's fiancée, played by Kathie Browne. Her last credit was an episode of *Hank* in 1966.

1.11 "The Boy from Pittsburgh"*.....................*November 29, 1959*
Directed by Frank Arrigo
Teleplay by George Tibbles
Story by John Larkin
Produced by John Larkin

Darren McGavin and Tommy Nolan from the episode, "The Boy from Pittsburgh."

The story begins ashore in July 1841, with Mr. Carter buying $50,000 worth of insurance on a cargo of diamonds he is transporting aboard the *Enterprise*. After the deal is transacted and the diamonds are given to the agent, he is pick-pocketed by Paddy Brit. Brit exchanges the small package for one which appears identical, and no one is the wiser. It is then revealed that Carter and Brit are in league to defraud the insurance company.

Boarding the *Enterprise* for the trip to St. Louis is Mrs. Rutherford, a widow. A boy also sneaks aboard as a stowaway as the boat steams out of port. Travis

*Historical Note: In the 1840's, the correct spelling of the city was *Pittsburg*.

eventually discovers him under a sack of potatoes and brings him to Grey's cabin. The boy confesses his name is Tom James and he is running away from an orphanage in Pittsburg(h). Grey promises to send him back on the return trip.

There is a good scene between Grey and Tommy in which Grey details his own past. As a boy growing up in Boston (!), his mother died when he was young and his father "did the best he could," he guesses. But Grey ran away although

A posed scene with Darren McGavin and Mona Freeman.

he shouldn't have, because a boy needs a home base. He stresses the fact Tommy needs an education and the best place for him is back in the orphanage.

Tommy "maneuvers" Grey into putting him to work, supposedly as a punishment, but he is thrilled over the chance to be part of the crew. He is assigned duty as a waiter and although he doesn't like the task, preferring to work with Carney in the engine room or piloting the boat, he is advised to make do with what he has.

Grey sits with Mrs. Rutherford in the saloon (dining room), and tries to talk her into adopting Tommy. But when the boy accidentally spills water on her, she reacts violently, hurting his feelings by the obvious rejection. Badly upset, Tommy runs away, hiding in a wardrobe of the cabin being used by Mr. Carter. He overhears Carter and Brit's plan to blow up the *Enterprise*. They are going to smuggle aboard a keg of powder disguised as a barrel of nails and ignite it to cover the fact they have the real diamonds.

Grey gives Louise Rutherford a tongue lashing for the way she rejected Tommy and she confesses that her own son died of scarlet fever. He hugs her and is sorry for her loss but believes another child in her life will help her wounds heal.

Tommy tries to tell Grey and Ben what he heard, but after all the grandiose stories he has told, no one believes him, Ben likening him to his "little brother." But Grey does decide they had better make sure they still have the precious stones. Against Ben's strenuous objections he opens the package and finds the diamonds there. Still suspicious, he attempts to cut glass with one, finding it does not leave a scratch. They therefore know the real diamonds have been switched.

When the boat docks, the consignment of nails is brought on board. Grey and Travis check them and find only nails. What they don't know is that the fifth barrel, containing the powder, has already been taken by Brit.

Carter and Brit prepare to blow up the *Enterprise*. Tommy stops them by throwing away the fuse, so Carter sees an opportunity to have the diamonds all to himself. He knocks his partner and the boy unconscious and starts a fire. Grey rescues Tommy and throws the keg of explosives overboard before it can explode.

Carter tries to escape in the rowboat, but loses his balance getting it lowered and falls into the river. Captain Holden laconically remarks that a rescue attempt will never find him in the darkness and that seals the thief's fate.

In St. Louis, passengers prepare to depart. Grey tries to talk Mrs. Rutherford into taking Tommy with her, but she makes the excuse he will be better off getting an education in the orphanage and leaves. She is almost to the wharf before she has second thoughts and calls Tommy to her. They embrace and the show finishes with a feel-good ending.

"The Boy from Pittsburgh" is the counter to "The Faithless." Where the former was light, uncomplicated and predictable, the latter was dark and psychologically intricate. Both stories worked and serve as an example of what Riverboat *could have been. One shared factor, however, is the idea that the series was not going to*

be character-driven. "The Faithless" could have been set anywhere and required little intervention by Ben or Travis. While Holden played a larger role in "The Boy from Pittsburgh," giving a glimpse into his background, there lacked any interplay between the regulars. Aside from the scene where Grey and Ben argued over the captain's right to inspect the diamonds (no such objection was made when Grey had Travis check the barrels for nails), this, too, could have been taken from the pages of an anthology series.

Above, facing page: Some of the most memorable scenes shot for Riverboat *involved Darren and the child actors cast in the series. His interaction with Tommy Nolan in "The Boy from Pittsburgh" was a shining example of such inspired moments.*

Perhaps more tellingly, the one significant scene between Holden and Frazer was contentious. With no camaraderie, it was difficult to develop any viewer loyalty. By the 11th episode, you didn't know whether you were going to get a Grey episode, a Ben episode, or a show requiring neither.

Contrast that to Gunsmoke, *which premiered in 1955, and was still using a half-hour format in 1959. While the producer presented episodes where the regulars were not featured, the show had already established a comfortable family feel in Dodge City.*

The regulars' positions were clearly staked but more critically, their relationships with one another became the backbone that would carry it through 20 seasons. Many of the stories on Gunsmoke *could have taken place on any TV Western, but the chemistry between Matt, Kitty and Doc is what created unprecedented viewer loyalty.*

Granted, Riverboat *was only in its first season, but the chances of it finding any comfort zone at this point appeared grim.*

GUEST CAST

Tommy Nolan *(b. 1/15/1948, Montreal, Quebec, Canada.)* Born Bernard Girouard, he was a familiar child actor in the 1950's. He made two *Thriller* episodes, "Child's Play" (1960) and "Paradise Mansion" (1961). He has only two additional credits for the 1960's, *Kiss Me, Stupid* (1964) and *Something for a Lonely Man* (1968). He retired from acting and became a writer.

Mona Freeman *(b. 6/9/1926, Baltimore, MD.)* Born "Monica" Freeman, she was signed by Howard Hughes and thrived in juvenile roles but never succeeded in graduating into major adult roles. She worked primarily in the 1950's, but in 1972 she played Mrs. Bristol in the TV film, *Welcome Home, Johnny Bristol.*

Robert Emhardt *(b. 7/24/1914, Indianapolis, IN; d. 12/26/1994, Ojai, CA, heart failure.)* The easiest way to conjure his face is by thinking of Roger, the coat-of-arms dealer in "The Knightly Murders" episode of *The Night Stalker* (1975). He studied acting in London and worked extensively on Broadway. He was usually cast as a villain.

King Donovan *(b. 1/25/1918, New York, NY; d. 6/30/1987, Hartford, CT, cancer.)* Married to Imogene Coca from 1960 until his death, his first credit was *Open Secret* in 1948. He appeared in five episodes of *It's a Great Life* (1954-56) and seven episodes of *The Bob Cummings Show* (1955-58, playing Harvey Helm). His last credit was *Nothing Lasts Forever* (1984). Horror fans will always remember him for playing Jack Belicec in the Kevin McCarthy classic, *Invasion of the Body Snatchers* (1956).

1.12 "Jessie Quinn" . . . . *December 6, 1959*
Directed by Jules Bricken
Written by Tom Seller
Produced by Jules Bricken

The story begins in Galena, Illinois, as two men blow up a mine, remarking, "That's ore which will never reach Sam Houston."

Aboard the *Enterprise*, an army lieutenant offers Captain Holden $5,000 to accept a shipment of lead and another $5,000 if he delivers it safely to Sam Houston at Texas Junction on the Red River. (This is a tremendously long trip, requiring the steamer to go down the Mississippi nearly to New Orleans before making a "V," and then going up the Red River and across into Texas.) The officer, Perry Quinn, states Houston can't win the war without ammunition and Galena is his main source of lead. Quinn will assign his best agent to guard the cargo. Grey reluctantly accepts, stating he is not doing it for the money but because he remembers the Alamo (1836) and "doesn't like the way Santa Anna runs a war."

Lieutenant Quinn warns Grey of one problem: he has an enemy who will stop at nothing to prevent the shipment from reaching Houston — his brother.

Quinn's agent is murdered by Johnny Hollister. His partner, going by the name of Beaumont Chandler, steals the agent's identity papers and boards the *Enterprise*, pretending to be the guardian of the shipment. Hollister also goes aboard in the guise of a traveling salesman. Grey immediately suspects Hollister as being in league with Santa Anna and confides in Chandler.

Also boarding the boat is Jessie Quinn, a matriarch from Texas who says she is returning home to her ranch. Although she is warned the "side trip" may be dangerous, she tells Captain Holden she fears nothing.

It is soon revealed that both Perry and Bo Chandler (actually Jody Quinn) are Jessie's sons, fighting on opposite sides of the war. Bo is already wanted for sabotage and Jessie can ruin him by revealing his true identity to Holden. She does not, although she put up the money for the shipment and it is in her best interest to do so.

Darren poses with Valerie Allen on the waterfront exterior.

When Hollister warns Bo that his mother has to be gotten rid of because she can compromise the mission, Bo sets him up by maneuvering Grey to check his bags. He finds incendiary material and the two get in a fight. Chandler bursts in and shoots Hollister because he was a threat to his mother.

When the *Enterprise* docks, there is a burial service for Hollister. Afterward, Bo tries to burn the ship but Jessie stops him. It is revealed mother and son are estranged and fighting on opposite sides of the war. Grey overhears their

Darren with Valerie Allen on the waterfront exterior, joined by Burt Reynolds.

argument and realizes that Bo is not the agent but a saboteur who means to prevent the cargo from ever reaching Houston. Bo flees the boat.

Realizing both Perry and Jody (Bo) are brothers, Grey confronts Jessie. She confesses that many years ago, she was a widow with two young sons. The Indians were attacking and a squaw, who had lost her own child, demands a replacement from Jessie. In order to save the weaker child, she gives over Jody. The boy escaped, but has never forgiven her for abandoning him. This explains

Burt Reynolds and Mercedes McCambridge, who played the title role in "Jessie Quinn."

why he has dedicated his life to defending causes that his mother and brother support.

The *Enterprise* reaches Texas Junction and prepares to unload the lead. Bo gets his mother off the boat; then his men overcome Perry's soldiers and take their uniforms. Pretending to accept the cargo, they overwhelm the crew and hold Grey and Perry aboard. Mrs. Quinn, who has escaped capture, manages to get Jody's gun and is in a position to free the captives. She cannot betray her

Darren McGavin with Clu Gulager.

son a second time, however, and drops it. Jody is overcome with emotion from the fact she actually loves him, and has a change of heart. He lets the prisoners go and is put under arrest.

Grey sees to it Jessie can free him and she does. Turning herself in, she expects to be arrested for complicity, but Grey says she saved the *Enterprise* twice and he owes her. Bo will now fight for the Texans and there is hope his reconciliation with his mother will heal past scars.

This was an interesting script, taking advantage of the earlier historical period in which Riverboat *is set. Most Westerns were usually placed in the early 1870's, so conflicts such as the war for Texas independence were a good way to differentiate the two.*

While, at first, a cargo of lead may seem trivial to the viewer, lead was actually one of the most important and lucrative cargoes a riverboat could transport. Lead mining at Galena did more to open the Upper Mississippi than nearly any other freight, passengers included.

Darren McGavin and Kevin Hagen stage a fight scene in front of an oft-used cord of wood. Note the production crew in the photo on the bottom. If this shot were used for publicity, the picture would have been cropped. Stills like these were also used for matching the actors so that various camera angles could later be edited into one smooth sequence.

Another still of Darren and Valerie Allen. Note the crew in the background and on the Enterprise *deck.*

The now-expected conflict between Grey and Ben continued. Frazer did not like the idea of Holden bringing bullet molds aboard to prepare the lead for immediate use and was nearly non-existent the rest of the hour.

The credit for musical score was given to Fred Steiner, and again, the score during the fight scene between Grey and Bo seemed inappropriate, almost jovial. This made it appear Bricken and Steiner were not on the same page or had conflicting views of the scenes that were meant to represent legitimate drama.

A plus to the episode was the rapport between McGavin and Mercedes McCambridge.

GUEST CAST

Mercedes McCambridge *(b. 3/16/1916, Joliet, IL; d. 3/2/2004, LaJolla, CA, natural causes.)* A radio actor before hitting the big screen, she created many memorable roles on the series *I Love A Mystery, Inner Sanctum* and *The Guiding Light* in the 1940's and 50's. She won an Academy Award for Best Supporting Actress in her film debut, *All the King's Men* (1949), and a nomination for *Giant* (1956). She performed the voice of the demon in *The Exorcist* (1973), and had to sue Warner Brother's because they originally failed to credit her for the role. She won, and new prints of the film had to be remade. In 1987, her only child, John Lawrence Fifield Markle, murdered his wife and children and then killed himself. Most of her episodic TV work was done in the 1960's.

Clu Gulager *(b. 11/16/1928, Holdenville, OK.)* Born William Martin Gulager and nicknamed for clu-clu birds, he is part Cherokee and is related to Will Rogers. Signed in the 1960's, this actor who never had fun acting appeared in hundreds of films and TV shows. He is most known for his work in Westerns (primarily as Deputy Emmett Ryker on *The Virginian*, 1964-68), but reinvented himself in the 1980's with such low budget films as *Nightmare on Elm Street, Part 2* (1985) and *The Return of the Living Dead* (1985).

Richard Gardner. Primarily a TV actor, his last credit was an episode of *The Invaders* in 1967.

Kevin Hagen *(b. 4/3/1928, Chicago, IL; d. 7/9/2005, Grants Pass, OR, esophageal cancer.)* The son of ballroom dancers, his father left when he was five and the family moved to Portland, OR. He served in the Navy and did not start acting until he was 27. Before that, he served in the US State Department in Germany, earning a degree in International Relations from the University of Southern California. His first credit was an episode of *The Gray Ghost* (1957). Usually cast as a heavy, this likable character actor had innumerable roles in Westerns, including *Gunsmoke* and the Warner Brothers slate of series. He appeared in two *Thriller* episodes, "Flowers of Evil" and "The Fingers of Fear." He is probably best known for the character of Dr. Hiram Baker on the series, *Little House on the Prairie* (1974-83). His last credit was in 1992 in an episode of *Amazing Stories*.

1.13 "Strange Request"............................ *December 13, 1959*
Directed by John Rich
Written by Clair Huffaker
Produced by Gordon Kay

Laurna Langton, famed actress, makes a strange request of Grey — she offers him $2,000 if he will immediately take the *Enterprise* upriver to Red Bluff. She is in a hurry and must leave right away, promising to explain her motives when the boat is underway. Captain Holden has only six men aboard, but the promise of easy money — and the thrill of transporting such a famous thespian and her agent, David Fields — on a well-paid adventure appeals to him and he accepts.

Also boarding the boat is a thug-type named Luke Cragg. It is clear from the outset that Cragg has nothing but contempt for Fields, calling him a "washed-up actor" living off a woman.

Once the *Enterprise* is underway, Laurna explains the rush. Six years ago, she and her husband, a schooner captain, were aboard his ship with their young son, Bobby. They were attacked by Indians and Mr. Langton was killed. The savages also stole her son and she has spent the intervening years advertising in St. Louis for anyone who has recovered a boy answering Bobby's description. She recently received a message from the Cragg family stating they have such a child but are unwilling to wait more than a short time for her to "pay up."

The boat arrives in Red Bluff and the Cragg family is introduced. They are a bunch of hillbillies, comprised of the father and four sons — Matthew, Mark, Luke and John. (TV hillbillies always seem to reproduce by parthenogenesis.) They are quick to talk business. The family group wants $5,000 for the boy, plus the $2,000 Laurna paid Grey to bring her to Red Bluff. Quick with their rifles, the sons keep Grey under guard as he and Laurna are introduced to the child.

Dressed in Indian garb with long hair, the boy is half wild. He barely speaks English and when Laurna tries to give him a peppermint candy he bites her. Grey speaks to him in Sioux, but he does not remember anything of his past life, so she has no proof he is really Bobby.

The Craggs take Grey aboard the *Enterprise,* planning on commandeering the boat. In a ridiculously easy ploy, Grey turns the gangplank on its side and the hillbillies tumble into the water. After they are rescued, he makes them work in the boiler room on the trip back to St. Louis.

Laurna cuts the boy's hair and dresses him in "white man's clothes," clearly responding to him in a loving way. But she makes it clear that if he is not Bobby, she wants nothing to do with him.

In order to facilitate his identification, Grey takes the child on a tour of the *Enterprise,* trying to elicit memories of his father's ship. Nothing works, but Grey is determined that even if he is not her son, he's a "nice kid," and she ought to adopt him.

The subplot involves Mr. Fields trying to dissuade Laurna from becoming attached to the boy. She has previously stated that if she finds Bobby, she will give up acting and devote her time to raising a son in the proper manner. Clearly, this runs counter to Field's best interests, as he has "devoted his life" to promoting her career.

When the boy starts to remember details — a yellow ship and white sails — Fields panics. He hits Carney over the head and frees the Cragg clan in an attempt to take over the *Enterprise*. Grey and Ben fight them off, and beat the staggering odds of two against six.

With everything in control, Grey brings the boy to the pilot house. Laurna begins singing a song she used to perform for Bobby when he was a baby, and when he remembers the lyrics, it is clear this really is her son.

"Strange Request" had all the ear-marks of a hastily written script and is a classic example of the strain of fleshing out an hour with a five-minute idea. Throw in hillbillies, the conflict of the Cragg clan trying to extort money, the take-over of the Enterprise, *the oft-used unscrupulous agent, the boy stolen by Indians and the actress willing to throw everything away for the sake of motherhood and the script represents a trite, thoroughly uncharming episode.*

Too many circumstances didn't work: the boy goes from savage to refined gentle-child between scenes. He suddenly started speaking (broken but fluent) English. The hillbillies were embarrassing. The agent's plight was shopworn. The conflicts over the Enterprise *being taken over were too easily solved. Grey's attempts to get Laurna to keep the boy even if he weren't Bobby were stock-in-trade and too similar to "The Boy from Pittsburgh."*

As before, the highlights of the episode came when McGavin had scenes with child actor Peter Lazar. Even with bland dialogue, Darren had a special rapport with children, clearly apparent here.

Of note, this is the first episode where Grey Holden's wardrobe changed. Until this point, he habitually wore a black shirt and a double-breasted navy jacket. In "Strange Request," he sported a white shirt, possibly so viewers could distinguish him from the bad guys if they hadn't already figured it out.

GUEST CAST

Jan Sterling *(b. 4/3/1921, Manhattan, NY; d. 3/26/2004, Woodland Hills, CA, from a series of strokes.)* Born into a wealthy family as Jane Sterling Adriance, her mother remarried and she was brought to Europe, where she was schooled in London and Paris. Developing a distinct British accent, she returned to New York, where she worked on Broadway for many years, primarily playing English characters. She appeared with Ruth Gordon in the 1942 production of *Over 21* and it was Ruth who urged her to change her name. She played beside Jane Wyman in *Johnny Belinda* and earned an Academy Award nomination for her work on *The High and the Mighty* (1954). She also worked the soap, *The Guiding Light* from 1969-70.

Rhys Williams *(b. 12/31/1897, Wales; d. 5/28/1969, Santa Monica, CA.)* A Welsh actor with an enormously familiar face and voice, he might most easily be recognized as playing Oates in *The Spiral Staircase* (1946) or Dai Bando in *How Green Was My Valley* (1941). He played Doc Burrage on *The Rifleman* (1959-60).

Lawrence Dobkin *(b. 8/16/1919, New York, NY; d. 10/28/2002, Los Angeles, CA, heart failure.)* He appeared in numerous feature films: *Patton* (1970) as Col. Gaston Bell; *The Ten Commandments* (1956) as Hur Ben Caleb; *12 O'Clock High* (1949) as Capt. Twombley, the group chaplain, but he will always be remembered for his role in the *Star Trek* episode "Charlie X" (1966).

Peter Lazer *(b. 4/12/1946, New York, NY.)* A child actor, his first credit was in an episode of *Robert Montgomery Presents* in 1953. His last credit was a *Felony Squad* episode called "Ordeal by Terror" in 1967.

Lee Van Cleef *(b. 1/9/1925, Somerville, NJ; d. 12/16/1989, Oxnard, CA, heart attack.)* He began his adult life as an accountant and served in the Navy aboard minesweepers during WWII. His first significant role came in the touring company of *Mister Roberts*, where he was discovered by Stanley Kramer and subsequently cast in *High Noon* (1952). Lee had one green eye and one blue eye and was missing the last joint of his middle finger. He became the most easily recognized of all celluloid villains and appeared everywhere in the heyday of the 1950's and 60's.

Glenn Thompson (d. 9/7/1983.) Another character actor/stuntman, most of whose accomplishments went uncredited. His last role was *The Silencers*, 1966.

1.14 **"Guns For Empire"**. . . . . *December 20, 1959*
Directed by Herman Hoffman
Written by Samuel A. Peeples
Produced by John Larkin

Captain Holden goes ashore, where he is set upon by thugs and dragged away, with orders from the boss that if they don't hear from him in four days, they are to kill Grey.

On the dock, a cargo is being brought aboard the *Enterprise*. Marked "farm tools," there are actually 500 rifles in the crates. It turns out Anthony Lorimer is smuggling guns. The Army has been watching him for months and now that they have found his cache, they are determined to make a case. A sergeant is sent with this message but Lorimer's henchman, Mr. Lansing, has the man murdered.

On the boat, it is revealed Ben has been dating a passenger named Rose. He thought their relationship was serious, only to discover she is not only familiar with Tony Lorimer but actually in love with him.

Ben refuses to put out until Captain Holden returns, but Lorimer reminds him they have a deal and he cannot wait for the captain to return. They are to steam 300 miles up the Red River to Lorimer City, where the namesake has established a colony. Ben remains obstinate and is informed that Grey is being held captive because he "might interfere with the plan." If they reach their destination in time, Grey will be set free.

In order to make the crew comply with orders, Lansing brings out a Gatling gun that he says he will use if they don't obey orders. Ben, Travis and Carney have a meeting and decide it is better to comply. In the meantime, Ben will try

Grey Holden saving the day with a Gatling gun from the episode, "Guns for Empire."

to find out where Grey is by getting the information from Rose.

She professes not to know and Lorimer explains his Grand Scheme: he is establishing an ideal community, where the settlers will be free from meddling politicians. He is a great man, a decider, and his rule will be law. He needs the guns to keep away any who would steal land (which he has stolen from the government).

In the boiler room, a steam gauge locks and the pressure builds, threatening to blow up the boat. Ben and Lansing fight, and Ben threatens to keep him in the boiler room, so they will all perish together. In terror, Lansing confesses that his plan is to kill Holden and the crew to keep them from interfering. At that moment, Carney unfreezes the gauge, the threat passes and Ben is forced to concede defeat.

Interspersed between scenes aboard the *Enterprise* are those of Grey being held captive in a shack. His jailers are bumbling idiots and he manages to free himself twice in two separate scenes, only to be recaptured.

Rose tells her story to Ben. She was raised along the river and made her way to New Orleans, where she "got along" working in saloons. It was there she met Lorimer, who took her away from her squalid life and promised to marry her. Ben accuses her of romancing him while really being a spy (presumably because she

was casing the boat prior to Lansing and his men taking it over), but she swears she believes in Tony's dream, and is only trying to make it come true.

When Rose tries to tell Tony that Lansing intends to kill everyone and ruin his plans, he makes a 180-degree turnaround and threatens to kill her, saying Lansing is more important to his plans than she is.

Rose tells Ben where Grey is being held captive and Ben jumps ship. He finds Grey and frees him, then the two return to the landing where the Gatling gun has been set out. Grey plays Tarzan, swinging on a rope to land beside the gun. He turns it on Lansing and his men and defeats them. Meanwhile, Rose and Tony quarrel in the dining room. They struggle over a pistol and the gun goes off. Lorimer staggers on deck where he falls over dead and Ben finds Rose where she fell, inexplicably killed by the same bullet that felled Lorimer.

The script ends with Grey remarking to Ben that he will get a medal for stopping the evil Lorimer and preventing the guns from reaching their final destination.

    This is the second episode to feature both McGavin and Reynolds and the first to give Reynolds a chance to really act. Unfortunately, most of his scenes were terrible, especially the fight in the boiler room, which reeked of bad acting by everyone involved. In fairness, the dialogue was atrocious, but the effect was nothing short of embarrassing.

    In fact, the episode featured poor acting by nearly everyone but George Macready, who did his best to play a megalomaniac.

This page, facing page: Two different angles of Darren McGavin posing with the Gatling gun. They provide a good look at the studio lot behind him.

Again, this script seemed overworked, with the action confusing and the time muddled. The character of Lorimer was wildly overdrawn and his emotional changes, as well as his motives and mad scheme, were unbelievable. The necessity of having a Gatling gun stretched credulity and seemed thrown in to add "flavor" to an otherwise unworkable idea. Lansing was the stock bad guy, not helped by casting Dennis Patrick in the role. Gena Rowlands seemed lost and barely made it through her scenes.

If regular viewers of Riverboat *are to go by what they see on the screen, then the year must have catapulted to 1879. The Gatling gun was not invented until 1862, and that version had six barrels. The one used by Holden had ten barrels. That style was not manufactured until 1879. Obviously, the director used whatever props were available — and it seems a petty point — but first, the idea of using a Gatling gun seemed over the top to begin with, and even the most elementary research would have made the writer aware that the gun was not invented until the decade after the series was supposed to be set.*

Ironically, the scenes with McGavin and Reynolds were the best to date. They appeared more comfortable together, without the usual contentiousness between characters and actors.

GUEST CAST

George Macready *(b. 8/29/1908, Providence, RI; d. 7/2/1973, Los Angeles, CA, emphysema)* Scarred on his right cheek from an auto accident, he achieved recognition as Rita Hayworth's husband in *Gilda* (1946). A U.S. gymnast, he claimed to be distantly related to the 19th century Shakespearean actor William Macready. A deep voice and distinguished personality always made him stand out, although his portrayal of Martin Peyton on *Peyton Place* (1965-68) is probably the one role for which he is known. He appeared in scores of TV episodes, most notably as Joe Smith on the episode of *Thriller* entitled "The Weird Taylor" (1961).

Gena Rowlands *(b. 6/19/1930, Madison, Wisconsin.)* A highly recognizable actress in the 1950's and 60's, she was married to John Cassavetes from 1954 until his death in 1989. Her work in *A Woman Under the Influence* (1974) and *Gloria* (1980) earned her Academy Award nominations for Best Actress. She played a recurring role in the TV series *Peyton Place*, playing Adrienne Van Leyden.

Dennis Patrick *(b. 3/14/1918, Philadelphia, PA; d. 10/13/2003, Hollywood, CA, house fire.)* Born Dennis Patrick Harrison, many of his character roles reflected his Irish heritage. He began his stage career at the age of eight in a production of *H.M.S. Pinafore*. He played a vampire in a 1950 episode of *Stage 13*, and then went on to play Jason McGuire and Paul Stoddard in the TV soap *Dark Shadows*. He also played Sheriff Patterson in the film *House of Dark Shadows* (1970) and appeared as Vaughn Leland in *Dallas* (1979-1984).

1.15 "The Face of Courage" . . . . *December 27, 1959*
Directed by William Witney
Written by Bob and Wanda Duncan
Produced by John Larkin

The story begins in St. Louis, where the *Enterprise* has taken aboard a contingent of soldiers, horses and ammunition. Their destination is Fort Union,

An action shot with Darren McGavin showing off the knife he wore sheathed behind his back. It was part of the costume change which occurred at mid-season.

"the last port on the Missouri." Captain Holden believes the trip will be nothing out of the ordinary until he witnesses a band of Indians following the riverboat. Sergeant Carmody, the officer in charge, reluctantly informs him there has been serious trouble with what Grey describes as "Stone Age savages." Holden is greatly angered that the true state of affairs wasn't made clear to him and threatens to cancel the contract at the first sign of trouble.

Going along for the ride are two women, expecting to get positions in the nearby dance hall and subsequently, husbands.

The first stop is Atkin's Landing, where Grey expects to take on wood. The settlement is deserted and an investigation soon reveals that all the people are in hiding. None of them want to help the crew load wood and Homer Atkins, a widower with a young daughter, explains that if Grey is transporting soldiers, that can only mean trouble. The Indians are on the rampage up north and with the added company of soldiers, there is likely to be war.

This convinces Grey to turn back and he offers to bring the settlers with him.

Another action shot taken on the studio lot credited to the episode "The Face of Courage."

They agree and start to board when the Indians attack. Men and women are killed, and the settlement is burned.

Among the settlers boarding are Joshua McGregor and a small boy named Chip. When Chip's dog is inadvertently left behind, Grey risks his life to save the spotted "Andy Jackson." He is then forced to tell Chipper that his parents "aren't coming," because they were among the ones killed.

After Grey informs a gravely wounded Sgt. Carmody that he is compelled to turn around, the soldier summons Corporal Simmons. He enjoins him to leave the boat and take dispatches to the commanding officer of Fort Union. The corporal breaks down and cries, stating he doesn't have the courage for such a mission.

Because of the importance of the dispatches and the need to re-supply the fort, Captain Holden changes his mind and determines to forge ahead. In a touching scene with Grey and Chip, the captain recruits the boy to help aboard the boat. Chip confesses that he would like to assist but he is afraid of Indians. Grey explains that it's all right to be afraid, but that when you're a man, you have to keep going. Corporal Simmons overhears this and resolves to be braver.

Joshua displays amazing talents, stating he fought in the War of 1812 and also did some trading with the Indians. This experience makes him invaluable and he, too, is recruited in the effort to help protect the *Enterprise*.

One passenger who won't fight is Homer Atkins. It is his belief that once before, when he raised his hands in violence against his fellow man, God punished him by having his wife die. Kitty, one of the saloon girls, overhears his protest and stands by him.

Because they do not have enough wood to fight the upstream current, Ben loses control and the steamer crashes into the bank. This puts them at the mercy of the Indians and their position is perilous.

Forced to take a party ashore to gather wood, Grey witnesses one of the Red Men doing a war dance to inspire the war party to courage. Afterwards, they attack and Travis is killed. His lifeless body is carried back aboard.

Feeling they cannot defend the boat, Grey gets the passengers ashore, and then orders Ben to burn the boat if it appears they will be overrun. Better that than allow the supplies to fall into enemy hands.

He has an idea how they might drive the Indians off but it requires an almost suicidal risk. Corporal Simmons volunteers to go with him, having found courage. They take a keg of gunpowder and plant it by the log where the Indian war chief performed his dance, hoping that by blowing him up, the rest will flee. Unfortunately, the medicine man dances on a different log and is too far away for them to kill. Simmons rushes up, grabs the keg with the lit fuse and hurls it at the Indian. Simmons is wounded, but, with Grey's help, succeeds in scaring away their enemy.

For his heroic effort, Corp. Simmons can now feel like a man and Grey earns the sobriquet, "Big Thunder" for the blast that scared away the Indians.

In a feel-good ending, Homer and Kitty ask Grey to marry them and the newly orphaned Chip becomes cabin boy aboard the *Enterprise*. Joshua, who also has the distinction of having served for two years aboard the Memphis Belle, is also hired as a new crewmember.

"The Face of Courage" might more accurately have been titled, "In With the Good, Out With the Bad." Apparently the producer, John Larkin, was not insensitive to McGavin's rapport with children and hoped that by introducing a boy to the family aboard the Enterprise, *he would give the series a warmer feel. He also changed the configuration of the crew by writing out William Gordon as Travis and introducing the multi-talented recurring character of Joshua McGregor, played by Jack Lambert.*

Ironically, the character of Travis typically had more lines and more screen time than any of the cast except McGavin. He appeared in 13 out of 15 episodes, including those featuring Burt Reynolds, and often served as pilot, making his sudden expulsion even more surprising.

The most outstanding (in a peculiar way) feature was the brief, nearly nonchalant way in which the authors chose to do away with Travis. Aside from an extremely minor scene when Carney reacted to Travis' death, absolutely nothing was made of his demise. Typically, when a series regular is written out, he either disappears into thin air or the producer takes the opportunity to milk the circumstance (in this case, the death) for

The boys of the Enterprise *pose with Joanna Moore, although neither one of them "got the girl" in the end.*

all it's worth. The fact Travis was killed and never mentioned again (not even given a tearful burial) underscores the idea they sacrificed poignancy for brute fact: he's out, the new characters are in. Take it or leave it.

Further complicating (confusing?) matters, Ben was conspicuously absent from the earlier fight scenes, making it clear the series was in flux, without any clear direction. This would continue to plague Riverboat *for eight more episodes, until a complete restructuring would take place.*

It is also interesting to note that in the main titles the three guest stars are listed as "Co-starring." This is the first time "co-starring" has been added.

GUEST CAST

Joanna Moore *(b. 11/10/1934, Americus, GA; d. 11/22/1997, Indian Wells, CA, lung cancer.)* A beautiful, likeable actress who made the rounds of such shows as *The Fugitive* and *Run For Your Life*, she was born Dorothy Cook. Orphaned as a child when her mother and younger sister perished in a car accident and her father died a year later from complications of the same accident, she won a beauty contest and went to Hollywood. Married to Ryan O'Neal, they had a very difficult relationship, in part because of her alcoholism and drug addiction. She is the mother of Tatum O'Neal. After a divorce in 1967, she disappeared from sight, later losing three fingers on her left hand from an auto accident. Her major roles were *Walk on the Wild Side* (1962) and *Son of Flubber* (1963.) She also played Sheriff Andy Taylor's girlfriend on *The Andy Griffith Show* in 1960.

Tom Drake *(b. 8/5/1918, Brooklyn, NY; d. 8/11/1982, Torrance, CA, lung cancer.)* Popular actor who worked from the 1940's into the 1970's, he played Bobby Drake in *Raintree County* (1957) and appeared with McGavin on an episode of *The Night Stalker*, playing Don Kibbey in the episode "The Energy Eater" (1974).

Doug McClure *(b. 5/11/1935, Glendale, CA; d. 2/5/1995, Sherman Oaks, CA, lung cancer.)* A seemingly ageless leading man, he earned fame as Trampus in the Western *The Virginian* (and later *The Men from Shiloh*). UCLA-educated, he started his career with uncredited roles in *Friendly Persuasion* (1956) and an episode of *Death Valley Days* in 1957.

Tracey Roberts *(b. 12/2/1914, Little Falls, NY; d. 2/8/2002, Los Angeles, CA.)* Born Blanche Goldstone, she adopted the stage name Tracey Roberts from two actors she admired: Spencer Tracy and Robert Montgomery. Her favorite film was *Actors and Sin* with Eddie Albert (1952). Never successful as an actor, she went into teaching, where she opened her own acting school. She taught, directed and produced many local productions. She made a number of TV guest star appearances and also appeared in the film *Queen for a Day*, with McGavin.

Paul Birch *(b. 1/13/1912, Atmore, AL; d. 5/24/1969, St. George, Grenada.)* The original "Marlboro Man," he began his career as one of the original members of the Pasadena Playhouse. He bore a resemblance to President Grant and often played him in film and TV roles. He also found himself frequently cast as General R.E. Lee and enjoyed the dual challenge of playing wartime opposites. He starred alongside William Campbell in the syndicated TV series *Cannonball* (1958) about over-the-road truckers. To fans of *The Fugitive*, his face immediately comes to mind when identified with his recurring character of Captain Carpenter, Lt. Philip Gerard's immediate superior.

1.16 "Tampico Raid". . . . . *January 3, 1960*
Directed by Richard H. Bartlett
Written by Richard N. Morgan
Produced by Richard H. Bartlett

The year: 1843. Forty miles off Tampico lay a Mexican prison called Diablo Corazon, meaning "Heart of the Devil." There, political prisoners who have run foul of the Spanish authorities are kept to rot.

So explains Captain Holden's opening narration. The Teaser reveals that several men and one woman are incarcerated and desperate to get out. Joanie Norris has a plan: the men cut a hole in the roof and she climbs through it to the outside. Jumping down, she scampers into the woods — and then surprisingly allows herself to be recaptured.

Act One begins in New Orleans. Grey is sending Chipper off to boarding school, explaining that he will be running produce up and back from Piquanto for the next several months so nothing exciting will transpire. As Joshua escorts the boy away, the same woman we saw in the Teaser approaches Grey, asking for passage. She does not have the $10 fare, so he refuses her

Later that day, she is seated around a bar table with Ben, Carney, Pickalong and Pickalong's pet monkey, Petie, trying to convince them to get her aboard the *Enterprise.* She explains that her father, a Frenchman who went through the French Revolution, and eleven others, had heard about a similar struggle in Tampico and traveled there in hopes of aiding the cause for freedom. Given ten more years they might have succeeded, but the Spanish authorities threw them in Diablo Corazon for their trouble.

Joanie explains that she was also a prisoner but escaped and let herself be recaptured so she could be brought to the Commandant. She offered him a bribe: let her go to America where she will raise $10,000. When she pays him off, he will let her father and the others go free. She intends to raise the money but not for a pay-off. Rather, she intends to put together an army and free them by force.

Pickalong, who also sings and plays guitar, regales the company while Carney suggests they can put up the passage fare for her. Ben has a better idea. If Grey will only hear her out, he will aid her cause.

The crew try to make the captain listen, but he flies off the handle and refuses. Although in the opening scene he would have taken her for $10, now he declares that he has had trouble with women. "They bat their eyelashes" at the crew and suddenly the boat is "driven into a reef." His attitude, Ben explains, is because "they have been robbed more than once by women," so he can't really be blamed.

Joanie pretends to be mugged on the dock and a produce fight ensues. Grey yells "Fire on the dock!" to get his men's attention and they break off, but not before Ben smuggles Joanie aboard.

Continuing the light-hearted mood, Grey complains that berries for his dessert have disappeared. Pickalong, the cook, feigns innocence, and then brings them to Joanie where she hides in the hold. Carney fetches her bedding and with Ben in attendance, they plot how they are going to help. She hides when Grey tracks down his missing crew, and then emerges to scream that they are only trying to help. Unmoved, Holden states she is just like Ellie Jenkins ("The Race to Cincinnati") and Laura Sutton ("Escape to Memphis" — called Laura Winters in the dialogue): both equated with "murder, mayhem and robbery." (An interesting pair, since he had "love affairs" with both.)

Ben is incensed when Grey orders him to put the stowaway ashore, and refuses. He owns a piece of the boat and that gives him a say. Grey retorts that he is still the captain and Ben threatens to sell out, which is all right with Holden. Grey relents, however, and agrees to hear Joanie out.

Holden takes Miss Norris to his cabin where she relates her goal: raise money, get up an army and save her father. She wishes Grey were more like Ben, so Grey challenges her by saying there is only one way to compare them — by kissing. They have a long kiss before she slaps him and they get into another shouting match.

When things calm down, Grey states there is no money to be raised in Piquanto because the crops are bad, leaving one to wonder why he was going there for the next several months to transport produce. Being the great schemer he is, however, he comes up with a plan. He has a gambler friend in New Orleans. If Joanie promises to split the profits, he will arrange a fundraiser for her. She agrees, and Grey admits that he knows her father so there is no reason for him to question her motives.

Meanwhile, Ben, Carney and Pickalong (whom we are told in a "thank you moment" is a cook who came aboard "three weeks ago" after they lost their previous cook) go ashore and blackmail the residents into giving them money for Joanie's cause. One sold Ben a bad compass; another sold them substandard cargo. They manage to extort an amazing $800 but succeed in running foul of the law. The sheriff wants them arrested but Grey pulls out of port, saving his crew.

Ben plans on repeating the same tactics all the way down the coast to Piquanto, but Grey points out the sheriff will ride ahead and tighten the purse strings. Nothing more is said of his scheme with the gambler (which would not have been affected by the extortion), but he comes up with another idea. They will steam all the way to Tampico and free the prisoners themselves!

This elicits a great gnashing of teeth as Ben protests he cannot navigate over the open water of the Gulf of Mexico and Joshua protests they could all get killed. But now Holden is the one who's hot on her cause and carries the day. Besides, he adds, there are 2,000 bales of cotton waiting at Galveston they can pick up on the way back, so it will be a profitable journey. (Presumably he is telepathic because he has had no outside communication about the cotton and if he knew it was there in the first place, why would he be wasting his time transporting produce from Piquanto, where the crops were bad?)

The weather turns foul. Interspersed with too many scenes of Petie, the monkey (adding a lilting effect to the episode which already featured too much), Grey has to save Pickalong, who has become frozen to his post somewhere inaccessible on the boat. He maneuvers down on a sling, unfreezes both crewman and valve (?) and saves the moment, if not the day.

Meanwhile, Joanie has gone goo-goo over Grey and fantasizes about being his "mate."

Miraculously, by the next scene the boat has reached their destination. Grey scales the wall of the prison, the crew follow, there is a fight and they manage to defeat two or three times their number. Then Grey breaks into the Commandant's office and has a sword fight with him, which he wins.

The prisoners are freed and the crew arrange for Joanie to nurse Grey (who hurt his hip in the sword fight) back to health, even if it takes weeks, even months! The script ends with Captain Holden howling in protest.

Richard N. Morgan, who did the story on "Race to Cincinnati" and both teleplay and story on "The Faithless" (two of the better Riverboat scripts), is given sole writing credit this time. He either needed the influence of other writers or must have been required to churn "Tampico Raid" out in an afternoon. Not only was the plot utterly implausible and filled with contradictions, the dialogue was uneven, even ludicrous, particularly that between the Mexican guards at the prison speaking high school Spanish. Grey's refusal to bring a woman aboard and his inexplicable turnaround were bad enough, but the "love story" had a "hide your head in a bag" feel.

Richard H. Bartlett produced and directed the episode and he should have left the direction to surer hands. He created a very uneasy mix of levity and seriousness and most of the scenes using doubles were obvious. The introduction of yet another two regulars, the monkey and the cook, called "Pickalong" (whom Lambert and occasionally Wessel persisted in calling "Piccolo") seemed ill-timed and awkward.

From here on out, the crew consisted of Ben (pilot), Carney (chief engineer), Joshua (man-of-many-talents-including-pilot), Chip/Chipper (boy), Andy Jackson (dog), Pickalong (cook) and Petie (monkey). The Enterprise now becomes a floating menagerie with too many animals, too many look-alikes (Carney and Pickalong) and too many accents (Carney, who mysteriously developed an Irish brogue and Joshua who used a Scottish one thick enough to cut with a knife). The series also advanced from July 1841 (episode 11, "The Boy from Pittsburgh") to 1843 (episode 16, "Tampico Raid") without explanation.

Worse for Bartlett, the acting in "Tampico Raid" was sub-par from top to bottom. Pat Crowley was especially weak (possibly from being misdirected), the actor cast as Pickalong (John Mitchum) unappealing (a fatal flaw in a series regular) and those cast as Mexicans shameful. Even in 1959, Bartlett could have found some native Mexican actors to play the parts with greater authority and authenticity.

Like the previous episode when the format was altered, the opening credit listed Pat Crowley as "Also Starring."

Of all the changes made (including Holden's wardrobe, where he now sported a pocket watch from his belt and a knife worn at the back), one glaring feature was carried over: the animosity between Grey and Ben. Again, they were on opposite sides for nearly the entire episode, becoming painfully obvious in the shouting match when Ben threatened to sell his share of the boat and Grey declaring himself the captain, who must be obeyed. With a few lines of dialogue changed, it would have been easy to imagine McGavin and Reynolds having a spat on the set.

On a historical note, the legal command order on Mississippi riverboats was not the same as on a sailing vessel. The captain had authority only while the boat was docked or maneuvering in or away from the wharf. Once the steamer was in open water, total authority fell on the pilot. He made the rules, he determined speed, course and whether the vessel pulled over at night or continued on during the hours of darkness.

Typically, "captains" were either "for hire" (earning a cut of the profits as well as a salary), or flat out owned the boat, and were little more than figureheads. On the river, they took orders from the pilot and by law, were not permitted to interfere. Grey's assertion, therefore, that as captain he had sole discretion to make decisions flies in the face of law and precedent.

GUEST CAST

Pat Crowley *(b. 9/17/1929, Olyphant, PA.)* Best known as Joan Nash in the TV series, *Please Don't Eat the Daisies* (1965) where she was billed as "Patricia Crowley," she usually played a strong woman character.

Edward Colmans *(b. 8/31/1908, England; d. 5/25/1977, Los Angeles, CA.)* Although born in England, he was usually cast as a Mexican or other "type." A sampling of his character names gives an idea what a casting director thought of him: Don Julio; "Hotel Clerk," "Spanish Priest," "Andrea Doria captain" (*Night Gallery*). Probably the most recognizable of his TV roles was as Professor Napolsky in the first season *Mission: Impossible* episode, "Short Tail Spy."

1.17 "Landlubbers" .... *January 10, 1960*
Directed by William Witney
Written by Tom Seller
Produced by John Larkin

The Teaser begins with Captain Klig and his men tearing the name off the *Enterprise,* replacing it with a new placard, identifying the boat as the *Dolphin.* He remarks that this will make it look as though the *Enterprise* had sunk and his boat, the *Dolphin,* is still intact.

Grey and Ben see the *Enterprise* adrift and race aboard. After a fight, they are dumped into the river. Captain Klig states it is now his boat and that Holden's steamer sank a month ago.

Grey had left three men aboard to guard the *Enterprise* while the rest of the crew were ashore, but all were murdered. This is the first and last time they will be mentioned, putting them in a category with the late, unlamented Travis.

Chip sees the placard of the *Enterprise* floating in the river and retrieves it. The crew must now travel overland, hoping to catch the steamer at Willow's Landing, 200 hundred miles by land and 500 by water.

The new crew of the *Enterprise:* Grey, Ben, Carney, Joshua, Chip, Andy Jackson, Pickalong, (Petie conspicuously absent) and Hoskins (the convenient, you-know-what's-going-to-happen-to-him crewman), gather for a pow-wow. Aside from Grey, none are overly anxious to travel overland, Pickalong complaining he was hired as a sailor. When offered the chance to back down, they reluctantly agree to participate in the venture and pool their resources, the bulk of their personal purses having been lost aboard the *Enterprise.*

With what money they have, Grey hires Barney Jones, a local, to be their guide. Before they set off, however, a woman named Miss Lanyon appears. She had booked passage to St. Louis and demands to be taken, even if that means by horse and wagon. Her urgent need to leave town is soon revealed in the person of Shag Ryan. It seems he bought her as a mail-order bride and considers her his property. He is determined to keep her at all costs, even murder. (At this point, if you were Hoskins, you'd consider a new livelihood, but he gamely carries on.)

The crew of the Enterprise *becomes "Landlubbers" as they attempt to catch up to their stolen riverboat.*

Privately, the not-so-trustworthy guide tells Shag the best way to get his woman back is to let him handle it. He is going to take the party through Echo Valley, an Indian burial ground. With a word of forewarning in the braves' ear, Barney anticipates they will murder the crew, while letting him and the woman escape. His treachery is explained by the fact Captain Klig paid him twice what Grey offered to make sure Holden & Company never make it to the refueling stop.

Darren McGavin's Grey Holden protects Gloria Talbott in "Landlubbers."

Pickalong entertains the group by singing in accompaniment with his guitar as they trudge along. Reaching Echo Valley, the crew see smoke signals and suspect trouble. Complicating matters, Ben has used his compass to determine they are going in the wrong direction if they intend to reach the river. (Presumably the sun never shone, explaining why the rest of the gang had no idea the direction in which they traveled.)

While Miss Lanyan tells Grey her life story, a huge boulder crashes down, nearly killing them. Afterward, the Indians attack and Hoskins complains of "ghosts." After surviving the attack, Grey trails Barney Jones and overhears him telling the braves the party desires to steal gold from their ancestors' burial sites, while he just wants to get away with the girl. Grey and Jones fight, Jones confesses his complicity and Joshua shoots and kills the guide.

This seems to put to rest the idea of ghosts, but just when they think the coast is clear — surprise — Hoskins gets an arrow in the back. Since it can't be Jones (he's dead) or Indians (they've left), it must be — ghosts!

Darren McGavin fights off Arthur Batanides and ghosts in "Landlubbers."

Andy Jackson goes missing (seemingly his best talent) and Grey goes off to the rescue. It turns out Shag Ryan has been shadowing them and has lured the dog away. Grey saves Andy, but they are now fearful lest Shag reappear out of nowhere and kill them before they reach the river. Miss Lanyon bravely volunteers to go back to him so the rest can live, but Grey gallantly refuses by saying his first responsibility is to his passengers, whether aboard the boat or on land.

They arrive at the wood stop just as the *Enterprise* steams up. Shag reappears and shoots Joshua. Grey performs surgery, and then stalks Shag. They fight; Shag wins and ties him up. Grey gets loose and kills Shag.

As the boat slows to a stop, Grey and Ben climb up the paddlewheel and get on board. The rest of the crew pretend to be bringing in wood and another fight ensues. Grey defeats Klig and determines to bring him to the authorities, where he will charge him with piracy and murder. They put the sign "Enterprise" back on the boat and throw the "Dolphin" overboard.

The story was actually a positive, but the implementation of it failed rather miserably. The death of Hoskins was nearly as predictable as Pickalong's singing, and this was only the second episode in which he appeared. The dialogue about ghosts came out of nowhere and was never really developed, so it seemed lame and a bit silly. The acting was generally good, although no guest star apparently merited being listed in the opening credits. The episode did feature some bad matching (not the first time), but no credit was ever given for script supervision.

Perhaps the most interesting point in "Landlubbers" was the fact that writer Tom Seller had Joshua shoot Barney Jones instead of letting Ben have the honors. This would seem to be a perfect set-up to feature the second-billed actor, but he was conspicuously absent.

GUEST CAST

Gloria Talbott *(b. 2/7/1931, Glendale, CA; d. 9/19/2000.)* Her great-grandfather founded the city of Glendale, where she grew up surrounded by the motion picture business. Her sister is Lori Talbott. Gloria founded her own dramatic play group and worked local clubs before breaking into the business proper. She made numerous TV guest star appearances and a number of low-budget horror films such as *I Married A Monster from Outer Space* (1958), *The Cyclops* (1957) and *Daughter of Dr. Jekyll* (1957).

Richard Devon *(b. 12/11/1931, Glendale, CA.)* He played Sgt. Alden in the TV series *Richard Diamond* (1959-60) and a recurring character in the syndicated *Space Patrol* in the 1950's. When he asked for a pay raise, his character was put in permanent suspended animation.

Kay E. Kuter *(b. 4/25/1925, Los Angeles, CA; d. 11/12/2003, Burbank, CA, pulmonary complications.)* Perhaps best known as playing the character Newt Kiley on *Petticoat Junction* (1964-70) and *Green Acres* (1965-70), he spent the latter part of his career doing voice-overs for commercials and films. He was the voice of the Hershey's Kisses commercials for 14 years and did character voices, including Grimsby on *Little Mermaid II* (2000).

Arthur Batanides *(b. 4/9/1922, Tacoma, WA; d. 1/10/2000, Los Angeles, CA, natural causes.)* A well-versed character actor, he made four *Police Academy* films playing Mr. Kirkland, the last in 1989, which also happened to be his last film. Appearing in hundreds of TV shows, he played D'Amato on the *Star Trek* episode "That Which Survives" (1969). He made several episodes of *The Wild, Wild West*, including "The Night of Miguelito's Revenge," and made two episodes of *Twilight Zone*, "The Mirror" and "Mr. Denton on Doomsday" (1959; playing Leader.)

Jerry O'Sullivan *(b. 3/6/1889, Pennsylvania, PA; d. 3/16/1978, Orange County, CA.)* Credited with only five TV appearances and three films, *Springfield Rifle* (1952), *Pickup on South Street* (1953), and *North to Alaska* (1960), all of which went uncredited.

Frank Warren. Probably best known for playing the recurring character of Art on *The Andy Griffith Show* (1961-62), he had few credits other than several episodes of *Sea Hunt* (1958-59).

1.18 "The Blowup"................................. *January 17, 1960*
Directed by Darren McGavin
Written by Al C. Ward
Produced by John Larkin

Two men are driving a wagon into town. A keg rolls off and explodes.

In town, Miss Martha Crane has hired Mr. Simon to help her ship a cargo of gunpowder. This peculiar substance is very unstable and liable to blow up at any time. He is concerned Captain Holden will put up an objection, but she gives him a knowing smile. "Leave him to me," she remarks and goes off to set the stage for Grey's acquiescence.

The crew of the *Enterprise* has gathered in the local watering hole. Ben, Joshua, Grey and Pickalong (sans Petie) are at the bar and Carney, already drunk, sits alone at a table. Miss Crane waltzes in (a shocking action for a lady in the 1800's, yet they accept this, although this is not the first time a female has done so on *Riverboat*), and begins flirting with Carney. Using his on-again, off-again Irish brogue, he happily obliges. This is the cue for four thugs (hired by Simon) to get fresh with her. Carney eagerly comes to her rescue and a fight ensues.

Grey smashes one of the brawlers over the head with a chair and comes up, face-to-face with the marshal. This abruptly ends the contest.

Back on the *Enterprise*, Grey complains that he is the only one freed, while the rest of his crew is in jail. Miss Crane happily informs him that she can testify his men did not start the melee and volunteers to pay their fines. She also generously offers Captain Holden a $5,000 fee for transporting 24 kegs of gunpowder 100 miles up the Arkansas River. When he expresses surprise, she explains it is for her father's work. He accepts, with the comment, readily believable, that she need not have gone to all the trouble of instigating a fight to secure his cooperation.

In a nicely staged but surprisingly protracted scene, shot upward from ground level to the outside balcony of a tall building, Grey spanks Chip, who hollers his lungs out. He is being punished for running away from Miss Wilkin's Boarding School. Dragged inside, Chip explains that he wants to go along on this voyage. The captain has "the itch," however, a reference to danger, and decides it is best the boy stay behind to get his education as a gentleman. Andy Jackson, however, is permitted to go. As they will only be gone a week to ten days, Chip shouldn't have long to wait for their return.

Boys being boys, Chip promptly stows aboard, sitting on the arm of the paddlewheel and waving good-bye to Miss Wilkins as the boat departs.

Affecting stealth, he scurries across the deck, inadvertently knocking over one of the kegs of gunpowder. It immediately begins to smoke. Simon sees the phenomenon and starts screaming. Grey assesses the problem and tosses the keg overboard. It sinks underwater but still explodes with tremendous force.

Shouting that the powder is ten times more powerful than ordinary gunpowder, Captain Holden threatens to throw the lot into the river. Miss Crane carefully explains he cannot: the substance will explode even when wet and cause great damage.

Joshua, the-man-who-knows-everything, has seen something like it years before. An army engineer developed a very powerful explosive but it proved highly unstable and unpredictable. Sometimes it could not be ignited and at others, for no apparent reason, it self-ignited and blew up. To substantiate his point, he rips the cover off the keg, revealing: US Army Ordnance" and across it, the word "Condemned."

This places Grey in an untenable situation. He can't dispose of the powder in the water for fear of having a keg harm a passing boat and he doesn't want it aboard. Joshua wisely advises him to "trust to luck."

In a comfortable, enjoyable scene, Chip explains to Grey, Ben and Carney how he escaped Miss Wilkins' clutches and is sent to his quarters to contemplate his sins while the rest laugh at his expense. This is broken short by Joshua's appearance. He announces they cannot stop for wood because if they do, the crew will mutiny. They are afraid of being killed and have no intention of staying aboard. Carney and Ben go off to argue with the boiler men while Joshua takes a stiff drink.

He, too, is "scared stiff" of dying. He explains to Grey that as a "Salem man," his dream has always been to buy some land, put down roots and have a wife waiting for him at the end of the day. Grey tries to comfort him and suggests he hold onto that dream.

Miss Crane apologizes to Grey for putting him in a bad position and he is uncharacteristically sympathetic. Her father is a wonderful man, a mining engineer, and it is he who needs this special powder for his operations. "That's all you need to know," and apparently it's good enough.

Unsatisfied by Carney, the crew confront Grey and demands to be put ashore. In a good, well-played scene, Captain Holden stares them down and refuses their demands.

Nothing else of consequence happens and the *Enterprise* pulls into the camp landing. No one is there to greet them and it is soon apparent why: the miners have all been murdered, each shot over twenty times. The site has been raided, the money to pay Grey stolen and the map to the mine taken. This is tragic news but Grey takes it calmly. He will simply get the powder off the boat and get away as soon as possible.

Miss Crane steals a pair of Grey's pants, four kegs of powder and two horses. When Grey realizes she's missing, he, Joshua and Carney go after her. She isn't hard to catch and when he tries to take her back, she reveals the true secret. Her father discovered a diamond mine halfway up the Mount Everest of Arkansas. She is determined to mine the precious stones herself and offers each man a generous share of the profit.

In an interesting scene not typical of a TV series featuring regular characters, Carney and Joshua break with Grey. Each has a great desire to become wealthy, Carney so he can be somebody and Joshua so he can buy his land and fulfill his dream. Grey observes that Joshua would fight him over the chance for riches. Not above a taste for wealth himself, he gives in to their demands.

Carney is sent back to the boat with orders not to tell anyone of their find (including Ben). In his place comes the hapless Jimmy to help scale the mountain and carry one of the four kegs. Like poor Hoskins before him ("Landlubbers"), it's no secret he's the one to be sacrificed to the gods of television drama.

Progressing up the mountain, the party come upon the body of a Mexican, shot twenty times, like the miners. They identify him as the brother of the infamous bandito, Juan Miguel. This explains who killed Mr. Crane and the miners at the camp site. It bodes trouble because the Mexicans have the map and a head start, but the intrepid band push on.

Tied to one another by safety rope, they scale the barren heights, precariously clinging to nearly invisible finger-holds. At one point Jimmy slips and Mr. Simon, Miss Crane's "bad luck piece" cuts him free, sending the crewman to his death. Undeterred, they proceed, bumping and banging the powder kegs strapped to their backs. Fortunately for the continuance of *Riverboat*, none explodes.

The team finally reach the heights and success is before them. But lo and behold, the Mexican gang appears and covers them with rifles. They are looking for gold but so far, haven't found the hidden mine opening. "Simon the Craven" bargains for his life, telling the banditos it isn't a gold mine, but contains untold riches in diamonds. Juan Miguel is unconvinced. He doesn't want "glass that shines," he wants gold.

Fearing the murderers will kill them all with ill-placed powder kegs, Simon attempts to escape and is shot in the back. In the confusion, Grey manages to get a gun and the outlaws hide in the cave. Not a good idea, as it turns out, for

Grey fires on a keg. It explodes, trapping the men inside and thus putting an end to their glorious careers.

Miss Crane still has a beautifully cut diamond the size of a walnut, so all is not for naught.

Back aboard the boat, Carney laments his lost chance and Joshua frets over the land he cannot buy. Grey cheers him up by the stiff upper-lip admonition to "hang onto his dreams."

If you can buy the idea of mysterious, unstable gunpowder that explodes at will with ten times the force of regular explosives, a barren mountain the height of Everest in Arkansas, and a diamond mine in the clouds, "The Blowup" had a lot going for it. Most of its strengths, however, came from characterization and some superb directing.

Darren McGavin directed and it was clear from the outset he had a feel for what Riverboat *could really be. The scenes with Chip (overlooking the protracted spanking) were top notch, warm and heartfelt. More importantly, McGavin, himself, given a chance to emote, shone throughout the episode, putting in, by far, his best performance to date. The scene where he stared down a mutinous crew was outstanding and the continuing interplay with Joshua — his fear, his dreams and his subsequent disappointment — were remarkable.*

Director McGavin also managed to make the trek up the mountainside tense and believable, not an inconsequential feat, considering he had only a backdrop and an interior to bring to life. The fight scenes in the bar and against the banditos were better than average and well put together, easily glossed over the more awkward plot. In fact, if writer Al C. Ward had abandoned the mine altogether and concentrated on the danger of the kegs exploding aboard the Enterprise *and the crew's personal desire for riches, this might have been the one gem in the series.*

Historically, it is interesting to note that in the 1840's, insurance companies excluded payment for damages due to gunpowder explosions. If Holden had the boat insured, he ran the risk of being unable to collect and being ruined if the kegs had gone off.

As usual, Burt Reynolds had little, if anything, to do. His absence during the second half of the episode when the party climbed the mountain was glaring, and the few scenes he had were more throw-aways than substantive. It might have been more interesting to see his reaction to a diamond mine and get his reaction to balancing wealth against improbable odds. But that was not where the series was going, and it suffered for it. Clearly, at this stage, Joshua was emerging as the primary co-star, with Carney getting more than his fair share of screen time. Mike McGreevey more than held his own as Chip, and by the fourth episode in which he appeared, had already proven both he and his character filled a sorely needed hole aboard the Family Enterprise.

GUEST CAST

Whitney Blake *(b. 2/20/1925, Eagle Rock, CA; d. 9/28/2002, Edgartown, MA, cancer.)* Real name Nancy Whitney, she worked out of the Pasadena Playhouse, and then graduated to TV roles. She guest starred in the premiere episode of *Perry Mason* (1957). With her husband/writer, Allan Manings, she created the sitcom *One Day at a Time* (1975). She will always be remembered for playing "Mrs. B" in the comedy *Hazel*, starring Shirley Booth (1961). Singer Whitney Houston was named after her; she was the mother of actress Meredith Baxter.

Dean Harens *(b. 6/30/1920, South Bend, IN; d. 5/20/1996, Van Nuys, CA.)* His career began in 1944 with a small film role in *Christmas Holiday*. He went on to play Noel Clinton on *General Hospital* (1965) and Dr. Charles Fuller on *The Brighter Day* (1960-61). He also played a recurring role on *The F.B.I.* as SAC Bryan Durant (1967-69).

Carlos Romero *(b. 1927.)* A familiar face in TV Westerns, he appeared as a Latin character in most of the popular series throughout a prolific career. He played a recurring role in *Zorro* as Sgt. Serrano. His last credit was an episode of *L.A. Law* (1989).

James R. Scott. *Riverboat* is his only listed TV appearance. Small roles in several films of the 1950's, all uncredited, round out his career.

John Day (aka John Daheim) b. 6/22/1916, Minnesota, MN; d. 9/22/1991, San Diego, CA.) Another nameless character actor whose contributions usually went uncredited, he appeared in hundreds of minor roles, many non-speaking. He frequently did stunt double work in films and TV.

1.19 "Forbidden Island" . . . . *January 24, 1960*
Directed by Sidney Lanfield
Written by Bob and Wanda Duncan
Produced by John Larkin

   A sister and brother team of Carolyn and Raoul Dupres are planning to attack the *Enterprise*. Unknown to them, a river pirate named Garnett is close on their heels with a scheme of his own.

   While the crew takes on wood, Captain Holden warns Joshua to beware of Cajuns. These bandits sank the Louisville Belle yesterday and he doesn't want any trouble. Ben, in the pilothouse, is also nervous.

   Despite this forewarning, the Cajuns row up to the boat in broad daylight, board and quickly subdue the crew. They demand and take the cargo belonging to Mr. Johnson, of Baton Rouge, Louisiana, before departing. It appears the theft will be accomplished without bloodshed, but immediately afterward, shots are fired. "Willie," only 18 years old and on his first voyage, is killed, along with another unnamed crewman. Grey wants revenge for the loss of $3,000 worth of cargo "and that," referring to the dead men.

   In Baton Rogue, he offers a $100 reward for anyone who can guide him to "Forbidden Island," where the Cajuns hide out, all the time wondering why the

Dupres gang took only that merchandise owned by Mr. Johnson. He doesn't get an answer but Grey does receive a threat from Johnson: either pay him the $3,000 or he will slap a lawsuit on him and sell the *Enterprise.*

Grey arranges a meeting with a man willing to take him to the Dupres family stronghold. While he waits, Garnett (a famous pirate, but unknown to Holden) approaches with a deal. If he supplies the men and Grey the boat, he will lead an expedition to the island. Grey refuses, finding it too dangerous and Garnett,

Darren McGavin and Pat Michon taking direction in the episode "Forbidden Island."

leaves but not before another thug secretly steals Grey's watch which he wears hanging from his belt.

While Pickalong sings with Petie at his side, Garnett goes to the riverboat and demands to see Ben. He lies, telling him Holden wants the *Enterprise* to maneuver through the swamps with his men on board so they can attack the Cajuns. As proof, he offers Grey's watch. Ben must believe him and they set out on this dangerous mission.

The guide (who turns out to be one of the Cajuns) brings Grey to the stronghold. He is met by Carolyn and Raoul, who tie him up. She haughtily explains she and her people only steal to buy food. The Cajuns are originally from Nova Scotia, having immigrated to Baton Rogue fifty years before. Two years ago, there was a great fever and many died. They mortgaged their farms to Johnson to pay for supplies. They were supposed to have five years to pay off the loans, but Johnson foreclosed after two years. This is why they stole only his cargo.

Aboard the *Enterprise* (in a scene destined to raise expectations that are never fulfilled in this episode), Ben confesses to Joshua that his father has recently died. His mother is taking the death hard and wants him to come home. He hasn't told Grey and wonders what to do. Joshua (less than helpfully) remarks that Ben must make up his own mind about leaving.

Garnett's idea is to have the crew of the *Enterprise* and the Cajuns kill each other off. He drives the boat into a riverbank and orders everyone out for the big confrontation.

Garnett's men open fire. Carolyn determines it is Garnett who has come to kill them and tells Grey that the pirate has been raiding riverboats for years and wants their island as a hiding place. She lets him loose and they go out to fight the pirates, unaware that Grey's crew is with them.

After a shootout, Grey realizes what is happening and calls a halt to the battle. Before they can recoup, however, Garnett appears and brags that it was his men who sank the Louisville Belle and blamed it on the Cajuns. He kills Raoul and locks the crew in a cabin. The pirates prove no better at standing guard than the *Enterprise* crew, for the boys knock out a portion of the wall and escape.

They manage to bypass even more guards, steal aboard the boat and regain possession. After pushing away from the mud bank, the boat returns to Baton Rogue. Johnson shows up with the authorities and a court order attaching the *Enterprise* for non-payment of debt. Grey makes a deal: if he recovers the cargo from the Belle, Johnson must accept it in exchange for a clean slate, wiping out Holden's debt and also allowing the Cajuns to go free.

After a nicely played but gratuitous scene with Chip, who once again stowed aboard, the *Enterprise* returns to Forbidden Island. Holden and the boys pick off the pirates one-by-one until only Garnett is left. While the pirate deserves to be taken to trial, convicted and hanged, Grey and Carolyn decide to abandon him alone on the island. He can't get off and no one will ever rescue him. Garnett crumples at this fate and begs to be taken off, to no avail. He's left there and there he will stay.

Aside from the teaser of Ben threatening to leave, the episode is forgettable. The guest stars (none of whom warranted a name in the title credits) were only so-so and the plot seemed repetitious and drawn out. There were too many fight scenes and too little substance, evoking no emotional response from anyone. For the third episode in a row, the Enterprise *loses crewmembers, which is a pretty high mortality rate. The series had also bilked the riverboat pirate idea too often to make this episode stand out. The idea of the Cajuns' plight was interesting, but not developed in a manner to arouse sympathy.*

It also stretches credulity that Holden did not know the name and face of a pirate raiding riverboats "for years," or have any previous knowledge of Cajuns living on a private island.

Additionally, it is questionable whether Holden could be held legally responsible for the loss of cargo taken at the hands of thieves. Shippers in the 1840's and '50's were required to insure their merchandise as protection against loss from river accidents or robbery, not go after the boat's owner.

Of note, for the first time the end credits, which traditionally combined the series' regulars and guest stars, has the heading "The Crew of the "Enterprise." In order, they were Dick Wessel, Jack Lambert, John Mitchum and Mike McGreevey.

GUEST CAST

Miguel Angel Landa. As his name suggests, he was usually cast as a Mexican or a Spaniard, with character names such as Miguel (*High Chaparral*), El Magnifico (*The Beverly Hillbillies*) and Pepe (*Gunsmoke*). Many of his later credits are Spanish language films.

Patricia Michon. Also billed as Pat Michon, she often played French or foreign characters. One of her better roles was as Yvette Dulane in an episode of *Thriller* (1961) entitled "The Prisoner in the Mirror."

Patrick Westwood. An actor primarily working in British productions or playing foreign characters, he appeared in an episode of *The Avengers*, entitled "Stay Tuned," and in *Space: 1999* as Hubert Daley, and as Dr. Shaw in "The Bringers of Wonder" on that series. He appeared in *Pit and the Pendulum* (1961) as Maximillian the butler.

1.20 **"Salvage Pirates"** . . . . *January 31, 1960*
Directed by Richard H. Bartlett
Written by Richard N. Morgan
Produced by Richard H. Bartlett

Over the scene of a schooner crashing into a reef, Captain Holden's narration states that, while times may be bad for some, everything is very well with the *Enterprise*. The boat is in the Gulf of Mexico near Cat Island, just returning from a trip to the west coast of Florida, where they had picked up a load of alligator hides. He figures this will be the most profitable trip he has ever made since first taking over "the old girl."

Pickalong and Petie are teaching Chip nautical terms and Joshua is piloting the boat. A youth joins him and identifies himself as Terry Blake. Although serving as a boiler man on this voyage, his father was a sea captain on a sailing ship and he has been on the water since he was a boy. Grey gave him permission to come up and watch. He immediately observes that the channel light warning of reefs is out of place.

The scene cuts to the schooner. A man and a woman have survived the crash. Jacques Termain sees the *Enterprise* and knows they will be rescued. He warns Louise, with whom he is ostensibly in love, to make up a story to their rescuers. She is to say her dowry went down with the ship and her father will pay the riverboat captain for salvaging a chest of pearls.

Grey jumps into the cold water and swims over to the survivors. He takes Louise back with him but in so doing, his hip "popped out" again and he is unable to stand. Lying on the deck, he and the crew listen to the story Louise tells. If he manages to collect the chest of pearls (worth $40,000), her father will give him anything else he manages to take off the wreck.

Grey points out that they are hardly in position to salvage the cargo as they have no tackle, but Carney leads the crew in protest. If they get equal shares of what's recovered, they are all for trying the operation.

Jacques refuses to leave the wreck because if he stays on it, that gives him first salvage rights. Holden sends Pickalong over to join him so both the mate and the *Enterprise* establish their claim. Holden will steam to New Orleans, hire a salvage vessel and return.

An obstacle immediately turns up. In the vicinity is a barge already carrying tackle. Joshua presumes the captain of that vessel moved the channel light to deliberately sink the ship and Grey remarks he has heard of a boat prowling these waters with just such a reputation.

Pickalong and Jacques perform dueling songs as Joshua and the crew row behind the barge with the intention of taking control. While they maneuver into place, the barge captain and his first officer try to lure Pickalong and Jacques off the wreck. When they refuse to leave, he shoots holes in their escape boat, forcing them to abandon the position. They swim over to the barge just as Joshua leads the attack. They are successful and Pickalong (again called "Piccolo" by Joshua) demands the pirates all be shot for luring unsuspecting ships to their doom. Joshua prevails and settles for tying up the crew after Mr. Savage, the barge captain, cravenly begs for his life.

Back aboard the *Enterprise,* the crew do not want to leave for fear the pirates will take advantage of their absence and ransack the schooner. However, the wreck is too deep for swimmers to hold their breath long enough to recover the treasure. Grey remarks that when he was in Boston (referencing his history of having come from Massachusetts in "The Boy from Pittsburgh"), he learned of a diving helmet that supplied air to divers. He thinks they can manufacture one aboard the *Enterprise* if anyone is brave enough to try. Terry Blake volunteers. If he succeeds, Grey promises he can become a cub pilot.

Terry also knows about craftsmanship and he helps forge two helmets. Other crewmen prepare bellows which will be used to force air through hoses into the helmets. The complicated and intricate tasks are completed within a short time and the boys try them out. Taking a waterproof lantern with them (!), they dive into the wreck. Everything works perfectly, but the helmets prove too bulky for the divers to maneuver through the wreck and they nearly drown in the cramped space.

While a new plan is considered, Jacques tells Louise he does not want to go back to sea. He wants the pearls so he can be rich. He and Louise lied about the fact the pearls constituted her dowry; actually, she is nothing but a serving girl who fell in love with him on the voyage. But if they can make this work, they may have a successful marriage.

Meanwhile, the barge pirates free themselves and decide to bring aboard a cannon they have waiting in the wings. They plan on blasting the *Enterprise* to bits and then recovering the wreck. After bringing the hardware aboard, however, they decide not to use it because the *Enterprise* also has a cannon (!) and they don't want to get into a shooting match.

With Grey in his quarters, he calls for Louise and quizzes her about her fiancée. She makes up a name on the spot: James Kincannon. The name sounds familiar and he consults the New Orleans "Blue Book" for further identification. Meanwhile, Terry and Jacques decide to abandon the helmets and use only the hoses for air. With the boys working the bellows, they try again and recover the chest.

Now that they have what they want, Joshua decides on some revenge. He sets a keg of powder out on a rowboat and settles it alongside the schooner. When the pirates try to haul it up with their block and tackle the keg explodes, presumably sinking the barge. They all have a belly laugh over this misadventure and declare that no one will try to alter the channel light again.

As the *Enterprise* steams into New Orleans, Jacques and Louise decide to escape so they won't have to share the pearls. Joshua and Carney stop them, however, and the woman is brought to Grey. He has figured out their scheme ("Kincannon" was the owner's name on the chest) and calls them liars. He declares full ownership of the pearls and has them locked up.

In New Orleans, Grey has Mr. Kincannon brought aboard and introduces him to Louise. Kincannon is an old man and clearly not her intended. Kincannon wants his property returned and hard bargains with Grey. In an act of generosity, Holden demands $1,000 for the lovers and $20,000 (half the value) for himself.

In the final scene, the crew, led by Carney, come into the captain's quarters and demand their shares. They can't wait for Kincannon to return because they want to go out and get drunk. When Grey protests he can't get up and walk to the safe, Joshua offers to crack it. On Holden's astonished interrogative, "What kind of a crew do I have?", Joshua retorts that whatever they are, he picked them. On their hearty laughter, the episode ends.

In this episode, Burt Reynolds has been removed from the opening credits and his name does not appear at the end titles. Under the newly established "Crew of the Enterprise*," the names listed now read: Jack Lambert, Bart Patton (Terry Blake), Mike McGreevey, Dick Wessel and John Mitchum. This clearly represents a total reevaluation of the series and the actors' standing. Reynolds is written out (his absence is not explained), Lambert and McGreevey move up, Patton is introduced and given second billing under Lambert, and Wessel is moved down.*

"Salvage Pirates" clearly demonstrates Joshua's new importance as he and Carney dominate the episode, having the bulk of dialogue and screen time.

The plot was interesting but again far-fetched, particularly in the fact the crew had the wherewithal to create diving helmets in a matter of hours. That said, most steamboats of the 1840's and 50's carried blacksmithing equipment with them in case of emergencies, so it is hard to believe but not inconceivable they could have rigged the helmets. The time factor is a problem, as were the breathing tubes. It was a common technique among television writers to use this device to save a star from drowning as late as the James Bond films, but the truth is, they don't provide enough oxygen.

"Salvage Pirates" had the look and feel of being uneven. Much of it was a throwaway; certainly the effort of the pirates to bring up a cannon, and not use it, stood out like a sore thumb. The excuse, "the Enterprise *also has a cannon," was not only dropped out of thin air, it was certainly inaccurate. If riverboats carried armament, they were used for ceremonial rather than aggressive purposes. The character of Jacques was also extremely unlikable, written more as a callous money-grabber than a legitimate lover.*

Perhaps the most glaring feel of the episode, however, is the prevailing callousness. Jacques and Louise are completely untouched by the grievous loss of life aboard the schooner. The Enterprise *crew, which first refused to shoot the pirates, end up blowing them to smithereens and having a good laugh over it. They are also unabashedly greedy, which, although a theme already developed in previous episodes (see "The Blowup"), does not make them likeable in any way, shape or form. The tag, when they stated the desire to romp around New Orleans, also leaves a bad taste. While not questioning the fact men are greedy and like their shore leave, it is hard for a TV viewer to develop any appreciation or loyalty for them.*

It is also interesting to note that with Reynolds gone, all the regulars (except Chip, the boy) are older men lacking physical attractiveness. None of them were likely to challenge McGavin as the male lead. The newest member, Terry Blake, is a handsome youth, but more of a bridge between McGavin and the Lambert/Wessel/Mitchum trio than Reynolds was.

GUEST CAST

Judi Meredith *(b. 10/13/1936, Portland, OR.)* Born Judith Clare Boutin, she was a child skater, performing in the Ice Follies until a series of accidents brought her into acting in 1956, when George Burns discovered her in a play and gave her a role in his show, where she played Bonnie Sue McAfee (1957-58). She made several episodes of *Ben Casey* (1966). Her last credit was an episode of *Emergency* (1972).

Richard Garland *(b. 7/7/1927, Mineral Wells, TX; d. 5/24/1969.)* Former husband of actress Beverly Garland, he played Constable Clay Horton on *Lassie* from 1954-56. While working primarily in TV, he appeared in *Attack of the Crab Monsters* (1957) as Dale Drewer and *Mutiny in Outer Space* (1965) as Col. Frank Cromwell.

Bern Hoffman *(b. 2/17/1913, Maryland; d. 12/15/1979, Sherman Oaks, CA.)* His forte appears to have been playing bartenders, for that character designation appears by Hoffman's credits for *Bonanza* (several times), *Dirty Sally*, and *High Chaparral*. His last appearance was on *Starsky and Hutch*, in 1975.

Johnstone White *(b. 8/4/1892, Oregon; d. 4/7/1969, Los Angeles, CA.)* Very few credits; his first known was in the film *Princess O'Hara* (1935). The *Riverboat* role was his last listed work.

1.21 **"Path of the Eagle"** . . . .*February 1, 1960*
Directed by Jules Bricken
Written by Halsey Melone
Produced by Jules Bricken

The scene: Independence, Missouri. The cast: Grey, Joshua and Chip, all dressed up in their Sunday best. Grey is in a surly mood and when he inadvertently bumps into a man hiring drivers for overland wagon trains, the two quarrel. Holden wins the fight, but cries, "Why did it have to happen here, right on this spot?" The "spot" he indicates is a marriage parlor.

Back on the *Enterprise*, Joshua observes that the captain is sore at the "muddy little town" each time they come. If he didn't know better, he would suspect Grey had a woman on his mind. He retorts, "Not a woman - a lady," and that sets the stage for a flashback which comprises the rest of the episode until the end.

The time: a year ago (before he met either Joshua or Chip). The place: Kingsport, in southern Illinois. The opening narration states that Holden is hauling freight in one of the best deals he ever made, but encounters unexpected opposition.

Aboard the boat, a man is seen escaping the *Enterprise* just as an explosion rips the vessel. The scene cuts to a mansion where two men, Henry Schofield and Gideon Templeton are talking. They are planning a grand expedition through Independence, Missouri, and then on to St. Louis, where their party of wealthy individuals plan on joining a wagon train to California. Schofield is in opposition, and later pleads with Templeton's daughter, Marion, not to cash in her $40,000 worth of bonds to stake her father's participation in the venture. As a dutiful daughter, she remains obstinate. If papa needs her money and support, she is all for the trip.

Bad luck seems to plague the party from the start, however, as a newspaper headline proclaims, "Boiler explosion destroys *Enterprise*." Templeton had chartered the steamer to take them to St. Louis and now he must make other

Beginning with "Path of the Eagle," Riverboat was moved to Monday night, in the 7:30–8:30 time slot. Numerous publicity stills — some of which actually made it to the newspapers — were taken. The ones with McGavin alone are easier to read, but the full shots give a better view of the riverboat in the background. The idea was a clever one, for riverboat captains used chalkboards or, in this case, large crates, to advertise their fares and shipping rates. Since Jack Lambert and Mike McGreevey, holding his dog, Andy Jackson, were to be featured, they were included in the shoot. Conspicuously absent, of course, is Burt Reynolds, who was already written out of the series.

arrangements. His assistant, Stephen Barrows, suggests another boat and arranges to have the captain brought in for an interview.

Grey and Ben read the same newspaper and the captain readily determines the truth. Their new stoker rigged the explosion and the newspaper article so he and his cohorts could steal Grey's contract. He storms off to the Templeton mansion and confirms his worst fears: Captain Jimmy Obanyon is ahead of him, cutting a new deal. The two fight and Grey throws him out. Miss Templeton

It was never safe to play the lady love of a series regular in the late 1950's and throughout the 1960's. Dianne Foster played Grey Holden's love interest in "Path of the Eagle," and her fate is apparent from the start.

is distressed by the violence and eventually Grey explains the hoax, saying that river thieves like Obanyon are all too common. Once the rogue had the party aboard his boat, not only would he charge them too much for passage, he would keep tacking on fees until her father ended up spending twice what Grey would charge. She apologizes and is appreciative for his help.

The Templeton party board the *Enterprise* and they steam down the Missouri River, a trip lasting four weeks until they reach Independence. Grey has a cabin

Darren McGavin's Grey Holden affects a faraway look while Dianne Foster's Marion Templeton is oblivious to her fate.

made up for Marion and is clearly attracted to her. This concern prompts him to try to dissuade her from going west. It is too dangerous, he says, and none of the party is equipped to face hardship.

Later, after listening to her read aloud to several children, he comments that he knows the author of the book: John C. Fremont. Once, he carried that army officer and his troops to Fort Leavenworth and got to know him well. She is duly impressed and they discuss another adventure book — this one a travel guide written by Landsford W. Hastings, called *The Emigrants' Guide to Oregon and California.* Grey knows Hastings, too, but has little confidence that any books have adequately prepared the travelers for what they will face.

The passengers discuss their plans. Templeton, a former state senator, has ideas of creating a Utopia in California. It is his opinion that the West needs educated people to settle there and establish a refined civilization. Grey considers Utopia "heaven on earth under a fig tree," and scorns the entire project, declaring that those whom Templeton styles "riffraff" have done just fine on their own.

Grey speaks to Marion privately in her cabin (finally a woman tells a man to leave the door open for the sake of propriety!) and proposes marriage. He wants her to live her own life and develop her own dreams, not blindly follow her father, who seems to want to make himself king of a new land. She reciprocates his feelings and accepts the proposal, but states it is her obligation to protect her father and his ideals.

When the *Enterprise* arrives in St. Louis (or Independence?), Ben remarks that he'd like to stay and be best man at Grey's wedding, but he has to get to New Orleans. This is the last of him in this episode.

While Grey goes off to buy a wedding ring, he is set upon by thugs and beaten. When he does not return to the boat, Barrows demands the ship proceed up the Missouri or lose the $3,500 contract. They oblige, leaving the captain to his fate.

Grey escapes and rides a horse to Wilmont's Landing, where he catches the *Enterprise* at a wood stop. Sneaking back aboard the boat, he orders Carney to arm the crew. They are not to fight when Obanyon mounts his attack, however, because Grey wishes to prove his point to Templeton.

When Obanyon and his men take over the *Enterprise,* it is revealed Barrows is in league with them. He plans on stealing all the passengers' personal belongings. Once that is established, the crew break out their weapons and a fight ensues. Barrows flees the boat and Templeton follows, eventually killing the traitor by smashing him over the head with a log.

The revelations convince Marion to call off the expedition and she and Grey plan their life together. Her father is willing to abandon his dreams, but then changes his mind. He pleads with his daughter to go with him. Predictably, she agrees and the party sign aboard a wagon train. As Marion promises Grey she will return, and he vows to wait for her, she tells a story about a previous pioneer who wrote about seeing clouds form in the image of an eagle with its wings spread all the way across the United States to the Pacific Ocean. This is her inspiration (and thus the title of the episode).

Before she leaves, Grey asks the name of the wagon train they have joined and she replies, "The Donner party."

On that grim note, the flashback ends. Chip asks if that's why Grey never got married, whereupon Grey tells him to mind his own business.

Beginning with this episode, Riverboat *moved to Monday night at 7:30-8:30, which may explain why it was shown out of order. Filmed before "Forbidden Island" and "The Salvage Pirates," "Path of the Eagle" was intended to be aired ahead of them. Not wanting to make too many changes at once, the producer held back, but the effort was ingenuous. Frazer appeared in this episode, but the decision to write him out had already been made. And he went with little fanfare. A casual comment of "going to New Orleans" ended Burt Reynolds' brief tenure on* Riverboat.

While "Path of the Eagle" should have had a lot going for it, there were multiple problems, not the least of which was geography. Because they needed to have the Templeton party depart the Enterprise *from St. Louis (where the Donner wagon train actually began its westward trek), the writer manipulated events to place them in the historically proper locale. However, the rest of the settings made absolutely no sense. The flashback began in southern Illinois. From there, the boat would have taken the Mississippi or the Illinois, depending on where Kingsport was, to St. Louis. From there she would have traveled the Missouri to Independence, and then retraced her path to St. Louis. And in the middle of all this, they ended up in Cairo, which is above Columbus on the Mississippi. A map would have greatly aided this confusing, roundabout and nonsensical trip.*

There is also the problem of chronology. Riverboat *began in 1841, jumped to 1843, and now leapfrogged to 1848. The Donner party left St. Louis on April 16, 1846. If Grey is telling the story in retrospect (and understanding the first news of the tragic fate of the wagon train did not reach the outside world for a year), that adds another twelve months. Clearly, time was not a concern for the producers, but is another example of inexplicable disregard for continuity.*

Additionally, the writers continue their penchant for unlikable characters. Gideon Templeton is hardly a sympathetic figure. He dismisses early pioneers as unfit to settle the uncharted territories and intends to set himself up as some sort of godlike supreme ruler of California. It is impossible to feel for his plight or agree with Marion to go with him on this harebrained scheme.

The reference to the book, The Emigrants' Guide to Oregon and California *is historically accurate, and considering Grey confesses to having some slight familiarity with the author Landsford Hastings, it would have been far more interesting for him to have gone into this in greater detail. The "guide," widely read, influenced many westward travelers to follow the path he set out. Unfortunately, Hastings had never tried the route writing only from sheer speculation. This came out later with details of the Donner debacle and Holden would surely have known it by the time he told the story. Bitterness over that would not only have explained the history to viewers unfamiliar with the circumstances, it would have given added pathos to Marion's implied death.*

Telling a story in flashback also ruins whatever suspense there might have been over Grey's romantic attachment. The outcome of the love affair, however hurriedly developed, is destroyed before it gets off the ground because the viewer already knows he never got married.

More time should have been spent between Grey and Marion, as that was really the most important aspect of the episode; but in reality, it played second fiddle to the subplots.

Complicating matters, the direction was unusually sloppy. Bricken did better work on his previous attempts, but in "Path of the Eagle," the fight scenes were poorly staged with obvious doubles standing in for McGavin and the thugs. And in keeping with recent tradition, no guest stars are listed in the main titles.

In summary, this was a wasted episode with great potential, falling victim to the all-too-familiar theme of a series regular falling in love and having a too-predictable excuse crop up to prevent a happy ending.

GUEST CAST

Dianne Foster *(b. 10/31/1928, Edmonton, Alberta, Canada.)* Of Ukranian descent, her real name is Dianne Laruska. She worked primarily in the late 50's through the 60's, playing girl friends and love interests. She turned down the role of Fred MacMurray's new wife on *My Three Sons* (taken by Beverly Garland). She appeared on the pilot of *Thriller* and a second season episode of *The Fugitive* called "Scapegoat." She is also the mother of actress Jody Foster.

Dayton Lummis *(b. 8/8/1903, Summit, NJ; d. 3/23/1988, Santa Monica, CA.)* He played the doctor (uncredited) in *The Bad Seed* (1956) and General Douglas MacArthur in *The Court-Martial of Billy Mitchell* (1955). Primary TV credits include two episodes of *Thriller* – playing Millard Braystone in the episode "Cousin Tundifer" and Clarence in "The Cheaters" (1960).

Myron Healey *(b. 6/8/1932, Petaluma, CA.)* One of the more prolific Western heavies, his first TV work began in 1950 on an episode of *The Lone Ranger*. Everything from *The Range Rider* to *The Roy Rogers Show, The Gene Autry Show, Annie Oakley* and *Cisco Kid* followed. He played Doc Holiday on the series *The Life and Legend of Wyatt Earp* (1958-59) and worked with McGavin on an episode of *The Outsider* ("I Can't Hear You Scream," 1968) and *The Night Stalker*, playing Col. Wright in the episode "Mr. R.I.N.G." (1975).

Wilton Graff *(b. 8/13/1903, St. Louis, MO; d. 1/13/1969, Pacific Palisades, CA.)* A long list of credits through the 1960's includes *The Sea Chase* (1955), *King Richard and the Crusaders* (1954) and *The West Point Story* (1950).

Grant Richards *(b. 3/23/1916, Raleigh, N.C.; d. 7/4/1963, Los Angeles, CA - from a car accident at the age of 47.)* He began his career doing radio work on the program *Gangbusters* and graduated to TV work with some motion pictures to his credit. He made appearances in the most popular series of the era, such as *Richard Diamond, Perry Mason, Bonanza, Death Valley Days.* His first film was *Hoppalong*

Cassidy Returns (1936) and his last work was on *The Untouchables* (1961-62) where he played Frankie Resco.

1.22 "The Treasure of Hawk Hill" . . . .*February 8, 1960*
Directed by William Witney
Written by Bob and Wanda Duncan
Produced by John Larkin

A boy runs into the cabin of his uncle George and warns him two men are approaching. Concerned, the man gives the boy a paper to hide, instructing him to go to his uncle's cabin at Three Forks. Under no circumstances is he to tell anyone what he has.

The child escapes as two unwelcome guests break in. They accuse George of holding out on them. During a recent robbery, he was entrusted with the $60,000 the gang stole. Word is George has hidden it and made a map of the location. They have come for the map. When he refuses to give it over, the leader, Murrell, directs his associate (nicknamed the "Paymaster") to shoot him.

Aboard the *Enterprise,* Captain Holden is in a testy mood. He refuses Pickalong's demand that he serve pheasant to the paying passengers and ignores the cook's mumbling that the boat won't make any money this trip and that they need passengers for a successful voyage.

In the pilothouse, Joshua and Terry are navigating when they spot a boy on a raft. Grey orders him picked up; they bring aboard Sam Dexter, the thirteen-year-old from the Teaser. Sam is all fuss and feathers, identifying his late father and his Uncle George as members of the famous Murrell gang. His mother died of the fever awhile back and he is on his way to another uncle, this one living in Tennessee. Grey assigns Chip to take him to his quarters for a bath and a good meal.

Chip and Andy Jackson feed the youngster and a rapport quickly develops between the two boys. Sam makes Chip swear not to tell anyone a secret, then shows him his pirate map of buried treasure. Since Sam cannot read, Chip goes over the simple diagram which is clearly set in a cemetery. Sam's idea is that they escape the riverboat as soon as it lands to go in search of the gold. Chip is not so sure that's a good idea, but he knows the captain needs money. This seems like the opportunity of a lifetime to make a contribution, so he reluctantly agrees.

Later, he speaks with Grey and reveals the fact Sam has a treasure map. Grey scoffs at the idea, declaring that it is probably fake. In another nice scene between McGavin and McGreevey, Holden laments the fact Chip has no boys his own age with whom to play. He says he would like to keep Sam aboard but warns that as soon as they reach shore, he must turn him over to the authorities. Sam needs a family to love him and there are folks in Hadleyville who don't have kids of their own and would be glad to take him in.

Chip worries that Grey's "disposition hasn't been very good, lately," because he's worried about money. If the map really did show where a fortune was hidden, he would like to get it and save the *Enterprise*. Grey softly reminds him that finances are his worry and not to bother about it.

Despite the admonition, Chip does worry and at the first opportunity, the boys escape. Unknown to them, their actions are observed by an old man sitting on the dock.

Sheriff Bates comes aboard and speaks to Holden. He has heard the boat picked up a boy and fills Grey in on the true facts. Sam's uncle was, indeed, a member of the Murrell Gang and did steal $60,000 from the ruthless leader and paid for it with his life. Word has it Murrell is after Sam because he has the map. When informed the boys have left, Grey orders Joshua to get a pair of horses so they can track them down.

Meanwhile, the informant reports to Murrell what he has seen, adding that soon after the boys left, two men on horseback went out to search. Murrell determines Sam is probably going to another uncle's house who lives at Three Forks. He has his "Paymaster" shoot the spy and goes after the boys.

Sam and Chip arrive at Uncle Arden's cabin. Having already heard the story about the map from Sheriff Bates, he ushers them inside where his wife, Aunt Samantha, is happy to see her nephew. Arden demands the map but before he can get it, Captain Holden and Joshua McGregor arrive. Arden chases them away at gunpoint and after they leave, he decides to follow them back to town.

Grey and Joshua have not left, however, and they prepare to confront Mrs. Dexter just as Murrell and his associate ride up. They barge in, demanding to know where Sam is. While they are talking to her, the boys flee out the back.

The Paymaster is going to beat the truth out of her but Grey and Joshua sneak into the cabin, and a fight ensues. They manage to chase the gang members off, but Murrell threatens that if they ever meet again, he will blow Grey's brains out.

Mrs. Dexter is suspicious of the river men, but realizing she has no choice but to trust the pair, she explains that Sam inquired about a town called Hawk Hill. She can see no point in the query, however, as the town died several years ago and nothing is left but the old church yard. With nothing better to go on, Grey and Joshua get directions and set out.

Arden soon returns, having discovered he was tricked. His gold lust is in high gear, and he tells his wife that he's sick and tired of being poor. Because his brothers were well-known thieves, no one would ever loan him any money to improve the farm and now he sees their loot as a reward for his suffering. She is shocked by his assertion and tries to talk him out of it by saying with Sam to help, the three of them can have a decent life. Hardly persuaded, he, too, goes after the boys.

Murrell and the Paymaster spot Arden and stop him. Because he is driving a wagon, they presume he intends to return carrying something heavy. The three quickly made a deal: if Arden leads them to the boys, they will give him 40% of the gold.

At Hawk Hill, Chip and Sam follow the directions and begin digging at the "X." Grey and Joshua get lost (despite Joshua bragging that he once advised a general on how to reach his destination) and are set back. Thus, Arden and the Murrell "gang" reach the cemetery first. They lock the boys in a shack and continuing digging in the hole.

Murrell subsequently shoots Arden, which turns out to be a good thing because Grey hears the shot. This guides them to the scene where a gunfight between the opposing factions breaks out. Grey kills the Paymaster then sees through Murrell's ruse when he pretends to surrender and shoots him, too.

Always ready for a fight, Grey Holden peeks over a slightly less than protective log, ready to shoot whatever bad guys come his way.

After rescuing the boys, Sam believes his uncle is dead. He is only wounded, however, and they make up before returning to the cabin. The treasure is recovered and both boys earn a reward.

Back aboard the *Enterprise*, Chip wants to pledge his money to Grey, but he tells him they will put it aside for his education. On shore, Sam and his new family wave good-bye and all's well that ends well.

This episode was meant to follow "Forbidden Island" and "The Salvage Pirates." Terry Blake was part of the crew, Burt Reynolds' name had been removed and the end credits ran the title, "Crew of the Enterprise,*" listing the actors in the same order: Lambert, Patton, McGreevey, Wessel and Mitchum. Again, no guest stars were listed in the beginning.*

"The Treasure of Hawk Hill" could be considered the first "Chip episode," and as such, was agreeable. Little Mike McGreevey held his own and Steve Wooten as Sam was well up to the task of playing his sassy and determined friend. The plot, although a little tedious with all the comings and goings, was solid, and William Witney worked in some good characterization between the regulars and guest stars.

As noted in the Introduction, character names were not given in the end credits, so it is unclear if the gang leader's name was "Morrel" or "Murrell." In the first instance, the name was surely a corruption of the latter and if the second, the notorious character had already been used in episode 1.5, "The Unwilling." In either case, it might have been wiser to have given the bandit another name.

On a historical note, it is a common misconception, perpetuated here by Pickalong, that first class passengers were the life's blood of a riverboat. In reality, that was not the case. Although cabin passengers paid a great deal for their fare, feeding these people and putting them up in well-maintained staterooms was a tremendous financial burden that in many cases did not cover the expenses outlaid. The main object in offering luxury accommodations was for the prestige of the line and to provide an aura of respectability that would lure shippers to use that boat for transport.

The real money actually came from ferrying cargo (which required no upkeep) and deck (or hold) passengers. While these travelers' fares were usually only a few dollars, a boat typically carried ten times their number and did not provide food or entertainment. That made them as inexpensive as cattle or merchandise and cost the owner nothing.

GUEST CAST

Steve Wooten. A child actor, he has only four listed acting credits, including *Young at Heart* (1954), *The Californians* (1958) and *Steve Canyon* (1959). He went on to work as a stuntman. His last credit is *Daredevil* in 2003.

Kent Taylor *(b. 5/11/1907, Nashus, Iowa; d. 4/11/1987, Woodland Hills, CA.)* Born Louis Weiss, his stage name was the inspiration for Jerry Siegel and Joe Shuster's name choice for Superman's alter ego, Clark Kent. (The first name came from Clark Gable.) Having a small role in every film no one ever knew the name of in the 1930-50's, he also played the recurring character Carlos Murietta in the 1950's series *Zorro*. His last credit was *I Spit on your Corpse!*, in 1974.

Richard Hale *(b. 11/16/1892, Rogersville, TN; d. 5/18/1981, Northridge, CA, cardiac arrest.)* Primarily a Western actor who frequently found himself cast as an Indian, he played Professor Latimore on the *Thriller* episode "The Incredible Doktor Markesan" and Goro on "The Paradise Syndrome" episode of *Star Trek*. His last credit was as an "old man" on the miniseries *How the West Was Won* (1978) with James Arness.

Virginia Christine *(b. 3/5/1920, in Stanton, Iowa; d. 7/24/1996, Los Angeles, CA, heart disease.)* Real name Virginia Christine Kraft. She will always be remembered for playing Mrs. Olsen, the Folger's Coffee Lady in TV commercials over a 21-year span, but she had a long and successful career as an actress. Her first film was *Edge of Darkness* in 1943. She is also noted for her work on *Invasion of the Body Snatchers*, and a number of Stanley Kramer's films, including *Guess Who's Coming to Dinner?* (1967). Her last credit was *Scooby-Doo and Scrappy-Doo*, (1979, voice).

1.23 "**Fight at New Canal**" . . . . *February 22, 1960*
Directed by R. G. Springsteen
Written by Tom Seller
Produced by John Larkin

The action begins with a government surveyor showing Captain Holden a map. He explains that by putting in a canal, he can shorten travel around a bend in the river by 92 miles as well as eliminating 14 miles of rapids. Grey is all for the project and promises to lend his support when a shot rings out and a voice from cover yells, "Get off this land! You'll never build that canal!"

Aboard the *Enterprise*, Joshua and Terry are navigating. Grey explains that he is going to oversee the building of a canal; the government has given him the financing and the river men voted him in charge. The plan is for Grey, Joshua, Chip and Andy Jackson to set up a camp while the rest of the crew steam up and down the river seeking diggers for the project.

While Holden waits for the new engineer to arrive, he sits beside a very attractive woman who immediately catches his attention. He begins flirting with her when he notices her wedding ring. She implies that need not be an impediment when her husband, Frank Paxton, arrives. Paxton, the canal engineer, introduces them, then announces that he has been unable to hire horses and wagons because the only two men in town who own such items are against the project. They go to set matters straight.

Mr. Harper and Mr. Dunnagan run the local stagecoach line and it is their belief the canal will ruin their business. Currently, they ferry passengers over the peninsula to the other side of the river where they then book passage on another boat. Eliminating the need for that will ruin them. They warn of trouble if the endeavor is not stopped.

Their threats are ignored and Grey manages to obtain wagons and horses somewhere else. Paxton goes ahead and his wife, Tracie, rides with Grey, making it clear she has a romantic interest in him. He tells her she is "trouble he doesn't want."

The wagon train is ambushed along the trail and there is a shoot-out. One man is killed and three severely wounded. It is subsequently revealed that Harper and Dunnagan were behind the attack. Dunnagan, in particular, hates river men because his wife died in a steamboat accident and he blames all river men for her death.

At the camp, Mrs. Paxton continues her pursuit of Grey, showing off a new dress for him. He advises her something conservative would be more appropriate and she remarks that she is not allowed to be useful, only decorative. When Paxton comes in, Grey warns that if Tracie were his wife, he'd be afraid to leave her alone. Frank ignores the advice and continues to work well into the night.

Rather than accompany him, Grey teaches Chip his geography and spelling lessons, noting that he never misses a day. Chip is not prepared, however, and is sent to bed. Before he goes, however, he sees a bear in the window. Grey finds no trace of the animal and believes the boy is only trying to get out of studying. Later, a bear enters the cabin and attacks Tracie, forcing Grey to shoot it.

Bixby, one of the teamsters in camp, turns out to be an employee of Dunnagan and Harper. He steals a keg of powder and plans to blow up a nearby waterfall, thus flooding the camp. He nearly succeeds, but Paxton discovers him just in time, pulls out the fuse and chases him off. When he comes back to tell Grey what happened, he finds the captain and Tracie kissing. Being a neglectful but jealous man, he takes his wife and storms off, declaring he is through with the canal.

When the Paxtons arrive in town to book a stagecoach out, the owners see opportunity and grab it. Well aware that Paxton's leaving will not solve anything because the government will just send another engineer, they capture Tracie and tell Frank that if he doesn't sabotage the project, they will kill her. Having no choice, he returns to camp and steals another keg of powder. Grey catches him and hears out the story.

He develops a new plan: Paxton will go back to town and tell the men Grey has abandoned the project because "he knows when he's licked." He will arrange for the wagons to be brought back as proof. When the kidnappers buy this story, they will go out and investigate. He will have the crew of the *Enterprise* waiting for them and they will finally put a stop to those two murderers.

Everything goes nearly as planned and there is a big fight at the camp. With Chip cheering his boys on, they defeat Dunnagan and Harper. With the pair out of the way, the canal can be built.

Back aboard the *Enterprise*, Pickalong sings (without his monkey), and it is announced Dunnagan was hanged and the rest, including Harper, got five years in jail. While the crew celebrate, Grey gives Chip a final quiz: spell "Philadelphia."

He recites, "Philadel-fia." The captain starts to protest, repeats the spelling in his mind and decides that is correct.

This episode might as easily have been titled, "The Panama Canal in Miniature," for it tells the story of the need for and building of the land cut-through. This tale has the added intrigue of local opposition, a neglected wife and a jealous husband, but succeeds in being entertaining.

The best scenes deal with the series' regulars, in particular the time Grey spends with Chip. This underscores the fact producer John Larkin finally got the message that viewers wanted some positive camaraderie with Family Enterprise. *Tom Seller, one of the better staff writers, took full advantage and created some stellar moments. Cutting back on Joshua, Carney and Pickalong's time, he concentrated on Grey and Chip. By cleverly weaving them throughout the script, he managed to make the episode palatable.*

The relationship between Grey and Tracie Paxton was a bit more involved and perhaps not as innocent as the usual fare of late 1950's episodic television. It was easy to imagine that without Paxton on the scene, the two would have developed more than a casual relationship. Depending on your point of view, it added or detracted from the whole. But it did give McGavin some better dialogue and he rose to the occasion.

Director R. G. Springsteen, making his first appearance behind the Riverboat *cameras, might have been better off using a wolf to attack, however, for even in 1959-60, a man in a bear suit stood out like a sore thumb. To his credit, however, he limited the exposure and nearly pulled it off.*

Alexander Courage (who would immortalize himself by writing the theme for Star Trek *just a few years later) worked on his second episode (the first being "The Salvage Pirates" 1.20, with Albert Woodbury) and did a masterful job. The music was startlingly different and particularly effective. No guest stars were listed in the title credits (although Charles Aidman certainly warranted this), and the end credits included the line, "The Crew of the* Enterprise" *over the five regulars.*

GUEST CAST

Charles Aidman *(b. 1/21/1925, Frankfort, IN; d. 11/7/1993, Beverly Hills, CA.)* A prolific, distinctive actor who had meant to be an attorney before being bitten by the acting bug, this left-hander appeared on every TV show imaginable. He served as the narrator for the 1985-87 rendition of *The Twilight Zone*, and assumed Ross Martin's place as Jim West's partner on the *Wild Wild West* as Jeremy Pike when Martin was absent for several months from illness. He played a remarkable Captain Leo Winwood in the *Night Stalker* episode "The Zombie" and his role in a *Thriller* episode "The Terror in Teakwood" (1960) still stands as a masterpiece.

Jean Allison *(b. 10/24/1929, New York, NY.)* An attractive blonde, she made the rounds of the studios in the 50's and 60's, appearing in Westerns and Warner Brothers episodic TV. Her credits include *Gunsmoke*, *Highway to Heaven*, and *Perry Mason*.

John Maxwell. An actor from the 40's and 50's, his last credit was an episode of *Coronado 9* in 1961. He appeared primarily in films, having small roles in *Them!* (1954; as Dr. Grant) and *The Court-Martial of Billy Mitchell* (1955; as a court-martial judge).

John Archer *(b. 5/8/1915, Osceola, Nebraska; d. 12/3/1999, Redmond, WA, lung cancer.)* He played the young male lead, Richard Dennison, in *The Bowery at Midnight* (1942) opposite the great Bela Lugosi. He also starred opposite McGavin in an episode of *The Outsider*, entitled "Service For One."

1.24 "The Wichita Arrows" . . . .*February 29, 1960*
Directed by William Witney
Written by Bob and Wanda Duncan
Produced by John Larkin

The Teaser begins with two woodcutters at Mulligan's Landing discussing a commission Captain Holden has given them. He pre-ordered 15 cords of wood and left instructions that the *Enterprise* pick up a cargo of beaver pelts in town. He will meet the boat later at Willow Landing. They are then shot in the back by arrows, presumably from an Indian attack.

Aboard the *Enterprise,* Joshua and Terry are navigating the river. Captain Turner warns of snags and they resent the intrusion. Turner remarks that when Captain Holden put him in charge, he runs the *Enterprise* like his own boat. And the reason he is there, Joshua adds, is that the crew is unfamiliar with the Red River (not surprising as the Red River is in Oklahoma and excused by the fact that Joshua and Terry were not in episode 1.12, "Jessie Quinn," where the *Enterprise* steamed up and down it). That established, they look forward to retrieving Grey, who will be waiting 50 miles upriver. Joshua is not sure he likes Turner but Terry happily declares, "I like him."

That settled, Pickalong, Petie and Chip discuss the fact one of their passengers, Miss Holly, isn't eating. After the obligatory song by Pickalong, Captain Turner goes to find out why Miss Holly is fasting. She explains she is too worried about her sister, whom she is to meet in the next town. Something is terribly wrong with Julie's marriage and she needs to find out what has gone awry.

They arrive at Mulligan's Landing and find it burned. The crew disembarks to assess the damage. Turner does not find the cargo that was supposed to be delivered and determines to go into the Red River settlement and find out where it is. Before he can leave, a youth attempts to steal one of their horses. They capture him and he identifies himself as Rico, a Wichita Indian. He speaks with a Mexican accent, explained by saying he was captured as a boy and raised by Mexicans (before presumably escaping and rejoining his tribe).

Rico is wanted for murder and he pleads with Turner not to turn him over to the authorities for they will hang him without a trial. A posse rides up and

Turner, well known to the locals, denies seeing him. They ride off and Turner takes Miss Holly into town.

While Holly goes off to find her sister, hard-nosed Turner warns the merchant to bring the beaver pelts to the landing and live up to his contract.

Holly and Julie reunite. Julie wants her sister to turn around and go home but won't say why. Her husband, Albert Scott, arrives and appears affable and pleasant. He is a tin peddler, not worried about Indian uprisings. After a meal shared

Dan Duryea's Captain Turner shakes hands with Jack Lambert's Joshua in a publicity still from "The Wichita Arrows." Happy smiles make it appear all is well on the Enterprise, *but that was far from the case.*

with Turner, the Scotts take Holly back to their cabin, inviting the captain to visit them later in the day after he completes some business.

The posse returns, having captured Rico. The sheriff tells Turner he is determined to put an end to all the recent murders by hanging the boy. Turner protests this will only incite an Indian war, but the lawman won't listen. Even though Rico is an admitted thief, he professes innocence of the killings. He confesses to Turner he stole a knife from Mr. Scott and found $5,000 in his money box. How could a mere traveling salesman have that kind of money?

Turner leaves Joshua and Terry to guard the jail and goes off to the Scott house. He gets lost and stops in at the widow Hawkins'. She gives him directions and remarks how much she likes Mr. Scott, for he always sells things so cheaply.

At the homestead, Julie finally confesses that something is terribly wrong with her husband. He loves money more than anything and the pair have lived a nomad's life, never staying long in any one place. There are always Wichita raids where they live and no one ever survives the attacks. She suspects he is involved. Turner determines to take both women back to the boat and orders them to pack.

Meanwhile, Scott shows up at Mrs. Hawkins' home, finds out where she keeps her cash and steals it. He then kills her with a bow and arrow and torches the building. Turner appears on the scene and is also shot. Returning home, Scott immediately determines his dirty little secret has been found out and takes the women hostage. He will move on to Texas and continue his thefts and murders there.

While Turner is treated by the doctor, the townsmen gather. They want to wipe out the Wichita tribe for their crimes. Turner tells them the Indians are innocent — it is really Albert Scott who is to blame. He fails to convince them and they demand Rico for hanging. Rico escapes and goes off to get his tribe.

Turner, Joshua and Terry follow the wagon tracks and come upon Scott. Scott sneaks up on Terry, holds him hostage and the other two surrender. Scott brags he has killed Julie and Holly and will do the same to them. "Look at his eyes," Terry warns. "He's mad." Taking a page out of Dave O'Brien's classic performance in "Reefer Madness," Don Haggerty offers a wide-eyed, wild stare to convince the crew he is, indeed, off his rocker. Before they can act on this, Rico leads the Wichita in an attack. Julie (who turns out not to be dead) is hit by an arrow but Scott manages to single-handedly hold them off by dead-eye shooting half a dozen whooping and circling braves.

He finally runs out of ammunition and asks Julie to reload his pistol. Why she doesn't just shoot her would-be murderer-husband is a mystery but she doesn't. It is later revealed she did not reload the gun, however, and Turner eventually fights Scott and manages to subdue him. Rico appears with a white flag and demands Scott for punishment. They take him away and unpleasant things are in store for the madman.

Back aboard the *Enterprise* with the cargo of beaver pelts, Carney and Pickalong play cards. In the pilothouse, Terry and Joshua give a blast on the boat's whistle, signaling Grey they are about to come into Willow Landing and pick him up.

"Wichita Arrows" is the first of two episodes in which Darren McGavin did not appear. He was in a contract dispute with the studio and rather than stop production, producer John Larkin went ahead by casting Dan Duryea in the series lead. Other than a few lines describing Grey's absence (and the tacit promise he would return "next week") nothing was done to change the script. Duryea merely played Grey Holden with a different name.

Although having a long list of credits, Duryea appeared uncomfortable in the role. Some of the scenes, especially in the pilothouse (teaser and tag filmed consecutively), were played over the top and in the rest of the episode he merely went through the motions. The end credit revealed "Tonight Starring Dan Duryea."

The script was a basic Western plot without much going for it and typically seemed more like a five-minute idea stretched out over an hour. It was another "anthology idea" which could have been played out without the Enterprise or the crew. The highlight was an appearance by Robert Armstrong as the sheriff.

GUEST CAST

Dan Duryea *(b. 1/23/1907, White Plains, NY; d. 6/7/1968, Hollywood, CA, cancer.)* Cornell University educated, he first worked on Broadway, earning praise for his performance in *Little Foxes*. He also reprised his role of Leo Hubbard in the film version (1941). Although he made many film and TV appearances, his appearance on *Twilight Zone* episode, "Mr. Denton on Doomsday" (1959) is probably one of the most remembered. He also played Eddie Jacks on *Peyton Place* (1967-68).

Betty Lou Keim *(b. 1938, Malden, MA.)* She debuted in the TV series *My Son Jeep* (1953) and went on to do numerous juvenile roles before graduating to playing Fran McCord on *The Deputy* (1959). She married and retired that same year.

Don Haggerty *(b. 7/3/1914, Poughkeepsie, NY; d. 8/19/1988, Cocoa, FL.)* Not to be confused with Dan Haggerty of *Grizzly Adams* fame (as the chairman of the Hollywood Walk of Fame did when ordering Don's star), Don was primarily a character actor who played toughs in Westerns and crime stories. His last credit was *Legend of the Wild,* in 1981.

Robert Armstrong *(b. 11/20/1890, Saginaw, MI; d. 4/20/1973, Santa Monica, CA, cancer.)* He grew up in Seattle and was an infantryman in World War I before studying law at the University of Washington. Brought to RKO by David O. Selznick, he had a good role in *The Most Dangerous Game* (1932). The following year, he immortalized himself as the wisecracking producer Carl Denham in *King Kong*. Continuing a successful career, he appeared in *Mighty Joe Young* (1949). His last credit was *For Those Who Think Young* in 1964.

Eve McVeagh *(b. 7/15/1919. Ohio; d. 12/10/1997, Los Angeles.)* Her first credit was *High Noon* (1952). She made two *Thriller* episodes ("'Till Death Do Us Part" and "The Hollow Watcher"), and an episode of *The Outsider* called "Tell it Like it Is… And You're Dead" (1968). Her last credit was *Square One TV*, in 1987.

Roy Barcroft *(b. 9/7/1902, Nebraska; d. 11/28/1969, Woodland Hills, CA, cancer.)* Real name Howard H. Ravenscroft. Signed to an exclusive contract with Republic, he made many TV serials, including *Manhunt of Haunted Harbor* (1944), *Mystery Island* (1945) and *The Purple Monster Strikes* (1945). He is cherished as playing Roy, a regular on *Gunsmoke*.

1.25 "Fort Epitaph"...................................*March 7, 1960*
Directed by John Brahm
Written by Richard N. Morgan
Produced by Richard H. Bartlett

In the opening narration, Captain Turner explains the riverboat is on the Missouri River delivering cannon and gunpowder to Fort Wilson. He adds, "I thought I was on the *Enterprise* for one trip, but my friend Captain Holden asked me to make one more trip for him."

Joshua, Terry and Turner are in the pilot house when they see smoke. It is soon revealed that the fort is under attack and burning. They break out the cannon (which at first seemed to be a reference to the ordnance mentioned in "The Salvage Pirates" but wasn't) and Turner gives the savages a taste of grape shot. The Sioux flee and Lieutenant Tom Henshaw comes out to greet their rescuers.

Henshaw informs Turner the fort is commanded by Major Luke Daniels, a disciplinarian who goes "by the book." The Indians, normally peaceful, have been on the warpath because Daniels had the heads of two squaws shaved. These young women were in love with soldiers and sneaked in to see their lovers. Daniels caught them and inflicted the terribly humiliating punishment meant to rile the braves.

The lieutenant, a former river man, adds that out of fifty soldiers, only 15 are left. Gravely disturbed, Captain Turner meets Major Daniels. Sarcastically remarking the riverboat was four days late, Daniels promptly impresses the crew of twenty into military service, using the Act of War to justify his action. Sergeant Matthews is put in charge of the crew; Pickalong is made cook and Chip an orderly while the rest are assigned guard duty. Although Henshaw is the only artillery officer left, Daniels declares him the "worst officer he ever had" and orders him to assist the cook.

Barbara Daniels, the major's wife, clandestinely meets Henshaw and bitterly complains about her husband. She says that as long as Daniels remains in command, they will all die. As though to confirm her fears, the major orders the *Enterprise* burned so his new recruits will not be tempted to escape. He would have gotten away with this act of barbarism but the Sioux also realize the significance of the escape vessel and put out the fires.

The soldiers have had no sleep for three days and are literally dropping at their posts. One remarks to Joshua that they call the outpost "Fort Epitaph" because that's what it is. Sgt. Matthews killed the two men who were in love with the squaws and many more followed them to the grave after the uprising.

In Daniels' quarters, Barbara has to endure her husband's tirade that she is barren. He has no son, nor any other male heir to carry on his name. Nor can he divorce her because those in Washington who determine promotions frown on such action.

Joshua gives one of the privates permission to sleep on duty, but Matthews catches him. There is a heated argument and Henshaw comes to Joshua's defense. When Daniels learns of this, he strips Tom of rank and gives Matthews a field promotion to lieutenant.

An Indian youth pole vaults over the wall of the fort and sneaks into the major's room, where he cuts his cheek with the tip of his knife, marking him with the highest possible insult, worse than scalping. He is caught before he can escape, however, and is identified as the son of Chief Running Bear. Daniels determines to use him as bait the following morning.

Henshaw will not speak out against his superior but when Barbara joins him, he tells Turner that the major started this war for his own glory. He knew shaving the heads of the women would result in an all-out attack and that is precisely what he wanted. He had counted on defeating them with the four cannon being delivered by the *Enterprise*, but as the boat was late, Daniels paid a heavy price in loss of life. Now, despite protestations to the contrary, he does not want reinforcements from a neighboring fort because that would mean admitting his own miscalculation.

Captain Turner declares Major Daniels unfit for command and asks the summoned troops to take a vote. He explains that the Army manual has specific rules governing this. All but Henshaw agree to relieve the major of command and Matthews is placed in charge. Afterward, Turner announces his plan to release the Indian boy and make his way to the *Enterprise* when he will take everyone away.

At sun-up, Turner addresses Running Bear. The chief sees that Daniels has been marked by his son and honor is satisfied. He makes peace and the white men are free to leave.

Aboard the riverboat, Daniels is placed under arrest. Barbara pleads his case to the captain, however, saying his actions are a direct reflection on her. If she had been able to deliver him a son, his unfettered ambition to make a name for himself would have been appeased. She asks Turner to release him and grant Luke the dignity of presenting himself for arrest when they reach the next fort. Turner agrees and visits his prisoner, launching into a speech about how the West needs soldiers like Major Daniels and that he deserves another chance.

While Pickalong sings, a drunken Matthews is confronted by Daniels. The two men fight and end up shooting one another. Barbara decides Luke actually committed suicide because he had no son and thus no future.

In the tag, Henshaw decides to quit the army and return to the river. Joshua says he will put in a good word for him with Captain Holden.

In "Wichita Arrows," producer John Larkin obviously expected Darren McGavin to return in time to shoot the next episode. As contract negations dragged on, however, the studio opted to film a second episode with Dan Duryea as Captain Turner.

To underscore this impatience (and perhaps as a threat), the opening and end titles of "Fort Epitaph" read "Starring Dan Duryea," as opposed to "Tonight Starring."

The official line given out by the studio, as printed in TV Guide, *in its February 6, 1960, issue, stated, "Dan Duryea has completed two episodes of* Riverboat *as a replacement for DARREN McGAVIN, injured in an auto accident."*

In keeping with the sentiment, the tag scene between Joshua and the likable Tom Henshaw strongly implied that were McGavin not to return, the clearly established "river man" character could easily be written in to take Grey Holden's spot as a member of the Enterprise. *The supposition appears even more likely when viewed by the fact Richard H. Bartlett was brought in to produce "Fort Epitaph." He had already produced "Tampico Raid" where Pickalong was introduced and "The Salvage Pirates" where Terry Blake came aboard.*

Other than that, there is little to say about "Fort Epitaph." It was a basic Western plot that might have been written for any number of series, although the subplot of Luke Daniels' obsession with having no heir to carry on his name was handled in a more brutal and honest way than was typical in 1960's TV fare. In that light, however, Captain Turner's assertion when he released the major from confinement that he was "a great officer needed by the army" is patently hypocritical. A man who purposely starts a war, miscalculates his ability to win that conflict, loses 35 out of 50 soldiers on a personal vendetta and threatens to torture an Indian youth can hardly be considered "great" or "necessary." It was an odd scene, oddly played, and out of character for Turner/ Holden. It represented a complete turnaround in sentiment and reflected unfavorably on the captain who either retrospectively approved Daniels' motive or served as a cheap writer's ploy to have the officer released in time for the equally implausible "suicide."

GUEST CAST

Dan Duryea (see episode 1.24, "The Wichita Arrows," page 148).

Joan Camden *(b. 6/3/1929, Los Angeles, CA; d. 12/25/2000, Los Angeles, CA.)* Her career primarily was centered in the 1950's where she played roles from Betty Earp in *Gunfight at the O.K. Corral* (1957) to episodes of *Richard Diamond*, *Perry Mason* and *The Outer Limits*.

Brad Weston. Primarily a TV actor, he appeared with McGavin on the episode of *The Outsider* entitled "Love is Under L," and also had a small role in the McGavin film, *Hot Lead and Cold Feet* (1978). He played Ed Appel in the *Star Trek* episode "The Devil in the Dark."

Charles Cooper. His claim to fame is that he appeared in *Star Trek: The Next Generation*, and *Star Trek V: The Final Frontier* (1989).

Mark Allen. One of the original cast from the TV soap *Dark Shadows* (1966), he played Sam "Pop" Evans. He played a trucker in "The Judgment, Part 1," the first of two episodes ending *The Fugitive* (1967).

Stuart Randall *(b. 7/24/1909, Brazil, Indiana; d. 6/22/1988, San Bernardino, CA.)* He co-starred in *Laramie*, playing Mort McCoy from 1960-63, and is known primarily for his TV guest star work, usually in Westerns such as *Bonanza, The Virginian*, and the Warner Brothers' oaters. His first TV appearance was an episode of *The Lone Ranger*, on 11/16/1950, and his last film appearance was *True Grit* (1969) in an uncredited role.

Ronnie Rondell, Jr. Primarily a stuntman or a second unit director, he appeared in many TV episodes and films in small roles, seldom given character names. Film credits include *Thelma and Louise* (1991), *American Outlaws* (2001), and several of the *Star Trek* films. He also acted as a stunt man for McGavin on the *Mike Hammer* series.

1.26 "Three Graves" . . . .*March 14, 1960*
Directed by William Witney
Written by Al C. Ward
Produced by John Larkin

Pickalong is singing as the *Enterprise* pulls into Green City. All the crew is dressed up for shore leave. The men are planning to drink and visit the ladies and even Chip has his eye on Geraldine. Grey is shocked by the revelation until they explain Geraldine is a girl dog, and it is actually Andy Jackson who is romantically involved.

As the boys prepare to depart, they are in for a rude shock: the town is deserted. With Captain Holden in the lead, they investigate, finding three freshly dug graves in the center of the street. Behind them is a sign reading "Get Out While You Can."

A more thorough examination reveals the townspeople left in a hurry. Meals are set on tables and in the saloon, poker chips and cards remain on the tables. Joshua determines the exodus occurred two or three days ago.

Since Grey bought the cargo of grain and seed with his own money on contract, he is determined to find the buyers and have them make good. He and Carney walk to Exeter, a neighboring town, in hopes of discovering answers. Along the way, they are attacked by a gang of men on horseback. Carney is wounded. The leader, Tom Bison, approaches with an explanation. He is sorry for the rude warning, but no outsiders are permitted in Exeter. He offers Grey his horse to take Carney to the local doctor who lives just outside town.

The physician greets the pair with a rifle but Grey barges in, to discover the shooter is a woman named Nora James. Dr. D. James was her father, who has recently died. A very embittered person, she explains that her intent had always been to work with her father. Being unable to obtain a medical education in the United States, she went to Vienna and only returned several days ago, to discover those in Exeter won't let her practice medicine. Grey is less than sympathetic.

Tom Bison rides up and announces that anyone recently in Green City will be shot if he dares enter Exeter. He says plague broke out there and the citizens of Exeter cannot afford to permit carriers into their environs. Grey remains obstinate, saying he needs to be paid for his cargo and Bison rides off. Dr. James is impressed by the captain's bravery, stating that everyone else is afraid of Bison.

Nora returns to Green City and the crew disinters one of the three graves so she can perform an autopsy. The river men rebel at the delay, particularly "Stoney," who speaks for the rest when he says the men want to get away as soon as possible. Joshua warns he's threatening mutiny and Grey gets in a fist fight with the dissident. Holden whips Stoney into submission and orders him locked up.

Terry comes to fetch the captain — the doctor has a report to make. She confirms the individual has recently died and states he does, indeed, carry bubonic plague.

This is bad news but it need not be fatal. Her father studied in China and saw this type of sickness. Dr. James developed a theory that the fever was not spread by man-to-man contact but by the fleas on infected rats. Grey decides to err on the side of caution and take the boat away when he hears a gunshot and rushes into the street. Pickalong has shot a man he caught skulking around the land deed office. One of the papers on the body is a Federal decree, stating the land will revert to the government unless improvements are made. Before he dies, the thief confesses: he was the one who killed Nora's father and made it look like an accident.

Chip is upset that something terrible will happen, explaining to Grey the crew is the only family he's got. Grey responds that Chip is the only boy they've got and makes him feel better. Holden then tells Nora her suspicions were correct: Dr. James was murdered. Nora goes berserk and he has to restrain her before she can go out with a rifle to shoot Bison and his men.

After being reminded she is a physician, Nora goes back to work, inspecting the men for fleas. They are all required to remove their shirts and complain bitterly about having to disrobe in front of a female. Joshua is the only one who does not comply, "fleeing" the scene in terror.

Dr. James announces none of the crew is infected. This leads Grey to infer the disease must have been brought in by outsiders because there are no rats in town as food left on the tables is untouched. Nora agrees, then laments that she once had a dream of a home and family but grew up "fighting off animals in the guise of men" who continually pawed her. If that weren't bad enough, the rest of her time was spent pulling her father out of a bottle. She quotes Keats to Grey and he recites a passage from Longfellow to the effect that men and women are worthless without one another.

Reading from a ten-day-old newspaper, Grey learns that three sailors came to Green City intending to settle down. He infers they must have been the ones who brought in the plague. Determined to get more information, he walks to Exeter and enters the local saloon that is doing a rip-roaring business. Cozying up to one of the locals, he is told the three sailors were friends of Bison and spent some time with him before returning to Green City.

Grey rifles through Bison's room and discovers the land speculator owns secondary rights to the homesteads in Green City. If the locals don't come back in two days, he obtains full ownership. Bison knew the sailors were infected and sent them back to Green City to frighten away the citizens.

Bison enters the saloon and sees Grey. He denounces the stranger and orders him killed. Holden counters by saying if they shoot him, his blood will spatter everywhere and contaminate them all. They back off and he escapes.

The men from Exeter form a gang and ride into Green City, determined to kill Grey for going into their town. Stoney is let loose to help repel them and subsequently becomes one of the few named crewmen who lives to tell the tale.

Grey gets a telescope and asks Nora to look at Bison. She readily identifies end-stage bubonic plague in the townsman, and diagnoses that any excitement will probably kill him. To bring this about, Grey hops off the boat and knocks off one of the townsmen. Conveniently finding his name on a document, he calls out, identifying himself as that man and claiming he's scared. In a great feat of dexterous being-in-many-places-nearly-at-once, he runs from one hiding place to another, calling out in each that he's scared and wants to leave. The tactic convinces Bison his men are about to run in panic.

Afraid to have his grand scheme ruined, Bison runs into the street where Nora draws a bead on him. Before she can send him to his reward, the fever up and takes him and he dies on the street, thus saving her from a cold-blooded act.

When the truth comes out that plague can't be spread by human contact, the dwellers of Green City return and pay Grey for the cargo they ordered. They also decide to let Nora James be their town physician. Grey presents her with a sign, "Dr. N. James" and she kisses him, re-quoting Longfellow. He promises to drop back every once in a while and see her.

As the boat prepares to steam away, Andy Jackson barks good-bye to Geraldine. She turns out to be a white terrier, far too formidable for him. Nora picks up the dog with the implied threat that when Holden comes back to visit, Geraldine will be waiting for Andy.

"Three Graves" picks up where "Fight at New Canal" left off, without mentioning Captain Holden's absence for the past two episodes. McGavin's name once again appeared in the opening credits and everything went on as normal.

This episode had a lot going for it (not the least of which was Beverly Garland) but doesn't bear close inspection. If the townspeople of Green City were so terrified that they fled (leaving food on the table), why did they bother burying the three dead sailors in the middle of the street? It is also farfetched to believe abandoned cats, dogs, hogs or wild raccoons (to say nothing of rats — what Western town didn't have rats?) wouldn't have broken in the houses and eaten the food, thus spoiling the reasoning used to identify the sailors with the disease.

Grey waltzes into Exeter totally unchallenged, even though he and Carney were spotted earlier in the episode by an entire gang of men from miles away. And life was pretty spicy in Exeter despite the legitimate fear of plague, a rather unusual reaction by men passing laws declaring that interlopers will be shot on sight. He also has a long "thank you" conversation with one of the locals, who surely would have taken him for a stranger. Where was the suspicion?

And the scene with Holden taking the identification off one of the thugs (what did he find — a driver's license?) and then popping in and out of innumerable places was just plain silly. Granted, it gave McGavin a chance to show off his prowess and added a genuinely amusing touch to the script, but it was out of place at a time of crisis.

Nora James' history and her unmitigated anger was an interesting touch, but would have worked better if done with more sensitivity. Grey's offhanded unconcern counterbalanced whatever sympathy she might have garnered and her story only got stale in repetition.

The historical mention of bubonic plague being studied in China by Dr. James (the father) was a good touch, as the Black Death was more common in the Orient. Symptoms included black spots on the body (thus the name) around the third day. Clearly, if Bison had been infected ten days ago, his condition would have been apparent even to an untrained eye. (It is interesting to note that in the Lexicon Medicum *or Medical Dictionary,* Harper & Brothers, New York, 1842, *the word "plague" is not included, nor is there any reference to the Black Death, there being no outbreaks to merit inclusion.)*

We also have to wonder how the three sailors (presumably exposed in the Orient) survived the nearly year-long voyage to Green City. If they did carry fleas, the entire crew of their sailing vessel, to say nothing of the crew of the steamer (which brought them to Green City) would likely have been infected. Terrible loss of life would have resulted and the original carriers would have been long dead before ever reaching the United States. Even ignoring that obvious fact, the sailors spent time in both towns before dying. Likely, more men than Bison would have been infected.

In the first episode after McGavin returns, John Larkin abandoned recent efforts to cast secondary actors in featured roles and hired Beverly Garland to headline the cast, for which she received co-starring credit in the opening titles.

GUEST CAST

Beverly Garland *(b. 10/17/1926, Santa Cruz, CA; d. 12/5/2008, Hollywood Hills, CA.)* Everyone who watched TV in the 1960's, from *My Three Sons* to *The Fugitive*, knows Beverly Garland. She frequently played the love interest of the star and you could count on her to give a great performance. Born Beverly Lucy Fessenden, she did a lot of horror/science fiction films in the 60's (*Twice-Told Tales* with Vincent Price; *The Alligator People*) but long before that, she starred on "Decoy" (1957), playing the first female detective – and incidentally, becoming the first female to star in a dramatic series in television history.

Robert Bray *(b. 10/23/1917, Kalispell, MT; d. 3/7/1983, Bishop, CA, heart attack.)* Passing on a chance to co-star in Joshua Logan's film *South Pacific* (to his everlasting regret), he eventually landed the role of Corey Stuart in the TV series *Lassie* (1964-68). He also appeared in *Bus Stop* (1956) as Carl, the bus driver with Marilyn Monroe.

John McKee. A character actor who spent most of his career in small, undistinguished roles, he habitually played characters with designations such as *Third Miner, Second Cavalryman, Outlaw Guard* and *Posse Leader.* He played Adm. William Leahy in *MacArthur* (1977), and Corp. Olds in *Pork Chop Hill* (1959). His last credit was as "Actor," in the 1983 film *Dempsey.*

Harry Ellerbe *(b. 1/15/1901, Atlanta, GA; d. 12/2/1992, Atlanta, GA.)* Working mostly in the late 1950's through the 60's, he moved back to Georgia as his career wound down. Early credits include *The Fall of the House of Usher* (1960), playing Bristol, and appearances in *The Fugitive* ("The Devil's Disciples") and *The Outer Limits* ("The Man with the Power").

Will White *(b. 5/9/1925; d. 4/23/1992.)* An actor usually regulated to small roles, he appeared in the *Twilight Zone* episode "To Serve Man" as a reporter. His character names were usually "Robber," "Constable," "State Trooper," "Al, the mechanic," and once, "Fancy's gunman."

1.27 "Hang the Men High" . . . .*March 21, 1960*
Directed by Hollingsworth Morse
Written by Jerry Adelman
Produced by John Larkin

Jim Madden lies dying in the street, a knife protruding from his chest. He begs Sue Parker to run for a doctor but it is too late. Realizing he is dead, she goes directly to the saloon, screaming "Murder!" Approaching Jeb Randall, who is playing poker with the boys, she delivers the startling news that the banker has been murdered and that his dying words were "Jerry did it."

Aboard the *Enterprise,* two young men, Jerry Madden and Brad Fallon are enjoying the scenery. If one or both of them has just committed murder, it isn't apparent from their demeanor. Continuing the theme of Joshua having done everything and been everywhere, he mentions to Jerry that he met his father, Mr. Madden, in 1834 and considered him a good man.

Back in Scottsville, Sue enlarges her story: Jerry knifed his father, and then stole some money. A man reports he saw the boys board the *Enterprise.* The locals debate what to do. The sheriff is out of town and the circuit judge won't be around for two months. Jeb decides they must take matters into their own hands. They will bring the boys back and hang them.

Tom Fowler argues against such rash action. He insists that Jerry and Brad be given a fair trial. Jeb gives in and decides if the self-appointed posse rides across country, they can catch up to the riverboat at Benton's Landing. They rush off.

On the boat, Chip is practicing target shooting with a pistol. He misses every one and Grey gives a demonstration of his own ability, easily hitting the bottles. But he explains shooting bottles is not the same as shooting men and thinks Chip ought to wait until he's older to handle a gun.

Captain Holden meant to bypass Benton's Landing but when he sees a passenger flag outside, he orders the boat over. At the same time, Carney warns him the crosshead is frozen and will require repairs.

At the dock, Jeb and the posse confront Grey. Jeb identifies himself as a deputy and demands the suspects be turned over to him. He has no papers to prove his authority, and suspecting a lynch mob, Grey refuses the request, even though the youths agree to surrender. A shoot-out ensues but when it is apparent the *Enterprise* is incapacitated, the posse holds its fire. During the gunfight, Chip grabs a rifle and tries to help. Grey takes the weapon away from him and sends him to his quarters as punishment.

Jeb sneaks aboard and while Grey and Carney are attempting to unfreeze the crosshead, he comes upon them, gun drawn. He demands the killers, and Jerry comments that Jeb is a "fanatic about murder." He always tries to get on jury duty any time a killer is being tried. That doesn't prevent Jerry from giving himself up and Jeb takes the suspects away.

Holden leaves Carney in charge as he and Joshua go after the boys, the captain feeling it is his duty to protect his passengers. They run across Miss Parker on the trail and she repeats her eyewitness story. Neither believe her.

The crew catch up to the posse as Jeb suggests they string up the murderers. Tom Fowler insists they have a fair trial, however, and he reluctantly agrees.

By the time Grey and Joshua reach Scottsville, the trial is underway. The local drunk, Sam Bridges, has been voted judge and twelve men appointed jurors. Tom stands as Jerry and Brad's council. Grey and Joshua barge in and listen as Sue gives her testimony. She is reluctant to say anything against Jerry because they were engaged to be married, but Jeb presses her to tell the truth. She repeats the same story, adding that she witnessed the killing and the subsequent robbery. Not surprisingly, the jury reaches a verdict of guilty.

It turns out Jeb is in love with Sue but she preferred Jerry because his father was rich. It might have worked out, too, but Jim Madden and the other self-righteous men of town did not approve of "her kind." He talked his son out of the engagement and sent him and his friend to New Orleans (explaining why they were aboard the *Enterprise*). She and Jeb are both bitter about people who hold themselves over the less fortunate.

Part of Jeb's anger against killers stems from the fact he saw his own father gunned down. Ever since, he has hated murderers and wants to see them all punished. (Reference Dunnagan in "Fight at New Canal," 1.23.)

The boys are taken to a barn outside town to await hanging at sunrise. Grey sneaks in to see Miss Parker and gets her to confess she was lying. He hurries her toward the barn, hoping to convince the townsmen not to commit a terrible miscarriage of justice.

As dawn approaches, the boys are afraid. Jerry repeats the Lord's Prayer. Grey brings Sue up just in time but she reneges on her promise and insists the boys are guilty. By this time, however, the posse has second thoughts about the hanging and urges Jeb to wait for the sheriff. But he is impatient and plans on hanging Jerry, first by putting a noose around his neck, and then having three men haul him off the ground.

Sue tries to hide her eyes, but Holden makes her watch and she finally breaks down and confesses. It was she who killed Mr. Madden because he scorned her and sent Jerry away. Jeb is incensed and becomes violent. Grey shoots him dead. Miss Parker is ordered held over for the authorities.

Back on board the *Enterprise*, Joshua is telling Chip how the boy helped the situation by praying. Grey observes that Chip ought to be punished for his stunt with the rifle at Benton's Landing and decides the proper course of action would be that Chip take apart and clean all nine of his pistols. That pleases everyone and the *Enterprise* happily steams away.

"Hang the Men High" was pretty standard Western fare: evil woman wants money. Evil woman kills for spite. Evil woman blames innocent son. (Mostly) good man in love with evil woman. (Mostly) good man seeks revenge. Very good series regular doesn't believe evil woman. Very good series regular gets evil woman to confess. Innocent boys are saved. (Mostly) good man dies. Evil woman punished. The intervening 50 minutes are fleshed out by "plot."

Stephen McNally (given a starring credit in the opening titles, but not in the end ones) was superb as Jeb Randall and his presence gave the episode a credibility it didn't deserve. James Nusser (in an uncredited role) as the town drunk/judge was up to his usual excellent standard and the supporting cast was adequate.

Continuing the tradition of having Joshua be the Everywhere Man, writer Adelman sneaked in a line about his knowing Mr. Madden in 1834 and was good for a knowing nod. The idea of hanging the boys by strangulation (pulled up by a rope) was odd, considering there were numerous discussions throughout the script of stringing them up from trees. In actuality, it was a plot to delay the executions until Grey could save the day and was obvious as such.

The "Crew of the Enterprise*" was listed as Lambert, Wessel, McGreevey. This marks the end of Terry Blake and Pickalong, who disappear without warning or further mention.*

GUEST CAST

Stephen McNally *(b. 7/29/1913, New York, NY; d. 6/4/1994, Beverly Hills, CA, heart failure.)* A successful attorney, he abandoned the law for acting, originally going under his real name, Horace Vincent McNally. In 1946, he changed his name to Stephen. Usually playing a character actor with few redeeming characteristics, he shone as Locky McCormick in *Johnny Belinda* (1948). His last credit was an episode of *Fantasy Island* (1980).

Karen Steele *(b. 3/20/1931, Hawaii; d. 3/12/1988.)* A former cover girl, she is most noted for her role in *Marty*, and also made numerous TV appearances, probably the most notable as Eve McHuron in the episode of *Star Trek*, "Mudd's Women."

Walter Sande *(b. 7/9/1906, Denver, CO; d. 11/22/1971, Chicago, IL.)* For Western aficionados, his appearance on the three-part episode of *Gunsmoke*, "Gold Train: The Bullet" (1971) would stand out as a role of major significance. He made the rounds of the TV Westerns of the day, and many of his film roles went uncredited.

Dallas Mitchell. A stunt man/character actor whose roles generally went uncredited or with character names such as "Cowboy." He made an episode of *The Outsider* with McGavin entitled "Tell It Like It Is... And You're Dead" (1968) and also co-starred in a first-year *Star Trek* episode "Charlie X," playing Tom Nellis. His last credit came in 1977 in a TV film called *Tail Gunner Joe,* playing a reporter.

Ray Hamilton. His two other credits beside *Riverboat* are *Bat Masterson* (1958) and *The Aquanauts* (1960).

1.28 **"Night of the Faceless Men"**. . . . .*March 28, 1960*
Directed by William Witney
Written by Bob and Wanda Duncan
Produced by John Larkin

Hooded men surround a terrified victim. The leader declares that the prisoner has been found guilty of a $5,000 theft from a stage robbery and is condemned to death. He orders several thugs, picked at random through a lottery system, to carry out justice. They fire, murdering the supposed criminal. Hooded riders then dump the body in town, announcing to the citizens that they stand for law and order.

Aboard the *Enterprise,* Captain Holden discovers no one in town will sell him any wood. He plans to go and seek the reason when more hooded riders dash up and toss Carney onto the deck. They warn Grey to "get this tub out of here," because they don't like strangers.

Danny Flynn, one of the river men, explains this used to be a good town before the "nightriders" took over. They profess to uphold the law, but mostly they want land cheaply and to cheat people. Taking Joshua with him, Grey decides to seek out an old acquaintance, Joe Oliver. If anyone can help them, Joe can.

They enter a very lively saloon, with music and dancing. Joe is behind a screen, kissing a woman. When summoned, he greets the pair as "old pals." He introduces his companion, Eileen, as his fiancée and she informs her astonished listeners Joe has turned over a new leaf and reformed. Formerly, he was a gambler Grey threw off the *Enterprise* "over a year ago" for running a crooked card game. Joe not only owns the saloon, now, he has built a school for the town.

What he can't do is procure wood for the boat. The locals only sell to those who pay extra for the privilege. Before he can explain further, a gang of hooded men come for him. A fight ensues, Joe is taken, Grey is beaten and Joshua, who

Hugh Downs made his only episodic television appearance in the Riverboat *episode "Night of the Faceless Men." In these two publicity stills, he poses with Darren McGavin in the pilothouse of the* Enterprise.

went after their friend, is pummeled and whisked away. When Grey comes to, he demands to know where the sheriff is so he can report the abduction. Eileen tells him there is no official law: the hooded men have taken over that responsibility. But she adds he might try Mr. Rogers, the lawyer.

Grey barges in and finds Rogers in the company of Mr. McLeish. Rogers can't help, and McLeish, who is in change of the "Committee," promises to do what he can but is doubtful of the outcome. Grey leaves, only to find a message placed over an empty hood and set through the tines of a pitchfork. It reads, "Sail by tonight and you get your man back. Stay and he dies." Grey takes it with him and returns to the boat.

Confronted by the problem, Carney decides they ought to leave, thus saving Joshua, as Joe Oliver is not one of them and they have no obligation to him. Although putting the choice to the vote, Grey then overrides it and decides to take the town apart in an effort to find the two missing men. Carney readily agrees.

The crew search the town. Eileen volunteers her services and goes with Grey to the Pauley house. Mrs. Pauley doesn't want "that kind of woman in her house," but relents and lets them in. The prisoners are not there but she gives them valuable information: the local men believe in the nightriders but the women haven't been fooled. Only they see the hooded men for what they are. Grey tries to convince her to take a stand but she is afraid.

Outside, a hooded rider attacks Grey and he fights him off. Before the man can run away, one of his own brotherhood shoots him in the back. Grey carries the body to Mrs. Pauley's where she discovers, to her horror, that the dying man is her husband. Harry was killed so he couldn't talk to Grey.

Grey leaves and considers canceling the effort. Eileen pleads with him to stay and help, when Rogers and McLeish appear. McLeish explains Joshua was taken by mistake. If Holden steams 20 miles downriver, he can pick up the crewmember at Crawley's Wood Station. But if he stays around until after sunset, it will be too late to see Joshua alive. Back on the *Enterprise*, Grey puts the decision up to vote again: do they stay and look for both men or do they leave and save only Joshua? They owe Joe Oliver nothing and decide to leave.

Eileen suspects Captain Holden will abandon Joe, so she appeals to Mrs. Pauley. If only they can make Grey "really mad," he will stay and continue the search. Mrs. Pauley finally realizes how much Joe means to the saloon woman and develops a plan. Aboard the *Enterprise,* she tells the captain Eileen is a bad woman; the saloon girl hatched the scheme to get Joe captured because with him out of the picture Eileen inherits everything. He appears unmoved, however, and the boat departs.

Around a bend in the river they run out of fuel and crash into the bank. While Chip laments the fact they are leaving Joshua behind, Grey reassures him. They are just playing a ruse. He intends to go back and surprise a few people. He and Danny dress as civilians and return to town. They hold Mr. Rogers at gunpoint and demand information. The lawyer pleads his case, saying he only pretended to be a nightrider, but actually he is against them. McLeish was the one who stole the $5,000 in the stage robbery and he runs the hooded men.

Chip, still distressed over affairs, slips off the *Enterprise* and goes in search of Joshua. Meanwhile, Grey sneaks into the hardware store and breaks into McLeish's safe, recovering the $5,000. McLeish finds him and they fight, Grey managing to escape with the loot. He runs to Mrs. Pauley, who protects him when McLeish follows. Grey leaves the money with her.

Chip finds a barn/warehouse outside town guarded by a hooded man. Sneaking a peek through the window, he spies Joshua and Joe hung to the ceiling by their

In an oddly staged (but dramatic) fight scene which never happened, Holden and crewman Danny Flynn fight it out on the streets of a Western town.

hands. Luring the guard outside, Chip tries to cut the captives down but doesn't succeed. He runs for help. On his way into town, he prays he doesn't get lost.

Grey confronts Eileen in the saloon and accuses her of having Joe change his will in her favor. She pleads her innocence but he doesn't believe the story. Outside, Grey is attacked and captured by the hooded men.

It nears sundown and the crew is restive. They can't find Chip and they don't know where Grey is. Time is growing short and things look grim. In town, Eileen

Hugh Downs' character entertains Grey Holden with his guitar, and poses on horseback to give an authentic Western flavor to a series about a Mississippi riverboat.

goes to Mrs. Pauley. She pleads with the widow to gather the women and march. If they band together, they can cause enough confusion to hold off the nightriders until the crew of the *Enterprise* come to help.

The hooded men assemble in the warehouse. The trial for the three captives has been held *in absentia;* all are found guilty. Joe will be executed first, with Joshua and Grey to follow. Before the sentence can be carried out, the league of women soldiers arrive. They pull open the doors and accuse the townsmen of being fooled by McLeish. Identifying them one-by-one, Mrs. Pauley carries her point and the men flee in shame. She unties Grey and he fights McLeish, beating him into a pulp. When the crew arrive, they find all is well and their assistance is not needed.

Eileen can now confess her ruse: she loves Joe and the story told by Mrs. Pauley was only to incite his anger. Grey is astonished that he was had, but finally acknowledges the truth and is glad all worked out for the best.

Back aboard the *Enterprise*, Chip, wearing a hood, flies out at Grey. He scares him and has a good joke, declaring it is October 31. Shouting, "Happy Halloween," he finally makes Grey laugh and all is well.

"Night of the Faceless Men" is the best script Bob and Wanda Duncan wrote for Riverboat. *Although another "Western theme," it was handled far better than others of the genre and made for good entertainment. For once, women were written in a dignified manner and the writers actually allowed them to save the day. This was strong writing for any period and especially for the 1960's. Both Eileen and Mrs. Pauley were positive characters and good acting made the story believable.*

William Witney was also on top of his game, and the direction stood out as innovative and effective.

There is little to nitpick in this episode. Having Joe recognize Joshua as a crewmember catapults the timeframe far into the future, making it at least 1848, so that in less than one full season, the series has advanced seven years. The worst transgression, however, was the reasoning used to make Grey "really mad." Sensing he could not be persuaded to save Joe by any humanitarian means, Eileen and Mrs. Pauley used his innate distrust of women to carry their argument. He too readily believed Eileen's greed as a factor in setting up Joe. As an excuse to stay and find the reformed gambler, it stood out as a sore point. Appealing to friendship, loyalty or decency would have been a far better tack for the writers to have used. As it is, they gave Holden a very unlikable character trait.

Casting a "name" actor as one of the crew also mitigated any suspense about Danny's welfare. Any savvy viewer would know Hugh Downs would not be killed off early in the episode. As it turned out, he had few significant scenes, so this hardly diminished the impact.

GUEST CAST

Hugh Downs *(b. 2/14/1921, Akron, OH.) Riverboat* is his only drama credit. The remainder of his career consisted either of playing sidekick or hosting talk shows, or playing himself in guest appearances. He is best known for working *The Tonight Show* with Steve Allen (1957-62) and for hosting the *Today* show, (1962-71).

Patricia Medina *(b. 7/19/1920, Liverpool, England.)* Always playing the damsel-in-distress, perhaps her greatest claim to fame was in her selection of husbands — Richard Greene (*Robin Hood*) from 1941-51, and Joseph Cotten (1960-94; his death). For horror fans, she made two episodes of *Thriller* – playing Victorine Lafourcade in "The Premature Burial" and Nadja in "The Devil's Ticket."

Jocelyn Brando *(b. 11/18/1919, San Francisco, CA; d. 11/27/2005, Santa Monica, CA, natural causes.)* Sister of Marlon Brando, she began her career on the Broadway stage at the age of 22. Her best known film role was playing the doomed wife of Glenn Ford in Fritz Lang's *The Big Heat*, (1953). In later years she played Mrs. Krakauer on the soap *Love of Life*, and Mrs. Reeves on the TV series *Dallas*.

Charles Gray *(b. St. Louis, MO.)* He played Bill Foster in the TV soap *The Young and the Restless* (1976). He appeared in *Ike* (1979) as Gen. Lucian Truscott.

Douglas Kennedy *(b. 9/14/1915, New York, NY; d. 8/10/1973, Honolulu, HI, cancer.)* After graduation from Amherst and a stint in the Signal Corps during WWII, he garnered bigger and better roles in Hollywood, usually as a supporting character or a thug. He played the title role in the TV series *Steve Donovan, Western Marshal* (1955) and was a policeman taken over by Martians in *Invaders from Mars* (1953). Later, Western fans fondly remember him as playing Sheriff Fred Madden on *The Big Valley* (1967-69).

Frank Ferguson *(b. 12/25/1899, Ferndale, CA; d. 9/12/1978, Los Angeles, CA, cancer.)* Probably best identified as Gus on *My Friend Flicka* (1959) or as Eli Carson on *Peyton Place*, his is as well-known a face as any character actor's of the era. His earliest credit was *Gambling on the High Seas* (1940) and his last playing Grandpa Macahan on *How the West Was Won* (1977), a reprise of his role on *The Macahans* (1976).

1.29 "The Long Trail" . . . .*April 4, 1960*
Directed by Hollingsworth Morse
Written by Oscar Saul
Produced by John Larkin

Grey Holden's opening narration begins by saying Indian Country is to the east and the Cherokee are being moved off their land "and sent on the long trail" west.

Over the scene of a Cherokee village, raiders ride in, shooting anyone and everything. After finishing their deadly deed, those Indians remaining come out of hiding, demanding to know from Colonel Tracker what he plans to do about punishing those guilty of the atrocity. The army officer dismisses their pleas by stating that even if he caught those killers, others would follow in their place.

Speaking to James, a college-educated brave, and his father Mark Evans, both of whom wear "white man's" clothes, Tracker informs them that the only way to stop the attacks is to move out. The government has set aside land for them to the west. They can either cooperate and agree to be moved, or die.

Holden's narration continues. The *Enterprise* is on the Tennessee River. He is well familiar with the Cherokee, one of the most highly educated tribes. On a prior trip, he brought in a printing press so there could even be an Indian newspaper.

As the boat docks, Colonel Tracker goes aboard. He wants to hire Grey to transport the Indians to their new lands. When the captain refuses, he presents orders from the "territorial general," demanding compliance. Holden may either wait where he is, or go with the colonel to hurry matters along. Because Grey is personally familiar with James and Mark Evans, he reluctantly agrees to accompany the Indians on the long trail.

The two men return to the village, Grey remarking that Tracker must have bad luck to be assigned this unenviable task. On the contrary, Tracker volunteered for it, knowing that a successful enterprise will earn him a general's commission.

Grey meets James, who refuses to shake his hand. Although once friends and appreciative of Grey's effort to bring them the press, which his father uses for the newspaper, James' attitude toward white men has changed. Although his mother was a white woman, he considers all Caucasians his enemies and all Indians his friends. Grey tries to talk sense to James' father, but Mark is a drunk and offers little resistance to his son's hostility.

James refuses to go along with the army plan to relocate, even though Chief White Bull has promised to sign a treaty, pledging compliance. He threatens to stay and fight. A council is called with James now in ceremonial dress. White Bull has second thoughts about the treaty so Tracker pulls him aside. He warns he has 1,000 soldiers only a day's march away. Sign, or be attacked. This gives him no choice and the deal is made.

The Indians must now march on an 8-10 day trek to the river, which the army officer demands be accomplished in five days. The Indians move out, with the weak and infirm suffering. One old man dies and is buried along the way.

James continues to complain, in open contention with White Bull. Finally, the leader pulls him aside. Although he does not like the youth because he wore white man's clothes and his mother was white, he does not want to completely alienate him. He divulges that he only signed the treaty because the Indians will be given money when they reach the river. With gold, he plans on buying guns for an armed resistance. This pacifies James and when the colonel demands they use a shortcut through a swamp to shorten the route, he must go along. This leaves Grey as the only antagonized party, for he believes White Bull has sold his people out.

Along the way, Mark gets drunk and threatens to write editorials against Colonel Tracker and White Bull. For the crime of bringing whisky into camp, Tracker orders him to receive 20 lashes and has his wagon burned, destroying the press in the process.

The party arrive at the *Enterprise* but the Indians refuse to board until being paid. The officer gives them some, but not all the money promised. They eventually accept what they are given and file into the boat. Tempers flair, however, and another council is called, pitting James against White Bull. The chief says his medicine is stronger than James' and to prove the Great Spirit is with him, he offers a desperate gamble: endure "self-inflicted torture" by having poisoned arrow tips cut his back and hang suspended by his arms until sunrise. If he survives, he will have nullified James' battle totem, a tomahawk.

White Bull manages to endure the torture and thus reasserts his authority. James must stand down, but when he learns the *Enterprise* has bypassed the Great Oaks Wood Stop (where the chief told him they were to buy weapons), he is very angry.

It is subsequently revealed that White Bull has, indeed, suffered grievously from the endurance test. His back is infected and his limbs weak. Knowing this, James refuses to honor the treaty and calls his braves to arms. If they erupt into warfare, both Colonel Tracker and Captain Holden will be turned over to squaws, who will torture them to death.

James also discovers that the chief has an added incentive for his ready compliance with the army. He made a private deal, receiving $10,000, choice land in the new territory and the promise he be made supreme chief of all displaced Indians. White Bull and Tracker get in a fight and both men fall overboard. No effort is made to rescue them.

Holden is now in full command of the boat. James threatens to shoot him but Grey argues that if he does, he only helps his enemies. He reluctantly makes up with Grey and Mark swears off whisky.

The *Enterprise* arrives in the Oklahoma Territory and the Cherokee disembark. They agree the new land seems promising and they will try and make a new start. All is not as peaceful as it seems, however, as an armed band of Pawnee approach and threaten the newcomers. They were there first and don't want any strange Indians. A gunfight breaks out and Grey shoots the Pawnee leader. He then promises James ten guns to use to defend the tribe.

This teaches James a lesson. Not all white men are his enemies and not all Indians are his friends.

As the *Enterprise* steams away, Grey tells Chip that he hopes someday there will be no more hatred.

However promising this script may have looked on paper, it was a dreadful, forgettable episode. Producer John Larkin must have had an open casting call: anyone who doesn't look Anglo-Saxon may apply for the three lead roles. The result was Perry Lopez as James, Abraham Sofaer as Mark Evans and Anthony Caruso as White Bull. In fairness, the latter actors were often cast as Indians, but seldom to good effect. While both were capable actors, put together with this script, the result was sheer humiliation and must have made them want to hide their heads in the sand. Harry Lauter wasn't any better as the stiff-necked, stereotypical colonel.

The plot suffered from the character of White Bull selling out his tribe. There was enough tragedy in the idea of Native Americans being displaced against their will without the unnecessary double-dealing. Sticking in Mark Evans' drunkenness seemed a nod of the head to the modern conception of the drunken Red Man and the scene at the end where the Pawnee tribe showed up just long enough to be shot by Grey had all the feel of a "thank you" scene so James could declare the expected, "Not all white men are bad and not all Indians are good" sermon.

The direction by Hollingsworth Morse was no better than adequate with some bad fight scenes and obvious doubles. The sets, usually acceptable (although obviously redresses from those used in every episode) were particularly bad, especially those of the Cherokee village. While making one sound stage into the exterior of an entire village is difficult, this one was cramped, brittle and lifeless. Subsequent scenes of the "long trail" were no better. Thankfully, Morse didn't bother filming the party going through the swamp or that would have been another painful embarrassment.

It is also historically interesting to note that many Indian tribes resisted being moved by steamboat because they believed the women and children would drown. The fear was not ungrounded and they did not go easily along with the forced westward migration and often put up stiff resistance.

GUEST CAST

Perry Lopez *(b. 7/22/1931, New York, NY.)* Most often playing Spanish or Mexican characters, the bulk of his work was done in the mid 1950's through the 1960's. Probably the most recognizable credit would be from the *Star Trek* episode "Shore Leave," where he played Esteban Rodriguez.

Abraham Sofaer *(b. 10/1/1896, Rangoon, Burma; d. 1/21/1988, Woodland Hills, CA, congestive heart failure.)* Usually cast as an Egyptian, an Indian or some other suspicious, nondescript character, he is probably best recognized from *Star Trek*, playing Melkotian in the episode "Spectre of the Gun" (1968), or *The Night Stalker*, as the Rakshasa Hunter in "Horror in the Heights" (1974). For those well-versed in TV anthology series, he would be easily recognized for playing "Nicolai" in an episode of *Thriller* entitled "The Weird Tailor" (1961).

Anthony Caruso *(b. 4/7/1916, Frankfort, IN; d. 4/4/2003, Brentwood, CA.)* Another actor from the Pasadena Playhouse (where he met and befriended Alan Ladd), he was often cast as foreign characters, or American Indians throughout his career, with character names such as "Rocco," "Chief Blackfish" and "Don Miguel Ruiz." He made frequent appearances on TV, including an episode of *Gunsmoke* entitled "Lynott" where he played "Talley" opposite Richard Kiley (1971). He also played Bela Oxmyx on the *Star Trek* episode, "A Piece of the Action" (1968).

Harry Lauter *(b. 6/19/1914, White Plains, NY; d. 10/30/1990, Ojai, CA, heart failure.)* With over 300 credits to his name (many of them *un*credited) and dating back to 1930 *The Family Ford*, he appeared in many TV episodes and films, including *Escape from the Planet of the Apes* (playing Gen. Winthrop; 1971) and the soap *Days of Our Lives* (1966) as Craig Merritt.

1.30 "The Quick Noose". . . . .*April 11, 1960*
Directed by Hollingsworth Morse
Written by Tom Seller
Produced by John Larkin

Carney is outside a fine old Southern mansion, determined to get inside. Behind closed doors, a terrible row is in progress. A young man named Barton Wingate is arguing with Amy Carstens, his fiancée. She tells him there will be no marriage and runs into the library, locking him out. Infuriated, he bangs on the door. Before he has a chance to beat it down, he is knifed in the back. The hapless Carney is arrested for his murder.

The *Enterprise* steams into dock with everyone eagerly anticipating the arrival of their engineer who has been gone for a month (visiting his brother). Nearby, a gallows is being constructed, promising a grim fate for some convicted felon. The town sheriff arrives and provides Captain Holden with the news: his officer is to be hanged tomorrow morning. He had a trial two weeks ago and was legally declared guilty.

Grey goes to the jail to get the story from Carney. Peculiarly resigned to his fate, Carney relates that he was drunk on the night in question. He was in the local saloon when Bart Wingate insulted a woman named Ruby. He pulled a knife on the brute but fell over a chair and lost his weapon. Bart took it with him as a trophy and Carney was only trying to get it back when the murder occurred. His presence at the house, coupled with the fact his knife protruded from Bart's back was enough to convict him of the crime.

Determined to get the truth, Grey goes to Judge Wingate's house. He is accosted by Jim, who pulls a gun, warning that everyone loves the judge and will do everything in their power to protect the grieving father. Unable to get an interview, Grey speaks with Amy, whose guardian is Judge Wingate. She hastily informs the captain to go back to his boat: Carney will not be allowed to hang, but in the interim, he is to do nothing to interfere. When he argues, Amy throws him out.

Miss Ruby visits Grey aboard the *Enterprise*. She defends Carney and gives Grey a list of those who might have committed the murder. Apparently, Bart Wingate was not well liked and any one of the people she enumerates, including Amy Carstens, may actually have perpetrated the deed. Bart was a barroom brawler and a card shark. She defends Carney but Joshua doesn't believe her, so she, too, gets added to the "list."

On deck, Chip is very upset and blames Grey for not freeing Carney. Joshua advises that the more he prays, the more it will help.

Grey begins his investigation with Lon Ogden, a bank clerk with heavy gambling debts. Pretending to have bought the man's IOU's, Grey threatens to show them to his employer unless he talks. Ogden says he was at the house during the night in question and confesses he and Amy are in love. A quarrel broke out when Amy told Bart she was breaking her engagement.

Holden determines there is a conspiracy of silence. He suspects many people know who really killed Bart but they are determined to protect the guilty party. He complains it is easier to kill one man than a whole town. Complicating matters, the sheriff warns Grey not to cause trouble.

Ignoring good advice, Grey returns to the mansion for another round of questioning. When Amy gives him a different story of where the judge was, he calls her a liar and she slaps him.

Convinced everyone is protecting the murderer, Grey and Joshua plan a breakout. Attaching a rope to the paddlewheel, they pull out the bars of the cell and free Carney. A fight breaks out in the street, with the captain and pilot making it back safely to the *Enterprise*. Carney, however, is not with them. Jim and company run a log through the paddle wheel so the boat can't pull out and Grey permits the townspeople to search, knowing the prisoner isn't there.

Amy finds the seemingly mortally wounded Carney and brings him to Ruby's room in the hotel to hide. They want to get him back to the boat but he moans and groans and insists on having his wound treated. Ruby goes to the *Enterprise* and solicits Chip's aid in getting the medicine chest from Grey's quarters. Grey discovers the box is missing but Chip won't say who came for it or why because he gave his word.

Guessing Miss Ruby was the woman who came aboard, Grey goes to her room where Carney is in a "delicate condition." It turns out the engineer has sustained no more than a flesh wound but he continues to act as though he's dying. Grey returns to the boat where he demands to speak with the judge. There is a confrontation with Jim, and Grey shoots him before he finally agrees to the meeting. Amy and Wingate arrive and they rehash the story yet again.

It turns out Barton was a bad apple; mean-spirited and vindictive, hardly the son the judge deserved. Wingate finally confesses he committed the murder and to demonstrate his prowess with a knife, throws it across the room, striking a small target. He says he never intended for Carney to take the blame and ultimately would have confessed.

Carney is exonerated and back on the boat; he is slow to convalesce. Chip waits on him and Grey admonishes that his crewman ought not to consider visiting his brother again for another three to four years.

This is the first of what might be called a "Carney episode." It had the look and feel of a 1940's Poverty Row mystery, with enough red herrings to make you look around the corner in anticipation of Bela Lugosi popping up as the prime (but innocent) suspect.

With little action, most of the hour was taken up telling and retelling the story that quickly grew stale in repetition. For an innocent man about to be hanged, Carney's resignation was a little hard to fathom and the scenes in Ruby's room where he believed himself to be mortally wounded bordered on the bizarre.

Except for William Bouchey who gave a very good performance as Judge Wingate, the guest stars were only so-so. Ed Nelson went in and out of a Southern dialect (a problem he had in several early TV shows, possibly because he had tried so hard to lose his native dialect and had trouble actually using it when called for), and Nan Leslie and Darlene Fields (as Amy and Ruby) were unremarkable. Dick Wessel (as was often the case) had trouble maintaining Carney's Irish accent and while his performance lived up to expectations, the characterization was out in left field. Mike McGreevey, as usual, shone as Chip, and his scenes were the only respite to a boring, confusing and ultimately flat script.

For this episode, the order of the "Crew of the Enterprise*" was changed to Lambert, Wessel and McGreevey, although in fairness, if they were listing them in order of screen time, Wessel deserved to be over Lambert, as he had been for most of Season One.*

GUEST CAST

Nan Leslie *(b. 6/4/1926, Los Angeles, CA; d. 7/30/2000, San Juan Capistrano, CA, pneumonia.)* Appearing in many Westerns in the 1940's and 50's, she also appeared in the TV series *The Californians* as Martha McGivern (1957-58) and *King's Row* (1955; playing Randy Monaghan). Her last credit was *The Bamboo Saucer* (1968).

Ed Nelson *(b. 12/21/1928, New Orleans, LA.)* Best remembered for his role as Dr. Michael Rossi on *Peyton Place* (1964), he began his career in 1955 when Roger Corman went to Ed's native state to shoot *Swamp Woman*. Nelson worked on the film in every capacity from location manager to alligator wrestler and went on to work in many Corman projects including *Attack of the Crab Monsters* (1957). Between this time and *Peyton Place*, he had two 1961 guest star roles in *Thriller* ("Dialogues with Death," and "A Good Imagination.") Another excellent role was a 1972 episode of *Night Gallery* called "Little Girl Lost." His last credit is *Runaway Jury* (2003).

Jack Mather *(b. 9/21/1907; d. 8/15/1966, Wauconda, IL, heart attack.)* His first role was in the film, *Up in the Air (1940)*. His career basically began and ended in the 1950's, however. His last credit was an episode of *Wagon Train* in 1962.

1.31 "The Sellout" . . . .*April 18, 1960*
Directed by Richard H. Bartlett
Teleplay by Ann Wesley
Story by R. Hamer Norris
Produced by Richard H. Bartlett

The episode begins during a terrible storm. With Grey and Joshua in the pilothouse, they observe the *Enterprise* is only two miles from Natchez but they have no cargo in the hold for ballast, so the going is rough. Logjams are coming at them all directions and ultimately one strikes the boat, tearing a huge hole in the engine room. With water pouring in, Carney warns that if water hits the engines, they will all blow up.

Fortunately, this dire prediction does not happen, although by the way the scene was directed, that would have been nearly impossible. In Natchez, Grey begins the rounds, seeking an $8,000 loan to have the *Enterprise* repaired. When no one will help him, he ends up at the Channing Brokerage. George Channing, the lender, refuses Grey's appeal, even on the strength of his reputation (which is good or bad, depending on the episode). He does, however, offer to outright buy the boat, remarking that with dock charges eating him alive and no money to pay his crew, Grey will be begging in a month to dispose of the boat for salvage.

Since Channing controls the town, he offers Grey no choice, but he refuses and storms off. This decision does not please Nanette Burns, Channing's partner, who declares that since George's "plan" did not work, she will try one of her own.

Back aboard the *Enterprise,* Joshua and Carney are concerned about the situation and puzzled why Grey did not make a more concerted effort to obtain financing. Chip wants to know if it's all right to pray for money. Grey replies, "I don't think anyone will mind."

Captain Nick Logan, an old friend of Grey's, comes aboard and they have a private conversation. Logan lost his boat six months ago and he still has a valuable cargo to ship. He knows Grey needs $8,000 for repairs and offers him a deal: he will pay to have the *Enterprise* repaired. In exchange, he leases the boat for two months to deliver his merchandise. The only catch is, Logan does not need Grey's crew but will pay them half salary for the time he is away. The two old pals yuk it up and Grey agrees to the terms.

It turns out Nick is engaged to be married to Nan, the mysterious woman who is also George Channing's partner. Logan feels bad for Grey, bemoaning the fact the river man will be lost without his boat, but she reminds him it will only be for eight weeks. He shrugs aside his objections, remarking she has brought new meaning to his life.

The deal does not sit well with Holden's crew, particularly Joshua and Carney. Joshua disdains the pay Logan offers and complains Grey has betrayed them. Chip approaches Grey as he packs to say good-bye. No one is taking him, so he plans to set out on his own. In a touchingly well-played scene Grey realizes the mistake and readily promotes Chip to cabin boy-first mate and agrees the two will stay together.

With the crew off the boat, Logan steams out of port, but it is only to go five miles up the coast. There he docks and unbeknownst to Grey, reconfigures the *Enterprise* into a gambling casino.

In town, Joshua and Carney get jobs as day laborers. Neither will have anything to do with Grey, bitter at the captain for the deal he made. Later, the local boys won't play with Chip, one in particular angry at the boy's "father." He says his uncle lost all his pay from the mines in a crooked game and Grey must be involved in the scheme. The uncle confirms the story, adding that the *Enterprise* is tied up at Clayton's Landing, where the operators are stealing money from poor working men.

Shocked by the assertion, Grey goes to the Landing to discover if the games are rigged. Nan sees him come in, however, and passes word to the dealers that they play fair with him. This apparently means letting him win (or he is extraordinarily lucky) for he takes away a large sum of money at blackjack.

Holden is not fooled, and goes to his former quarters, which have been feminized by Nan. Nick apologizes for the deception but explains he met Nan six weeks ago and now she is his fiancée. He didn't have a dime after his boat sank and he readily bought into her idea of establishing a gambling boat on the river. He denies men are being cheated and invites Grey to become a dealer.

It doesn't take Holden long to figure out the scheme. In order to convince the players the house is honest, they have men on their payroll "win." If losers are still sore, they give them back their losses, and then beat them up after they leave and take back the money. Back in town, Chip fights with his former friend's uncle after the man says the *Enterprise* is getting a bad name. When Chip complains to Joshua, he decks the offender.

Nan realizes Holden can ruin her plans so she begins to romance him. They have several kissing scenes before Nick catches on. Grey decides there can only be one captain aboard the *Enterprise* and he takes over, dealing Logan out. George Channing, who, along with Nan, stands to lose a great deal of money if the plan doesn't work, knocks Grey out and determines to carry on.

Joshua, Carney and Chip go up to the Landing and board the boat. Chip discovers Grey and Nick tied up and under guard. He runs for the crew, summoning them away from the gaming tables by telling Joshua, "Mama wants you — right now!" The men free Grey, who subsequently fights with Channing, ending by throwing him overboard. The rest of the gamblers are turned over to the sheriff.

In the end, Nick determines to change his fortunes by going to New Orleans. Grey hires him as a stoker, but when he complains Grey can't navigate, he is promoted. The rest of the crew come aboard and all ends well.

This script only works if you can believe an illegal gambling boat moored five miles off the coast of Natchez can make tens of thousands of dollars running crooked games. That seems pretty far-fetched because if it did work, everyone would be doing it. Why transport cargo and passengers when real riches were to be made dealing poker and blackjack?

It also stretches credulity that a river town like Natchez could possibly offer that many men with easy money to lose. There could not have been that many "miners" in all of Louisiana to make the venture pay off so handsomely in so short a time as two months. And if the only objection was that the Enterprise *would get a bad name, why didn't Logan simply change the name of the vessel? That way, when Grey got it back, no damage would be done to his reputation.*

Nor was any legitimate excuse given to Joshua and Carney for their intense anger at Grey for renting out the boat. Living hand-to-mouth, it is not unlikely he would find it impossible to raise the staggering sum of $8,000 to repair the boat. Had Logan's offer been a legitimate one, it would seem to have been a gift horse. Since Grey even bargained to have his crew paid half wages during their shore leave, it's hard to imagine a better deal. Instead of being bitter, they should have been the first ones to congratulate the captain. A two-month layover without incurring debt is as good as it gets, and probably better.

Historically, the crew's reaction makes even less sense. The low ratio of fixed charges to operating expenses encouraged the practice of laying up and discharging most of the crew when business was slow. During low water periods (winter and summer), all large boats sat at the wharves and the deck hands had to fend for themselves. Even tramp boats like the Enterprise *were occasionally grounded and most certainly would have discharged the crew. Steamboating was a hand-to-mouth business and no one blamed the captain/owner for saving money where he could.*

As usual, the scenes between McGavin and McGreevey were the highlight of the episode, particularly the one when Chip felt no one wanted him. It was tender and heartfelt and added a needed dimension to Holden's character.

Frank Overton, who played Captain Logan, received co-star billing in the opening and end credits and the "Crew of the Enterprise" *listed Lambert, Wessel and McGreevey.*

This episode ended Season One and although it finished on an upbeat note, one has to wonder at the co-starring credit given Frank Overton. Considering Richard H. Bartlett's propensity for producing episodes in which new characters were introduced, it raises questions as to what would transpire over the hiatus.

GUEST CAST

Frank Overton *(b. 3/12/1918, Babylon, NY; d. 4/24/1967, Pacific Palisades, CA, heart attack.)* Best identified by his role of Elias Sandoval in the *Star Trek* episode "This Side of Paradise" (1967), he played Major Harvey Stovall in the series *Twelve O'Clock High* (1964-67) and played Sheriff Heck Tate in *To Kill a Mockingbird* (1962).

Barbara Stuart *(b. Paris, Illinois.)* Early roles included playing Bessie, Gildy's secretary on the TV series *The Great Gildersleeve* (1955) and playing Alice, Howie's wife in the series *Pete and Gladys* (1960). Later film appearances included *Hellfighters* (1968) and *Airplane!* (1980).

Bartlett Robinson *(b. 12/9/1912, New York, NY; d. 3/26/1986, Fallbrook, CA.)* He began his career in 1933, performing on stage in NY before getting into films and television. He made many guest appearances from the 1950's-70's, including the famous *Twilight Zone* episode, "To Serve Man." His last work was in an episode of *Lou Grant* in 1982.

A wistful Grey Holden, in formal captain's attire, stares into the distance, with the waterfront exterior in the background in a First Season publicity still.

PART X.

CREDITS

(The designation "Guest Star," "Starring," or "Co-Starring" indicates the actor's name was listed in the front titles as well as the end credits unless otherwise stated.)

1.1 "Payment in Full" . . . .
     Guest Stars   Aldo Ray
                       Barbara Bel Geddes
                       Louis Hayward
                       William Bishop
                       Nancy Gates
                       John Larch
                       William D. Gordon
                       Barry Kelley
                       Charles Gray
                       Will Wright

1.2 "The Barrier" . . . .
     Guest Stars   John Kerr
                       Elizabeth Montgomery
                       William Bendix
                       Read Morgan
                       William Gordon *(no middle initial given)*
                       Peter Coe
                       Dick Wessel
                       Kenneth MacDonald
                       Tyler McVey

1.3 "About Roger Mowbray" . . . .
       Starring   Vera Miles
    Co-Starring   Cameron Prud'homm
                       Robert Vaughn
                       Madlyn Rhue
                       John Hoyt
                       Dick Wessel

Sandy Kenyon
Jon Lormer
Hank Patterson

1.4 "Race to Cincinnati" . . . .
      Starring   Anne Baxter
                     Monica Lewis
                     Lloyd Corrigan
                     Robert Lowery
                     Dick Wessel
                     William Gordon
                     Don Haggerty
                     Don Harvey
                     Charles Fredericks

1.5 "The Unwilling" . . . .
      Starring   Eddie Albert
                     Debra Paget

                     Russell Johnson
                     William Gordon
                     Dick Wessel
                     John Harmon
                     Ian MacDonald

1.6 "The Fight Back" . . . .
      Starring   John Ireland

                     Joan O'Brien
                     William Gordon
                     Tom Laughlin
                     Karl Swenson
                     Ken Lynch
                     Henry Danielle
                     George Mitchell
                     Robert E. Griffin

1.7 "Escape to Memphis" . . . .
      Starring   Jeanne Crain

                     Claude Akins
                     Philip Reed
                     June Dayton
                     William D. Gordon
                     Richard Wessel *(billed with his full name)*

Robert Burton
Forrest Lewis
John Holland

1.8 "Witness No Evil"...
    Starring   Vincent Price
                Barbara Lawrence
                (No other credits available)

1.9 "A Night at Trapper's Landing" ....
    Starring   Ricardo Montalban

                Peter Whitney
                Judson Pratt
                Stacy Harris
                Jack Lambert
                William Gordon
                Dick Wessel
                Raymond Bailey
                R.G. Armstrong
                Moris Ankrum
                Carol Daniels *(uncredited)*

1.10 "The Faithless"..
    Starring   Richard Carlson

                Bethel Leslie
                Bert Freed
                William Gordon
                Dick Wessel
                William Phipps
                Jeanne Bates
                Katie Sweet
                Bob Bice

1.11 "The Boy from Pittsburgh" ....
    Starring   Mona Freeman
                Tommy Nolan
                Robert Emhardt

                William Gordon
                Dick Wessel
                King Donovan
                Francis DeSales

1.12 "Jessie Quinn" . . . .
       Starring   Mercedes McCambridge *(listed as "Co-Starring" at end)*
                     Clu Gulager *(listed as "Also Starring" in end credits)*
                     Richard Gardner
                     Kevin Hagen
                     Valerie Allen
                     James Gavin
                     Charles Tannen
                     Richard Newton
                     Freeman Morse

1.13 "Strange Request" . . . .
     Guest Star   Jan Sterling *(listed as "Also Starring" in the end credits)*
   Also Starring   Rhys Williams *(not listed in the opening titles)*
                     Lawrence Dobkin *(not listed in the opening titles)*

                     Peter Lazer
                     William Gordon
                     Dick Wessel
                     Lee Van Cleef
                     Glenn Thompson
                     Larry Perron
                     Pete Dunn

1.14 "Guns for Empire" . . . .
     Guest Star   Gena Rowlands
          With   George Macready
                     Dennis Patrick
                     William Gordon
                     Dick Wessel

1.15 "The Face of Courage" . . . .
   Co-Starring   Tom Drake
                     Joanna Moore
                     Doug McClure

                     Dick Wessel
                     Jack Lambert
                     William Gordon
                     Mike McGreevey
                     Paul Birch
                     Tracey Roberts

1.16 "Tampico Raid"..

Also Starring	Pat Crowley
With	Dick Wessel
	Jack Lambert
	John Mitchum
	Mike McGreevey
	Edward Colmans

1.17 "The Landlubbers" ....
(no names in front)

Gloria Talbott
Dick Wessel
Jack Lambert
Mike McGreevey
John Mitchum
Richard Devon
Arthur Batanides
Kay Kuter
Jerry O'Sullivan
Frank Warren

1.18 "The Blowup"..
(no names in front)

With	Whitney Blake
	Dick Wessel
	Jack Lambert
	John Mitchum
	Mike McGreevey
	Dean Harens

1.19 "Forbidden Island" ....
(no names in front)
"*The Crew of the* Enterprise"

Dick Wessel
Jack Lambert
John Mitchum
Mike McGreevey

With	Bruce Gordon
	Pat Michon
	Miguel Landa
	Patrick Westwood
	Leonard Bell
	Saul Gorss

1.20 "Salvage Pirates" . . . .
  Co-Starring Judi Meredith *(at end only)*
 "*The Crew of the* Enterprise"
       Jack Lambert
       Bart Patton
       Mike McGreevey
       Dick Wessel
       John Mitchum

       Richard Garland
       Robert J. Wilke
       Bern Hoffman
       Johnstone White

1.21 "Path of the Eagle" . . . .
 (no names in front)
       Dianne Foster
       Dayton Lummis
       Dick Wessel
       Jack Lambert
       Mike McGreevey
       Myron Healey
       Wilton Graff

1.22 "The Treasure of Hawk Hill" . . . .
 (no names in front)
 "*The Crew of the* Enterprise"
       Jack Lambert
       Bart Patton
       Mike McGreevey
       Dick Wessel
       John Mitchum

       Steve Wooten
       Kent Taylor
       Virginia Christine
       Richard Hale
       Kenneth MacDonald
       Dennis Moore
       George Wallace
       Harry O. Tyler

1.23 "The Fight at New Canal" . . . .
(no names in front)
"*The Crew of the* Enterprise"
Jack Lambert
Bart Patton
Mike McGreevey
Dick Wessel
John Mitchum

Charles Aidman
Jean Allison
John Archer
Steve Mitchell
John Maxwell
Peter Brian
Richard Cutting

1.24 "The Wichita Arrows" . . . .
Tonight Starring   Dan Duryea
"*The Crew of the* Enterprise"
Jack Lambert
Bart Patton
Mike McGreevey
Dick Wessel
John Mitchum

Betty Lou Keim
Don Haggerty
Eve McVeagh
Victor Millan
Robert Armstrong
Roy Barcroft

1.25 "Fort Epitaph" . . . .
Starring   Dan Duryea
"*The Crew of the* Enterprise"
Jack Lambert
Bart Patton
Mike McGreevey
Dick Wessel
John Mitchum

Charles Cooper
Brad Weston
Mark Allen

                    Jon Locke
                    Joan Camden as Barbara Daniels

1.26 "Three Graves" . . . .
    Co-Starring   Beverly Garland
   "*The Crew of the* Enterprise"
                    Jack Lambert
                    Bart Patton
                    Mike McGreevey
                    Dick Wessel
                    John Mitchum

        With   Robert Bray
                    Harry Ellerbe
                    John McKee
                    Will J. White

1.27 "Hang the Men High". . . . .
    Guest Starring   Stephen McNally
         With   Karen Steele
   "*The Crew of the* Enterprise"
                    Jack Lambert
                    Mike McGreevey
                    Dick Wessel

        And   Dallas Mitchell
                    Clay Cooper
                    Walter Sande
                    Stuart Randall
                    Phil Chambers
                    James Nusser *(uncredited)*

1.28 "Night of the Faceless Men" . . . .
    Co-Starring   Patricia Medina *(at end only)*
         With   Jocelyn Brando
   "*The Crew of the* Enterprise"
                    Jack Lambert
                    Mike McGreevey
                    Dick Wessel

                    Douglas Kennedy
                    Charles Gray
                    Frank Ferguson
                    James Anderson
        And   Hugh Downs as Dan Flynn

1.29 "The Long Trail" . . . .
  "The Crew of the Enterprise*"*

	Jack Lambert
	Mike McGreevey
	Dick Wessel
With	Perry Lopez
	Abraham Sofaer
	Harry Lauter
	Anthony Caruso
	Robert Palmer
	Dennis Cross
	Peter Mamakos

1.30 "The Quick Noose" . . . .
  "The Crew of the Enterprise*"*

Jack Lambert
Dick Wessel
Mike McGreevey

Nan Leslie
Willis Bouchey
Jack Mather
Ed Nelson
William Hudson
Irving Bacon
Darlene Fields

1.31 "The Sellout" . . . .
  Co-Starring   Frank Overton
  "The Crew of the Enterprise*"*

Jack Lambert
Dick Wessel
Mike McGreevey

Barbara Stuart
Bartlett Robinson
Bill Henry
Walter Reed
Henry Rowland
Tom Monroe

Darren McGavin and Burt Reynolds pose together on the exterior set of the
Enterprise. *A lack of character development and dueling egos ruined what might
have been a promising team. The bad blood that developed between the two actors
nearly doomed the series, cost Reynolds his job and nearly saw McGavin replaced at
mid-season.*

PART IX.

PRODUCTION CREDITS

(Bold indicates the person's name appears in conjunction with other artists else-where. Note: There are no credits available for "Witness No Evil," episode 1.8.)

DIRECTORS

Frank Arrigo   1.11 "The Boy from Pittsburgh"
(see also under Art Director)

Richard H. Bartlett   1.2   "The Barrier"
1.5   "The Unwilling"
1.10 "The Faithless"
1.16 "Tampico Raid" *(also produced)*
1.20 "The Salvage Pirates" *(also produced)*
1.31 "The Sellout" *(also produced)*

John Brahm   1.25 "Fort Epitaph"

Jules Bricken   1.4   "The Race to Cincinnati" *(also produced)*
1.6   "The Fight Back" *(also produced)*
1.12 "Jessie Quinn" *(also produced)*
1.21 "Path of the Eagle" *(also produced)*

Felix Feist   1.3   "About Roger Mowbray"
1.9   "A Night at Trapper's Landing"

Douglas Heyes   1.1   "Payment in Full" *(also wrote)*

Herman Hoffman   1.14 "Guns for Empire"

Sidney Lanfield   1.19 "Forbidden Island"

Darren McGavin   1.18 "The Blowup"

189

Hollingsworth Morse   1.27 "Hang the Men High"
                       1.29 "The Long Trail"
                       1.30 "The Quick Noose"

John Rich   1.7   "Escape to Memphis"
             1.13   "Strange Request"

R. G. Springsteen   1.23 "The Fight at New Canal"

William Witney   1.15 "The Face of Courage"
                  1.17 "Landlubbers"
                  1.22 "The Treasure of Hawk Hill"
                  1.24 "The Wichita Arrows"
                  1.26 "Three Graves"
                  1.28 "Night of the Faceless Men"

WRITERS

Bob & Wanda Duncan   1.15 "The Face of Courage"
                      1.19 "Forbidden Island"
                      1.22 "The Treasure of Hawk Hill"
                      1.24 "The Wichita Arrows"
                      1.27 "Night of the Faceless Men"

Bob & Wanda Duncan   1.7   "Escape to Memphis"
(teleplay)
Richard B. Larkin *(story)*

Douglas Heyes   1.1   "Payment in Full" *(also directed)*

Clair Huffaker   1.13 "Strange Request"

Norman Jolley   1.5   "The Unwilling"
Samuel A. Peeples

Halsey Melone   1.9   "A Night at Trapper's Landing"
                 1.21   "Path of the Eagle"

Richard N. Morgan   1.16 "Tampico Raid"
                     1.20 "The Salvage Pirates"
                     1.25 "Fort Epitaph"

Richard N. Morgan *(teleplay)*   1.10 "The Faithless"
Richard N. Morgan &
Kate and Howard Phillips *(story)*

Samuel A. Peeples   1.14 "Guns for Empire"

William Raynor *(teleplay)*   1.4   "The Race to Cincinnati"
Richard N. Morgan *(story)*

Oscar Saul   1.28 "The Long Trail"

Tom Seller   1.2   "The Barrier"
             1.12 "Jessie Quinn"
             1.17 "Landlubbers"
             1.23 "The Fight at New Canal"
             1.30 "The Quick Noose"

Robert E. Thompson &   1.6   "The Fight Back"
Mel Goldberg *(teleplay)*
Robert E. Thompson *(story)*

George Tibbles *(teleplay)*   1.11 "The Boy from Pittsburgh"
John Larkin *(story)*

Al C. Ward   1.18 "The Blowup"
           1.24 "Three Graves"

Ann Wesley *(teleplay)*   1.31 "The Sellout"
R. Hamer Norris *(story)*

Hagar Wilde *(teleplay)*   1.3   "About Roger Mowbray"
Gene Coon *(story)*

PRODUCERS

Richard H. Bartlett   1.16 "Tampico Raid" *(also directed)*
              1.20 "The Salvage Pirates" *(also directed)*
              1.25 "Fort Epitaph"
              1.31 "The Sellout" *(also directed)*

Richard H. Bartlett &   1.5   "The Unwilling" *(Jolley also wrote)*
Norman Jolley   1.10 "The Faithless"

Jules Bricken   1.1   "Payment in Full"
             1.2   "The Barrier"
             1.3   "About Roger Mowbray"
             1.4   "The Race to Cincinnati" *(also directed)*
             1.6   "The Fight Back" *(also directed)*

Jules Bricken   1.9 "A Night at Trapper's Landing"
                 1.12 "Jessie Quinn" *(also directed)*
                 1.21 "Path of the Eagle"

Gordon Kay   1.13 "Strange Request"

John Larkin   1.7 "Escape to Memphis"
               1.11 "The Boy from Pittsburgh" *(also story)*
               1.14 "Guns for Empire"
               1.15 "The Face of Courage"
               1.17 "Landlubbers"
               1.18 "The Blowup"
               1.19 "Forbidden Island"
               1.22 "The Treasure of Hawk Hill"
               1.23 "The Fight at New Canal"
               1.24 "The Wichita Arrows"
               1.26 "Three Graves"
               1.27 "Hang the Men High"
               1.28 "Night of the Faceless Men"
               1.29 "The Long Trail"
               1.30 "The Quick Noose"

MUSIC
(sole credit)

Elmer Bernstein   1.1 "Payment in Full"
                   1.2 "The Barrier"
                   1.3 "About Roger Mowbray"
                   1.4 "Race to Cincinnati"
                   1.5 "The Unwilling"
                   1.6 "The Fight Back"
                   1.10 "The Faithless"
                   1.17 "Landlubbers"
                   1.19 "Forbidden Island"
                   1.22 "The Treasure of Hawk Hill"
                   1.26 "Three Graves"
                   1.27 "Hang the Men High"
                   1.28 "Night of the Faceless Men"
                   1.29 "The Long Trail"
                   1.30 "The Quick Noose"
                   1.31 "The Sellout"

RIVERBOAT THEME
(Music Score separate)

Elmer Bernstein 1.7 "Escape to Memphis"
1.9 "A Night at Trapper's Landing"
1.11 "The Boy from Pittsburgh"
1.12 "Jessie Quinn"
1.13 "Strange Request"
1.14 "Guns for Empire"
1.15 "The Face of Courage"
1.16 "Tampico Raid"
1.17 "Landlubbers"
1.18 "The Blowup"
1.20 "The Salvage Pirates"
1.21 "Path of the Eagle"
1.23 "The Fight at New Canal"
1.24 "The Wichita Arrows"
1.25 "Fort Epitaph"

MUSIC
(Main credit under: Riverboat *theme by Elmer Bernstein)*

ARRANGED AND ADPTED BY

Leo Shuken and Jack Hayes 1.9 "A Night at Trapper's Landing"

MUSICAL SCORE

Alexander Courage 1.23 "The Fight at New Canal"

Alexander Courage and 1.20 "The Salvage Pirates"
Albert Woodbury

Gerald Fried 1.18 "The Blowup"
1.24 "The Wichita Arrows"
1.25 "Fort Epitaph"

Ruby Raskin 1.13 "Strange Request"

Ruby Raskin 1.15 "The Face of Courage"
and **Albert Woodbury**

Ruby Raksin and Nathan Scott 1.14 "Guns for Empire"

Albert Sendrey 1.7 "Escape to Memphis"

Leo Shuker and Jack Hayes   1.16 "Tampico Raid"

Fred Steiner   1.11 "The Boy from Pittsburgh"
1.12 "Jessie Quinn"

Albert Woodbury   1.21 "Path of the Eagle"

DIRECTOR OF PHOTOGRAPHY

Ray Cory   1.6 "The Fight Back"
1.7 "Escape to Memphis"
1.10 "The Faithless"
1.11 "The Boy from Pittsburgh"
1.13 "Strange Request"

Ray Flin   1.24 "The Wichita Arrows"

Buddy Harris   1.15 "The Face of Courage"
1.16 "Tampico Raid"
1.17 "Landlubbers"
1.18 "The Blowup"
1.19 "Forbidden Island"
1.21 "Path of the Eagle"
1.22 "The Treasure of Hawk Hill"
1.23 "The Fight at New Canal"
1.25 "Fort Epitaph"
1.26 "Three Graves"
1.27 "Hang the Men High"
1.28 "Night of the Faceless Men"
1.29 "The Long Trail"
1.30 "The Quick Noose"
1.31 "The Sellout"

Lionel Lindon   1.2 "The Barrier"
1.3 "About Roger Mowbray"
1.14 "Guns for Empire"

Ray Rennahan   1.1 "Payment in Full"
1.4 "Race to Cincinnati"

John L. Russell   1.5 "The Unwilling"
1.9 "A Night at Trapper's Landing"

William A. Sickner   1.12 "Jessie Quinn"
1.20 "The Salvage Pirates"

ART DIRECTOR

Frank Arrigo 1.1 "Payment in Full"
1.2 "The Barrier"
1.3 "About Roger Mowbray"
1.4 "Race to Cincinnati"
1.9 "A Night at Trapper's Landing"

Raymond Beal 1.18 "The Blowup"

Howard E. Johnson 1.13 "Strange Request"
1.14 "Guns for Empire"
1.15 "The Face of Courage"
1.16 "Tampico Raid"
1.17 "Landlubbers"
1.19 "Forbidden Island"
1.20 "The Salvage Pirates"
1.21 "Path of the Eagle"
1.22 "The Treasure of Hawk Hill"
1.23 "The Fight at New Canal"
1.24 "The Wichita Arrows"
1.25 "Fort Epitaph"
1.26 "Three Graves"
1.27 "Hang the Men High"
1.28 "Night of the Faceless Men"
1.29 "The Long Trail"
1.30 "The Quick Noose"
1.31 "The Sellout"

John L. Lloyd 1.6 "The Fight Back"
1.7 "Escape to Memphis"
1.10 "The Faithless"
1.11 "The Boy from Pittsburgh"

John Meeham 1.12 "Jessie Quinn"

EDITORIAL SUPERVISOR

David J. O'Connell 1.28 "Night of the Faceless Men"
1.29 "The Long Trail"
1.30 "The Quick Noose"
1.31 "The Sellout"

Richard G. Wray 1.1 "Payment in Full"
1.2 "The Barrier"

Richard G. Wray 1.3 "About Roger Mowbray"
1.4 "Race to Cincinnati"
1.5 "The Unwilling"
1.6 "The Fight Back"
1.7 "Escape to Memphis"
1.8 "Witness No Evil"
1.9 "A Night at Trapper's Landing"
1.10 "The Faithless"
1.11 "The Boy from Pittsburgh"
1.12 "Jessie Quinn"
1.13 "Strange Request"
1.14 "Guns for Empire"
1.15 "Face of Courage"
1.16 "Tampico Raid"
1.17 "Landlubbers"
1.18 "The Blowup"
1.19 "Forbidden Island"
1.20 "Salvage Pirates"
1.21 "Path of the Eagle"
1.22 "The Treasure of Hawk Hill"
1.23 "Fight at New Canal"
1.24 "The Wichita Arrows"
1.25 "Fort Epitaph"
1.27 "Hang the Men High"

FILM EDITOR

Howard Epstein 1.23 "The Fight at New Canal"
1.27 "Night of the Faceless Men"
1.31 "The Sellout"

Marston Fay 1.14 "Guns for Empire"
1.15 "The Face of Courage"

Lee Gilbert 1.10 "The Faithless"
1.16 "Tampico Raid"
1.18 "The Blowup"

Edward Haire 1.9 "A Night at Trapper's Landing"
1.12 "Jessie Quinn"

Lee Huntington 1.1 "Payment in Full"
1.2 "The Barrier"
1.4 "Race to Cincinnati"
1.5 "The Unwilling"

1.6 "The Fight Back"
1.11 "The Boy from Pittsburgh"
1.13 "Strange Request"
1.25 "Fort Epitaph"
1.30 "The Quick Noose"

Danny B. Landres 1.20 "The Salvage Pirates"
1.26 "Three Graves"

Robert Leo 1.7 "Escape to Memphis"

Duncan Mansfield 1.17 "Landlubbers"

Stan Rabjohn 1.19 "Forbidden Island"
1.21 "Path of the Eagle"
1.22 "The Treasure of Hawk Hill"
1.24 "The Wichita Arrows"
1.27 "Hang the Men High"
1.29 "The Long Trail"

Irving Schoenberg 1.3 "About Roger Mowbray"

MUSICAL SUPERVISION

Stanley Wilson *All episodes*

SOUND

Stephen J. Bass 1.4 "Race to Cincinnati"

Earl Crain, Sr. 1.3 "About Roger Mowbray"

1.12 "Jessie Quinn"
1.14 "Guns for Empire"

John C. Grubb 1.15 "The Face of Courage"
1.17 "Landlubbers"
1.18 "The Blowup"
1.19 "Forbidden Island"
1.21 "Path of the Eagle"

Joe Lapis 1.13 "Strange Request"

William Lynch 1.9 "A Night at Trapper's Landing"
1.20 "The Salvage Pirates"

William Lynch   1.22 "The Treasure of Hawk Hill"

Melvin M. Metcalf, Sr.   1.10 "The Faithless"

John W. Rixey   1.23 "The Fight at New Canal"

William Russell   1.5   "The Unwilling"
1.6   "The Fight Back"
1.7   "Escape to Memphis"
1.11 "The Boy from Pittsburgh"

Frank Sarver   1.14 "The Wichita Arrows"
1.25 "Fort Epitaph"
1.26 "Three Graves"
1.27 "Hang the Men High"
1.28 "Night of the Faceless Men"
1.29 "The Long Trail"
1.30 "The Quick Noose"

Virgil Smith   1.16 "Tampico Raid"

Frank H. Wilkinson   1.1   "Payment in Full"
1.2   "The Barrier"
1.31 "The Sellout"

ASSISTANT DIRECTOR

James H. Barron   1.17 "Landlubbers"

Ben Bishop   1.26 "Three Graves"

George Bisk   1.9   "A Night at Trapper's Landing"
1.14 "Guns for Empire"
1.16 "Tampico Raid"
1.18 "The Blowup"
1.29 "The Long Trail"

Milton Carter   1.12 "Jessie Quinn"
1.13 "Strange Request"
1.31 "The Sellout"

Chuck Colean   1.25 "Fort Epitaph"

Carter DeHaven III   1.6   "The Fight Back"
1.11 "The Boy from Pittsburgh"

1.21 "Path of the Eagle"
1.30 "The Quick Noose"

Edward K. Dodds 1.27 "Hang the Men High"

William Dorfman 1.20 "The Salvage Pirates"
1.24 "The Wichita Arrows"

Frank Fox 1.4 "Race to Cincinnati"
1.7 "Escape to Memphis"
1.22 "The Treasure of Hawk Hill"

Charles S. Gould 1.3 "About Roger Mowbray"
1.5 "The Unwilling"
1.10 "The Faithless"
1.15 "The Face of Courage"

James Hogan 1.1 "Payment in Full"
1.2 "The Barrier"

Nate Holt, Jr. 1.19 "Forbidden Island"

Frank Losee 1.23 "The Fight at New Canal"

Wallace Worsley 1.28 "Night of the Faceless Men"

SET DIRECTOR

George Milo 1.1 "Payment in Full"
1.2 "The Barrier"
1.3 "About Roger Mowbray"
1.5 "The Unwilling"
1.9 "A Night at Trapper's Landing"

James M. Walters 1.4 "Race to Cincinnati"
1.6 "The Fight Back"
1.7 "Escape to Memphis"
1.10 "The Faithless"
1.11 "The Boy from Pittsburgh"
1.12 "Jessie Quinn"
1.13 "Strange Request"
1.14 "Guns for Empire"
1.15 "The Face of Courage"
1.16 "Tampico Raid"
1.17 "Landlubbers"

James M. Walters   1.18 "The Blowup"
1.19 "Forbidden Island"
1.20 "The Salvage Pirates"
1.21 "Path of the Eagle"
1.22 "The Treasure of Hawk Hill"
1.23 "The Fight at New Canal"
1.24 "The Wichita Arrows"
1.25 "Fort Epitaph"
1.26 "Three Graves"
1.27 "Hang the Men High"
1.28 "Night of the Faceless Men
1.29 "The Long Trail"
1.30 "The Quick Noose"
1.31 "The Sellout"

COSTUME SUPERVISOR

Vincent Dee   *All episodes*

MAKEUP

Jack Barron   1.4 "Race to Cincinnati"
1.5 "The Unwilling"
1.9 "A Night at Trapper's Landing"
1.13 "Strange Request"
1.14 "Guns for Empire"
1.15 "The Face of Courage"

Leo Lotito, Jr.   1.1 "Payment in Full"
1.2 "The Barrier"
1.3 "About Roger Mowbray"
1.6 "The Fight Back"
1.7 "Escape to Memphis"
1.10 "The Faithless"
1.11 "The Boy from Pittsburgh"
1.12 "Jessie Quinn"
1.16 "Tampico Raid"
1.17 "Landlubbers"
1.18 "The Blowup"
1.19 "Forbidden Island"
1.20 "The Salvage Pirates"
1.21 "Path of the Eagle"
1.22 "The Treasure of Hawk Hill"
1.23 "The Fight at New Canal"
1.24 "The Wichita Arrows"

1.25 "Fort Epitaph"
1.26 "Three Graves"
1.27 "Hang the Men High"
1.28 "Night of the Faceless Men"
1.29 "The Long Trail"
1.30 "The Quick Noose"
1.31 "The Sellout"

HAIR STYLIST

Florence Bush   *All episodes*

CHOREOGRAPHY

Miriam Nelson   1.5   "The Unwilling"

PART XI.
BIOGRAPHIES

ACTORS

Darren McGavin *(b. 5/7/1922, Spokane, WA; d. 2/25/2006, Los Angeles, CA, pneumonia.)* Although his real name was William Lyle Richardson, Darren McGavin is the name that will live forever in people's minds. Born in Spokane, Washington, the feisty redhead survived a tumultuous childhood, eventually making it to New York, where he trained at the Actors' Studio. His first film role was an uncredited part in *A Song to Remember* (1945). Like many actors of the time, he traveled from coast to coast, becoming an early TV star with his first series, *Casey, Crime Photographer* (New York; 1951; no copies known to exist). He achieved acclaim as a scene stealer in *The Man with the Golden Arm* (1955) and *The Court-Martial of Billy Mitchel* (1955), both directed by Otto Preminger. He became television's *Mike Hammer* before working concurrently on *Riverboat*, both for Revue. (Darren and his wife Melanie York owned a part of *Riverboat*, under the name Meladare Company Productions.) Mixing theatre with film work, some of his best acting triumphs were on episodes of *Route 66* ("The Opponent," 1961) and *Gunsmoke* ("Gunfighter, R.I.P.," 1966). In 1967 he starred as David Ross in the Universal series *The Outsider*, and in 1970 he headlined the first traditionally acknowledged made-for-TV movie, *The Challenge* with Mako. As Universal had once tried to replace him, McGavin assumed Tony Franciosa's role on *Name of the Game* when that actor was involved in a dispute. Under the auspices of his own production company (with his wife, Kathie Browne), they put out several films, including *Happy Mother's Day, Love George* (which he directed), and *Zero to Sixty*, which he co-wrote, using his real name, W. Lyle Richardson. He won an Emmy award for his portrayal of Bill Brown in the sitcom *Murphy Brown*, in 1990. His greatest theatrical release success came when he played the Father in *A Christmas Story* (1983), which has become a holiday perennial. In 1999, after beginning an episode of *The X Files*, he suffered a stroke, from which he never fully recovered. Darren was married to Melanie York, with whom he had four children, York, Megan, Graemm Bridget and Bogart. He married Kathie Browne in 1969 and they remained a couple until her death in 2003.

Burt Reynolds *(b. 2/11/1936, Waycross, GA)* Born Burton Leon Reynolds, Jr., his family moved to Florida, where he later he excelled in football. He was nearly drafted by the Baltimore Colts before injuries ended his sports career. Burt had three TV credits before being cast in *Riverboat* as Ben Fraser: *M Squad, Schlitz Playhouse of Stars* and *The Lawless Years* (all 1959). After his brief stint on *Riverboat*, he worked in episodic TV before landing a role on *Gunsmoke*, as the half-breed Indian, Quint Asper. Working with an established cast in a stable environment, he was well received and played that character from 1962-65. He had his own show, *Hawk* (1966) and eventually went into films, where he made a name for himself in such box office successes as *Deliverance* (1972), *The Longest Yard* (1974) and the *Smokey and the Bandit* trilogy (1977, 1980, 1983). He also scored in *Boogie Nights* (1996). He was married to Judy Carne and Loni Anderson.

William Gordon *(b. 1/4/1918; d. 8/12/1991, Thousand Oaks, CA; also billed as William D. Gordon.)* His first acting credits were in 1958 on *Maverick*. Fans of *Thriller* will immediately place both his voice and his name, for he worked extensively on that series in several capacities, doing the adaptations for "The Storm" and "The Premature Burial." He also played opposite Boris Karloff in the episode, "The Premature Burial." Other acting credits include *The Twilight Zone* and *The Virginian*. His first writing credit was a 1960 episode of *Startime* called "Jeff McCleod, the Last Reb." He was an associate producer on *The Fugitive*, and wrote five episodes for that classic series. He also produced *Twelve O'Clock High* (1965-66).

Dick Wessel *(b. 4/20/1913, WI; d. 4/20/1965, Studio City, CA, heart attack; also billed as Richard Wessel.)* His first credit was in 1935 in a film called *In Spite of Danger*, and was followed up by over two hundred roles, over half of them uncredited. He appeared in innumerable Westerns usually playing rough-and-tumble characters. He was a contract player at Columbia working in comedy shorts with The Three Stooges among others. *Riverboat* supplied him with his most steady work but he continued acting until the end of his life. His last role (released posthumously) was *The Ugly Dachshund* in 1966.

Jack Lambert *(b. 4/13/1920, Yonkers, NY; d. 2/18/2002, Carmel, CA, natural causes.)* Working on Broadway before getting into films, his first credit was an episode of *Stage Door Canteen* in 1943. Like Dick Wessel, many of his roles were uncredited and like Dick, *Riverboat* provided steady work for half a season, giving him a chance to establish his face with TV viewers. He appeared in one episode of *Mike Hammer* with McGavin ("Slab Happy") and made an episode of *Thriller* ("Masquerade," 1961), four episodes of *Wagon Train*, and seven episodes of *Gunsmoke*, including "The Badge," which was also his last credited work.

Mike McGreevey *(b. 2/7/1948, Phoenix, AZ.)* The son of John McGreevey, Mike (occasionally billed as Michael) worked solidly in television as a child actor from his first credit in 1959, *The Man in the Net*, until the 1979 film, *Mysterious Island of Beautiful Women*. Along the way he appeared in three episodes of *Lassie*, and on *Dr. Kildare*, *Wagon Train*, and several *Disneyland* episodes, including "For the Love of Willadean: Treasure in the Haunted House" (1964), "The Wacky Zoo of Morgan City" (1970) and "Michael O'Hara the Fourth" (1972). He also has a successful writing career, beginning with an episode of *Wonder Woman* (1976), including four episodes of *The Waltons*, ten episodes of *Fame* (1983-87), an episode of *Star Trek: Deep Space Nine* ("Babel" 1993) and the teleplay for *Bonanza: The Return* (1993). He also directed episodes of *Born Free* (1998) and *Mowgli: The New Adventures of the Jungle Book* (1998) as well as produced episodes of *Born Free*, *Tarzan* (1966) and *High Tide* (1982). Mike is currently working on documentaries.

John Mitchum *(b. 9/6/1919, Bridgeport, CT; d. 11/29/2001, Los Angeles, CA, stroke.)* He was the brother of Robert Mitchum, was a singer, songwriter and poet as well as an actor, and was a member of the Roger Wagner Chorale. His poem, "America — Why I Love Her" was nominated as the National Poem of the United States. His first credit was *The Prairie* (billed as Jack Mitchum) and his work ran the gamut from *Sky King* (1959) through *Thriller* ("The Cheaters" as the policeman), to five episodes of *Gunsmoke*, *The Munsters* ("Underground Munster," 1965), eleven episodes of *F Troop* and *The Outlaw Josey Wales* (1976). He also appeared in one episode of *The Night Stalker* with McGavin ("The Energy Eater" as the janitor). His last credit was *A Family for Joe* (1990). He also made the first three *Dirty Harry* films as Clint Eastwood's partner Frank DiGiorgio.

Bart Patton. His first acting credit was an episode of *77 Sunset Strip* ("The Kookie Caper," 1959) and from there he graduated to *Riverboat*. He also appeared in an episode of *Thriller* ("Cousin Tundifer," 1962), *General Electric Theater* and two episodes of *Hank* (1965). His last acting credit was *Silent Victim* in 1993. He produced *Beach Ball* (1965), *Wild Wild Winter* (1966), *Out of Sight* (1966) and *The Rain People* (1969) and served as first assistant director for *A Connecticut Yankee in King Arthur's Court*.

DIRECTORS

Douglas Heyes *(b. 5/22/1919; d. 2/8/1993, Beverly Hills, CA, congestive heart failure.)* A writer, director and producer, his name has to be familiar to anyone who watched television in the 1950's and 60's. His first writing credit was an episode of *Your Jeweler's Showcase* (1953) called "The Monkey's Paw." He had a long list of writing credits before *Riverboat*, including *The Adventures of Rin Tin Tin* (1954), *Cheyenne* (1955-56), *Circus Boy* (1956), *Tales of the 77th Bengal Lancers* (1956-57) and 11 episodes of *Maverick* (1957-59). He wrote three episodes of *Thriller* (1960-61) which include probably the best episode, "The Hungry Glass" with William Shatner, as well as "The Purple Room" and "The Premature Burial." He also wrote three episodes of *Night Gallery* (1970-71), and *The Barbary Coast*, again starring William Shatner. His last two writing credits are *North and South* (1985) and *North and South, Book II* (1986). He directed many of the episodes he wrote, as well as episodes for *77 Sunset Strip* (1958), nine episodes of *Twilight Zone*, three episodes of *The Bold Ones* (1969-72), and *Hunter*. His last credit as a director was *The Highwayman* (1987). He produced, among others, *Tales of the 77th Bengal Lancers, Circus Boy, Bearcats* (1971) and *The Barbary Coast*. He was married to actress Joanna Heyes, a familiar face in 1950's and '60's episodic TV.

William Witney *(b. 5/15/1915, Lawton, OK; d. 3/17/2002, Jackson, CA, stroke; aka, William Whitney)*. He began his career at Mascot, working on Poverty Row serials. In 1935, when Mascot merged into what became Republic, he became Hollywood's youngest director at age 21, helping to pioneer action-chase scenes. Some of his early work included *The Painted Stallion* (1937), *Zorro Rides Again* (1937), *The Lone Ranger* (1938), *The Lone Ranger Rides Again* (1939) and 29 episodes of *Stories of the Century* (1954-55). Like others in the *Riverboat* class, he worked on *Sky King* and *Lassie*, as well as *Frontier Doctor* and seven episodes of *Mike Hammer* with Darren McGavin. Staying at Revue, he also directed episodes of *M Squad, Frontier Circus, Tales of Wells Fargo, Laredo, The Virginian* and *Hondo* (1967, which co-starred Kathie Browne, who would later become Mrs. Darren McGavin). His last credit was *Showdown at Eagle Gap* in 1982. He also wrote a book, *Trigger Remembered*, about Roy Rogers' horse.

Hollingsworth Morse *(b. 12/16/1910; d. 1/23/1988, Studio City, CA)*. His first credit, as an assistant director, was *The Night of Nights* (1939). Before *Riverboat*, he directed 15 episodes of *Sky King* (1952), 50 episodes of *The Lone Ranger* (1950-53), 19 episodes of *Rocky Jones, Space Ranger* (1954) and a number of low-budget science fiction films. After *Riverboat*, he directed 38 episodes of *Lassie* (1959-62), *Flipper* (1964-65), *The Rounders* (1966-67), *F Troop* (1966-67), *Adam 12* (1968-69), *H.R. Pufnstuf* (1969-70), *Operation Petticoat* (1977-78) and *The Fall Guy* (1984-86) which were his last directorial credits.

Sidney Lanfield *(b. 4/20/1898, Chicago, IL; d. 6/20/1972, Marina del Rey, CA, heart attack.)* Going from vaudeville entertainer and jazz musician to gag writing for Fox Film Corporation in 1926, Lanfield debuted in Hollywood in 1930. Specializing in light comedy, he directed many of Bob Hope's films in the 1930's and 40's. A more recognizable film to *Riverboat* fans might be Basil Rathbone's *The Hound of the Baskervilles* (1939), one of only two Sherlock Holmes adventures set in the time they were written. In the early 1950's he became one of the first major film directors to try his hand at the new medium of TV. Like many others coming to *Riverboat*, he had established credentials at Revue, working on such series as *M Squad* (seven episodes) and *Bachelor Father* (five episodes). Standing out to those who grew their horror fangs in the 1960's is the series *The Addams Family*, for which he directed 18 episodes.

WRITERS

Tom Seller *(b. 8/27/1913; d. 10/28/1989, San Francisco, CA.)* By 1959, Seller had clearly established his Western credentials (notwithstanding his first credit, which was "Andy Hardy Meets Debutante" in 1940). He went on to *The Black*

Arrow (1948), 4 episodes of the fondly remembered *Sky King* (1952) and 37 episodes of *The Lone Ranger* (1949-57). Then followed *Casey Jones* (1957) and *Death Valley Days* (1958) among others, before *Riverboat*. He went on to write for *Laramie* (1962), *Bonanza* (1964), *Destry* (1964) and *Rawhide* (1961-65). His last credit is an *Ironside* (1970) entitled "The Laying on of Hands."

Bob *(b. 9/9/1927; d. 1/28/1999)* and **Wanda Duncan** *(b. 7/27/1925, Minco, OK; d. 6/16/2007; maiden name Wanda Louise Scott).* They were a collaborative husband-wife team whose first credits were *Riverboat*. They went on to write *One Step Beyond* (1961), two episodes of *The Virginian* (1963), three episodes of *Slattery's People* (1965), nine episodes of *The Time Tunnel* (1966-67) and five episodes of *Lost in Space* (1966-68) among other series. Their last credit was a segment of *Aliens from Another Plane* (1982) called "Visitors from Beyond the Stars."

Richard Neil Morgan. Like the Duncans, Morgan was a relative newcomer to television by the time he came to *Riverboat*. His only prior work was an episode of *Cimarron City* (1959), which was also shot at Revue. Afterwards, he wrote single episodes for *Bonanza* (1961) and *The Deputy* (1961; also Revue), *Adventures in Paradise* (1961), *The Andy Griffith Show* (1965), *The F.B.I.* (1966) and *Mission: Impossible* (1969). His last credited work was an episode of *Flamingo Road* in 1981.

PRODUCERS

Jules Bricken *(b. 1915, New York, NY).* His first production credit was an episode of *Footlights Theater* in 1953. He also produced a TV production of *The Miracle on 34th Street* (1955), three episodes of *The 20th Century Fox Hour* (1955-56) and two episodes of *The Schlitz Playhouse of Stars* (1957-58) before graduating to *Riverboat*. His last producer's credit was *The Train* (1964). He was also a director, beginning with *The Answer Man #1* (1946) and including *The 20th Century Fox Hour* (four episodes, 1955-56), three episodes of *General Electric Theater* and three episodes of *Thriller* ("The Devil's Ticket," "The Fingers of Fear" and "The Guilty Men," 1960-61). His last direction credit was *Danny Jones* (1972).

John Larkin *(b. 11/30/1901; d. 1/6/1965, Los Angeles, CA.)* His first producer's credit was *Handcuffs, London* (1955). He also produced one episode of *Fabian of the Yard* (1956), and 59 episodes of *M Squad* (1957-59). *Riverboat* was his last production credit. As a writer, he penned *Society Girl* (1932), *Charlie Chan at Treasure Island* (1939), *Charlie Chan in Panama* (1940), *Charlie Chan at the Wax Museum* (1940), and an episode of *M Squad*. *Riverboat* was his last writing credit.

Richard H. Bartlett *(b. 1922; d. 6/11/1994, Havre de Grace, MD, diabetes.)* His first production credits were *Silent Raiders* (1954) and *Cimarron City* (1958) before moving up to *Riverboat*. His first directorial credit was *Silent Raiders* and also included seven episodes of *Cimarron City* (1958-59), three episodes of *77 Sunset Strip*, and eight episodes of *Wagon Train*. His last directing credit was *The Great American Fourth of July and Other Disasters*, in 1982. As an actor he appeared in *I Was an American Spy* (1951), *Space Patrol* (1951-52) and *Silent Raiders*. His last acting credit was *The Lonesome Trail* (1955).

Norman Jolley *(b. 2/21/1916, Adel, Iowa; d. 8/13/2002, Scottsdale, AZ, cardiac arrest.)* Educated at the University of Wisconsin, he is probably best known for his work on *Space Patrol* (1950). As chief writer, he created many of the concepts used in that syndicated science fiction series. In 1958, he partnered with Richard H. Bartlett to form "Bartlett-Jolley Productions," where Bartlett directed the scripts Jolley wrote, with both producing. Jolley had one production credit before *Riverboat* (Cimarron City, 1958) and that was for Revue. He later went on as associate producer for *The F.B.I.* (1965-67) and *Ironside* (1973-74). As a writer, besides *Space Patrol*, he worked on *Science Fiction Theatre* (1955-56), *Cimarron City*, *Wagon Train*, *The Virginian*, and *The F.B.I.* His last writing credit was an episode of *Ironside*.

MUSIC

Elmer Bernstein *(b. 4/4/1922, New York, NY; d. 8/18/2004, Ojai, CA.)* No real introduction is needed for this prolific composer who was a protégé of Aaron Copland. His most recognizable scores were for *The Man with the Golden Arm* (1955, which co-starred Darren McGavin), his Oscar-winning *Thoroughly Modern Millie* (1967) and the theme for *The Magnificent Seven* (1960). A smattering of film titles include *The Ten Commandments* (1956), *The Birdman of Alcatraz* (1962), *The Hallelujah Trail* (1965), *The Sons of Katie Elder* (1965), *Airplane* (1980), and *An American Werewolf in London* (1981). Some of his TV work included *The Big Valley* (1967-68), the brilliant episode of *Gunsmoke* (1972) entitled "Hostage," and Jim Hutton's *Ellery Queen* (1975). His last music credit was *Cecil B. DeMille: American Epic* (2004).

PART XII.

SEASON TWO
1960-1961

The Season Premiere opens in Cincinnati on the close-up of a (painting) set-tlement, replete with houses, churches and plowed fields. A voice-over explains this is the "Paradise of the Prairie" — a beautiful colony where the soil is rich and the land sells for only $1.25 an acre. Camera pulls back to reveal Martinez Van-DerBrig offering his dream to any and all takers.

He has already sold many prime lots, but the settlers are getting restive, particu-larly a young woman named Tekla Kronen. She and her father, a newspaperman, are eager to be off. Mr. Kronen believes in the dream but his daughter, a self-described practical woman, is skeptical. Martinez sees the *Enterprise* in dock and sends her there, remarking they steam away the following day. Miss Kronen approaches Captain Holden to confirm the timetable, only to discover he knows nothing about passen-gers; he's planning to ship a cargo of wagon wheels down river. This does not sit well with her and she prays the dream VanDerBrig sells won't become a nightmare.

In the local saloon, Martinez offers a challenge. Filling a large stein to the brim, he promises that if the river champion can drink the beer without coming up for breath, he will buy drinks for all. Carney happens to be the "champion" and suc-cessfully wins the bet. Grey comes in to speak to Carney's companion, Mr. Blake. The captain wants to know why he isn't loading the cargo. Bill Blake explains the shipment has been held up in Pittsburg (see "The Boy from Pittsburgh" for a comment on the spelling). There is no other cargo anywhere in Cincinnati for them to consign.

Martinez next turns up in Grey's quarters aboard the boat, using the captain's shaving razor. They discuss Miss Kronen, who Grey says Martinez likes almost more than himself. Grey, too, is attracted to her. VanDerBrig offers a deal: consider-ing Holden has no cargo to ship, he suggests the captain take his twenty passengers downriver. He will not say where, but offers Grey sealed orders, to be opened two days into the trip. For $45 a head times 20 passengers, Holden agrees.

Season Two saw a significant change in cast. With Burt Reynolds gone, the producers apparently felt the need for Grey Holden to have a new antagonist, and he came in the form of Captain Bill Blake, played by Noah Beery, Jr. Like Ben Frazer, Blake was often at odds with Holden, but his "half partnership" in the Enterprise *gave him more of an even keel. The relationship between McGavin and Beery was decidedly better than that between McGavin and Reynolds, and Beery lent a somewhat older and more mature counter to Holden's new womanizing, beat-'em-up and occasionally speculative nature. The absence of Chip and the greatly reduced role for Jack Lambert was keenly felt, however, and the tone of the series, to say nothing of the writing, greatly suffered.*

The passengers (most immigrants with various dialects), come aboard. Among them is a Scotsman with his ill wife, a former miner named Red Dog Hanlon, and a "contessa," to whom Grey speaks French. Once they are settled, the *Enterprise* steams off.

After two days, Holden opens his sealed orders, revealing a map and the name of the colony: Rolling Stone. The passengers cheer, but Grey is concerned. He does not recognize the name nor do the directions make sense to him. He says

Darren McGavin and Noah Beery, Jr.

they have all been fooled: there is no colony and no fertile land for them to settle. Tekla accuses Grey of being in league with Martinez to steal their money.

In the pilothouse, pilot Bill Blake inspects the map. He thinks it will take them to the "Wabash." Grey had plans to turn around and go back to Cincinnati but reluctantly decides to plow ahead.

Tekla wants to repay Grey for his decision and kisses him. Immediately aroused, Grey passionately draws her close and kisses her (twice). She cries "That's not for me!" and hurries off.

Grey subsequently catches the "contessa" speaking in an American accent, revealing her for a fraud. She explains he has "found her out" and she's only trying to start a new life. He demurs by saying he knows nothing about her and calls her "Madam Contessa." Later, he serenades Tekla with "Shenandoah" and tries to get cozy, to no avail.

The *Enterprise* steams into "Rolling Stone." It is not as pictured. What buildings are there suffer from neglect. There are no churches, no tilled land. The passengers are angry. They blame Grey for cheating them. He offers to take them back but none have any money and nowhere to go, so they disembark. The dying Scot's wife has a hallucination of a beautiful settlement, exactly like the painting and then passes on to her reward.

Grey determines to return to Cincinnati and bring back Martinez with the promised cattle, mules and supplies. Bill Blake stays behind to help the settlers get started on their dream.

Back in the city, Grey finds Martinez with two lovelies, planning on making good his escape to the Southwest. Grey threatens bodily harm if he doesn't pay up, and accuses Martinez of being "a liar, a cheat and a scoundrel" — in short, a fraud. Martinez launches into a long speech about miracles and keeping faith. Although there is a "delay" in sending on the supplies, he professes complete innocence of any scheme. Grey makes him buy the supplies and returns with him to Rolling Stone.

At the settlement, Red Dog, who went from "eager to farm" to "eager to leave," incites the settlers. A fight breaks out and he is about to cut Bill's throat when the Contessa shoots him in the back.

The *Enterprise* arrives, they unload the animals and everyone cheers. Martinez admits others (who he presumably also scammed) tried and failed to make a go of it, but with inspiration, they can succeed.

Grey faces Tekla with the astonishing statement, "There's a share of my river for you if you want it," but she's a practical woman. She doesn't want to wait on a husband to come back from his river trips. She will settle in Rolling Stone — with Martinez, if he promises to stay. He does, and that settles that.

Mr. Kronen declares, "America — where anything can happen!" and the *Enterprise* steams away.

This episode can be critiqued with a brief summation:
Confidence Man sells a lot of hooey to faithful fools.
Confidence Man pays their one-way passage aboard Riverboat.

Faithful Fools blame Riverboat Captain when it turns out they're going nowhere (literally and figuratively).

Riverboat Captain discusses scheme with New Series Regular, AKA Master Riverboat Pilot Bill Blake.

Riverboat Captain has a love affair.

Riverboat Captain sets dreamers off in Nowhere Land and returns to make Confidence Man pay for his sins.

Confidence Man is also in love with Riverboat Captain's girl.

Confidence Man turns over new leaf, marries girl, establishes "The Paradise on the Prairie".

Possibly not the way Writer pitched idea to Producer, but pithy. Producer tries to spruce up episode by casting Name Actor to play lead role. Director uses a lot of new Stock Footage of Real Riverboat, throws in a few Fights and actually uses both Left and Right sides of the corridor to reveal passenger cabins. Only Returning Regular gets to do a Lot of Drinking, seemingly the only continuity to Season One ("The Quick Noose" where Carney was also drunk).

Perhaps a little unfair, but "End of a Dream" was a stunning departure from the tone finally established toward the end of Season One. In this season premiere, neither Joshua nor Chip appear (without explanation) and their loss is acutely felt. The character of Grey Holden has changed from a decent, hard-working river man with soft edges to a tough, extremely (over) confident sort, hardly recognizable (see further comments after episode 2.2). Bill Blake — as opposed to Terry Blake (Blake apparently being a popular "Old West" name immortalized by Amanda Blake; in this case played by Noah Beery) — appears as the pilot, totally without introduction and has a nominal role in this show.

The opening was radically changed. Instead of live-action shots of McGavin and the riverboat, the producer opted for a mere sketch (different than the one used during ad breaks in first season) of the Enterprise over which the names McGavin and Beery appear. There is a new, less-inspiring theme reworked by Gerald Fried, replacing Elmer Bernstein's memorable music and, not surprisingly, a different producer taking over the reins. Even small touches were changed: the voices now coming through the intra-boat communications were filtered, giving them a peculiar, surrealistic sound as though they were speaking over a telephone.

Grey continued to wear the same outfit of white shirt and swinging pocket watch but did not have the accompanying knife on the back of his belt, although that would reappear by episode 2.2.

Similar to Riverboat's premiere episode, "End of a Dream" was most certainly not intended to be the first episode, but was inexplicably shown out of order. Since the producer determined the order in which episodes were aired, the decision to run this before episode 2.2, "That Taylor Affair," lay at the feet of Boris D. Kaplan.

"End of a Dream" was extremely close to "Guns for Empire," in that a schemer sold a lot of gullible people on a "dream colony." It was a common theme for TV Westerns and did not play any better on Riverboat for the repetition. The character of Martinez VanDerBrig (and what kind of a name is that, anyway?) was wildly overdrawn and acted over the top by Cliff Robertson. Although it was obvious from the start that he had every intention of cheating the people (see in particular the scene where he told his *adoring lovelies he intended to go to the Southwest with his ill-gotten gains), he seemed a bit of a schizoid, alternately believing in "Rolling Stone" as a viable project.*

Things never got any clearer. After opening the sealed orders no river captain in his right mind would have accepted in the first place, Holden categorically states such a place does not exist. Then Bill Blake decides it may be "on the Wabash" and they go in search of it. (The Wabash, incidentally, is an Illinois-Indiana river running into the Ohio River. To reach it from Cincinnati, the Enterprise would have to steam past Louisville, Evansville and Mt. Vernon before making a "V" and going north.) Perhaps the most startling fact is that they find it when all indications were to the contrary.

The immigrants were wildly peculiar, made more so by the unusual and not-overly-effective casting. Accents varied between scenes and you were never sure who was supposed to be what. Susan Cummings was particularly weak as Tekla, having trouble with the dialect throughout the episode, as did Ben Wright. Unfortunately cast as a Scotsman, he would later shine as a Swede in a 1966 episode of Gunsmoke.

The character of Tekla (finally revealed as a Swede) was hardly the type of woman anyone would expect Grey to fall for and his "romancing" had the look and feel of convenience, if not an outright set-up. You never believed he was serious and at the end (like episode 1.21, "Path of the Eagle," where he proposes to Marion Templeton), his offer that "there's a share of my river for you" came out of left field.

Of course Tekla chooses Martinez, adding to the discomfort, because she has just spent the last hour trashing him to Grey and her father. There were also uncomfortable scenes between her and Grey (her reaction to being kissed stands out) that made you wonder about her sexuality.

"End of a Dream" was talky, with little action, and that contrived. Characters such as Red Dog changed at will and the (un)timely death of the woman after her psychic "vision" of Rolling Stone, being precisely as Martinez painted it, almost bizarre.

Gone, too, was the end title, "Crew of the Enterprise." Dick Wessel had his name included with the other guest actors.

GUEST CAST

Cliff Robertson *(b. 9/9/1925, LaJolla, CA.)* A prolific actor in the 1950's and 60's when television was new, he achieved stardom by his brilliant performance as *Charly* in the film of the same name (1968), for which he also won an Academy Award as Best Actor. Born Clifford Parker Robertson III, he was personally selected for the part of young JFK in *P.T. 109* by John F. Kennedy, himself. He was married to Dina Merrill from 1966-86. Other significant roles were *Man Without A Country* (1973), *Escape from L.A., Batman,* (playing Shame) and *Twilight Zone,* where he appeared as a ventriloquist in the 1962 episode, "The Dummy," and the episode, "100 Years Over the Rim." He made his film debut in *Picnic* (1955) and continues to work, his last credits including an appearance in the film, *Spider Man 2* (2004).

Susan Cummings: A fairly active actress in the late 50's and early 60's, she played Pat in the *Twilight Zone* episode "To Serve Man" (1962).

Robert J. Wilke *(b. 5/18/1914, Cincinnati, Oh; d. 3/28/1989, Los Angeles, CA.)* An actor equally adept at playing sheriffs as outlaws, he had a face that both jumped out from a crowd, yet remained undistinguished. He was the type of actor that made two episodes of *Riverboat* and stood out in neither, yet gave strong, credible performances. He played Captain Mendoza in the TV series *Zorro* (1959) and also appeared as a recurring character on *The Range Rider* (1951). An proficient golfer, it was said he made more money from that game than his extensive motion picture career.

June Vincent *(b. 7/17/1920, Harrods, OH.)* This hard-working blonde, born Dorothy June Smith, found work primarily in TV. Her first credit was *The Selfish Giant* (1939) and her last an episode of *Maude* in 1976. She made appearances on *The Fugitive*, "Death is the Door Prize" and "When the Bough Breaks," as well as well as five episodes of *Perry Mason*.

Ben Wright *(b. 5/5/1915, London, England; d. 7/2/1989, Burbank, CA, heart attack.)* The voice of *The Outer Limits* (1963), he did many voice-overs, including Grimsby on *The Little Mermaid* (1989) and *One Hundred and One Dalmatians* (1961) playing Roger. He appeared in several episodes of *Hogan's Heroes* and opposite McGavin in an episode of *The Outsider*. Perhaps his most memorable role was as Birger Engdahl, a Swedish barber, in a 1966 episode of *Gunsmoke* called "The Newcomers."

2.2 "That Taylor Affair" . . . . *September 26, 1960*
Directed by Allen H. Minor
Written by Allen H. Minor
Produced by Boris D. Kaplan

In the teaser, Grey and Bill Blake are dressed to their eye teeth. Holden explains he has a plan of multiplying his $1,000 cash tenfold. Two lovelies meet him in a carriage (similar to the opening scene with Lt. Devereaux in "A Night at Trapper's Landing") and he goes off to play poker.

At the gaming table, he is again surrounded by lovelies who fawn over him. Astonishingly, he has won $10,000 and decides to bet it all on one last hand. He catches his opponent dealing from the bottom and gets in a fight. Grey is beaten and taken away.

Act One begins in Baton Rouge with Grey having a discussion with Bill Blake. Now that Holden is broke, he needs a partner with a ready influx of cash. "Everyone on the river knows Bill has been trying to get hold of the *Enterprise*" — here's his chance. Owning a piece of this riverboat is like the gold rush in California (1848-9); and just as surely, they know the newly elected president Zachary Taylor means flush times."

Blake drives a hard bargain. He wants 50% ownership, a contract saying his services as "master pilot" cannot be cancelled and while Holden is off the boat, he is to be considered the captain. Grey "steams off" without accepting.

A commotion occurs outside. Sheriff Stone's men are putting a log with a chain and a padlock through the *Enterprise's* paddlewheel. The sign by the boat declares, "The *Enterprise* is being Sold at Public Auction as ordered by the Court." In a brief cameo, Joshua and Carney attempt to fight the deputies off, but fail. Grey protests, saying he needs more time to pay off his debts but the sheriff remains obstinate, saying Captain Morgan of the *Tennessee* is coming in tonight. He and Morgan are old friends, as evidenced by the fact Stone raised

This page, facing page: The new, debonair Grey Holden, decked out in his "shore leave clothes," found plenty of women ashore in Season Two. Here, Darren McGavin poses with Arlene Dahl, as a teaser of what audiences could expect in the coming episodes.

Morgan' son. But now it's time for the younger Morgan to have a command of his own and Holden's boat will do nicely.

Without a choice, Holden accepts Blake's offer and demands the cash. Bill decides he will hold onto "our money" until Grey has cut a deal with the sheriff, so off he goes again.

It evolves that Sheriff Stone has helped get Zachary Taylor elected. In return for the favor, Taylor has promised one delegate from town may attend his inauguration (March 4, 1849). The locals are holding an election to see who is going to represent Baton Rogue. Unfortunately for Stone, mortician Billingsford Pierce is chosen. Afterward, in a bad mood, Stone refuses to accept Grey's offer of $10,000 to settle his lien. This means the captain will have to come up with a plan.

He lies by saying the *Enterprise* is going to transport the president-elect to his inauguration. If Stone will release her, Grey will permit the sheriff to go

along. This way he can get the honor so richly deserved and spite the mortician in the bargain. He agrees.

In the captain's quarters, Bill is making himself comfortable. In a rather heated exchange, reminiscent of the contentious relationship between Holden and his former pilot, Ben Frazer, Grey complains about Blake taking over. Being half partner, however, he has every right, and things are left unsettled between the two men.

Grey had originally bid on the contract to transport Taylor but lost out to Morgan. He determines to steal the plans and "usurp" the lucky winner by "shanghaiing" the president. A "hostess" named Lucy Belle wants to work on the *Enterprise*. To prove her mettle, she finagles her way aboard the *Tennessee* and romances Captain Morgan. During the night she steals the "passport" and also sets back his clock so he won't notice the deception until after the *Enterprise* has steamed away to pick up Zachary Taylor.

Going to Spit Head Point, Grey gives the signal of four blasts on the whistle and the presidential party arrives on the dock. They unknowingly board the

Noah Beery, Jr., Arlene Dahl and Darren McGavin "discuss" plans for how the captains are going to transport the new President to his inaugural in "That Taylor Affair."

wrong boat just as the *Tennessee* steams up. Grey brags that Morgan will do him a great favor by bad-mouthing him in Baton Rogue as that will only enhance his reputation.

When Governor DeWitt complains the president has been shanghaied, Grey explains Taylor came aboard of his own free will. Taylor agrees and as a reward for the clever subterfuge, permits the *Enterprise* to bypass Baton Rogue. That means Mortician Pierce will not get to accompany the president and the sheriff gets his dream-come-true.

Without doubt, "That Taylor Affair" was meant to serve as the season premiere as it not only established Bill Blake, but gave his reasons for standing as co-captain of the Enterprise. *It can only be surmised that Boris Kaplan felt Cliff Robertson was a stronger guest star with whom to begin a new season. Jack Lambert had a few lines as Joshua in this episode, and he and Dick Wessel shared a separate credit in the end titles, but without the heading "Crew of the* Enterprise."

This episode clearly established the new Grey Holden. More of a devil-may-care character, he is now a rogue in rogue's clothing, and much more of a lady's man, as evidenced by the bevy of females following him from the Enterprise *and surrounding him at the poker table. Testosterone choked the air and McGavin put Ricardo Montalban to shame with his performance.*

How Holden suddenly became $10,000 in debt was never explained, and the sheriff's refusal to accept the cash Grey later obtains from Blake to pay off the lien defies law. Saying he wants to put the boat up for public auction merely serves as plot convenience, although how the riverboat became a hot commodity between seasons remains a mystery.

The series (now moved up to 1849) has a new co-captain but the producer seems determined to carry over the theme of first year by establishing an argumentative relationship between the principal regulars. This serves as yet another step away from "Family Enterprise," *setting a new, intentionally edgy tone. If the intent was to establish loner "Mike Hammer on the Mississippi," thus recreating McGavin's success on his previous series, it was a bad decision. Darren's strength as an actor came from portraying complex, multi-dimensional characters with strong interaction with those around him (see, for example, his brilliant creation of Joe Bascome on an episode of* Gunsmoke *called "Gunfighter, R.I.P.")*

Later producers would try the same technique as Kaplan in The Outsider, *where Darren played a private eye. Giving McGavin no recurring characters with whom to relate, and failing to capitalize on the actor's flair for humor, the series lasted only one year and disappeared from sight. Only in* The Night Stalker *(where McGavin, himself, strove to create a family atmosphere in the newsroom), did the combination of humor, intensity and charm permit his talent to shine through. The same could be said for the 1983 film* A Christmas Story *where, as the Old Man, he used those endearing characteristics (which were, incidentally, totally devoid from the script or the author's intent) to mold a remarkable, enduring legacy.*

Writer/director Allen H. Minor used more shots of the working riverboat to good effect and the script was original, if not a bit overcomplicated. The changes in Holden's personality, the introduction of Noah Beery (another actor not likely to challenge McGavin's male lead) and the limited scenes with Joshua and Carney, however, mark less appealing and uncharted waters for the Enterprise.

GUEST CAST

Arlene Dahl *(b. 8/11/1928, Minneapolis, MN.)* Of Norwegian descent, she always wished to be a musical comedy star. She made over thirty films including *Journey to the Center of the Earth* (1959) and appeared numerous times on *Love, American Style* and *Rowan & Martin's Laugh-In*. She was married to Fernando Lamas and is the mother of actor Lorenzo Lamas. She was also the Reingold Beer Girl for 1946.

Robert Ellenstein *(b. 6/18/1923, Newark, NJ.)* Before playing a Federation Council president in *Star Trek IV*, he appeared frequently in such Westerns as *The Wild, Wild West* and *The Big Valley*. He earned a Purple Heart in the Air Corps in WWII, and then returned to NY where he became part of early television, including a live episode of *Robert Montgomery Presents*, playing Quasimodo in "The Hunchback of Notre Dame" (1950).

Stanley Adams *(b. 4/7/1915, New York, NY; d. 4/27/1977, suicide.)* The first things most people think about when they hear his name is the *Star Trek* episode "The Trouble With Tribbles" (1966) and the fact that he shot himself to death. Tragic, considering he had a substantial career and appeared with McGavin on several projects, including an episode of *The Outsider*, the first *Night Stalker* film (1972) and the series episode "The Devil's Platform."

Paul Fix *(b. 3/13/1901, Dobbs Ferry, NY; d. 10/14/1983, Los Angeles, CA, kidney failure.)* Two words: *The Rifleman*. He played lawman Micah Torrance on that series and forever engrained himself into television lore. Working continuously in TV and films, the other major role that summons his face to mind is the character of Dr. Mark Piper on the original *Star Trek* pilot, "Where No Man Has Gone Before." Friends with Clark Gable and John Wayne, Peter Paul Fix was the son of a German-born brewmaster. He served in the Navy in WWI and started his acting career in silent films.

Gilman Rankin *(b. 4/17/1911, Massachusetts; d. 10/31/1993, Orange County, CA.)* A character actor most recognizable as a waiter or someone standing in the background, his characters had names such as "waiter," "horse trader" or "man on tractor." He made several episodes of *Gunsmoke*, including playing Purvis on the 1966 episode "The Wrong Man." He appeared in the film *Midnight Cowboy* (1969) and his last role was *Assualt on Precinct 13* (1976). His appearance on *Riverboat* was uncredited.

Milton Frome *(b. 2/24/1908; d. 3/21/1989, Woodland Hills, CA, heart failure.)* He played Lawrence Chapman on *The Beverly Hillbillies* from 1964-67 and offered many comedy roles in the 50's and 60's, including playing Mr. Blooker on *The Addams Family* episode, "Morticia, the Breadwinner" (1965).

2.3 "The Two Faces of Grey Holden" .... *October 3, 1960*
Directed by R. G. Springsteen
Written by Kathleen Hite
Produced by Boris D. Kaplan

The Teaser begins in New Orleans, an exotic setting where anything can happen…

A young woman stands on the dock, appraising the *Enterprise*. Carney hopes her attraction is for him. No. Bill Blake hopes her attention is for him. No. Grey smugly assumes she has eyes only for him and is proven correct when she beckons him down. He obliges and she throws herself in his arms with the astonishing statement, "I knew you would come!"

She subsequently calls the captain "Gabriel" (pronounced "Gab-ree-EL") and invites him to go "home" with her on a carriage she has provided. Titillated by the prospects, he readily agrees, waving good-bye to the astonished bystanders, who remark such behavior is not unexpected from Cajuns, and presumably Grey Holden, himself.

Stopping by a pond, Marie, between kisses, persists in calling Grey "Gabree-EL," and declares, "We are for always. We are forever." This seems peculiar to the intrepid captain, but he is willing to be called whatever she desires in consideration of future perks.

They arrive at the Cajun village where Marie joyously introduces Grey to her mama and papa as the returning Gabriel. The deception begins to wear thin as her parents are all too ready to accept he is who Marie says he is, despite protestations to the contrary. Papa takes the newcomer into the house and begins addressing events in Gabriel's life, which, of course, Holden does not remember. No problem, papa explains: it will all come back to you, and besides, Marie is a beautiful woman. Even Pape Roget identifies Grey as his long-lost brother, and the entire community prepares to welcome home the prodigal.

Everyone wants Marie to be happy and if she believes Grey is Gabriel, they are perfectly willing to go along. Sebastian, clearly in love with Marie, reluctantly approves the deception and warns Holden that from now on, he is to be Gabriel. Grey tries to dissuade him by saying this is not the way to cure the woman's sickness, but his words fall on deaf ears.

That evening there is a great celebration with dancing and wine. Grandma Jo tells a story of men and wolves to frighten the local children, then gives Marie a love potion she has made of dried lizard powder.

The fun wears off quickly and Grey tries to escape during the night. Sebastian clunks him on the head and brings him back.

The following morning, when Grey wakes from his unnatural sleep, Pape explains that Gabriel Roget was the pride of the village, engaged to Marie from an early age. He left on a trip to Arcadia (Louisiana, between Shreveport and Vicksburg) aboard the riverboat *Comet* to negotiate business for the village. Grey notes the *Comet* exploded a year ago and burned to the waterline, killing all aboard. Unable to accept Gabriel's demise, Marie has gone to New Orleans fifty

An early, but significant role for Suzanne Pleshette, she played the delusional Marie, who "mistakes" Grey Holden for her long-lost fiancé. The chemistry with McGavin was unmistakable, but nothing could have saved this "format" episode.

times in the intervening months, waiting for her intended to return. She has had the opportunity to bring many men back and ultimately chose Grey. Now he must accept the situation and marry her.

Father Paul is coming to perform the service. Grey sets him straight as to the true state of affairs and he is willing to denounce the deception, but the captain does not wish to be cruel. He has a plan to dissuade Marie from wedding a ghost.

Everyone wants Marie to be happy with the return of "Gabriel," but Grey Holden. Here, he fights with Thomas Gomez in a futile attempt to escape.

Back aboard the *Enterprise,* Captain Blake is highly annoyed at Captain Holden's absence. Grey has been gone two days when he should have spent his time more usefully obtaining two tons of cargo for the boat. He tells Carney he must now go out and consign cargo. After that, he will wait no longer for the gallivanting co-owner.

Back at the Cajun settlement, Grey dresses in Gabriel's clothes and bursts in to a gathering of women who are dressing Marie for her big day. Affecting

drunkenness, he embraces her with a rough uncouthness that she finds objectionable. This snaps her out of her delusion and she calls off the wedding. Grey then turns her over to Sebastian.

The newly engaged (married?) couple drop Grey back at the *Enterprise* that fortunately has not steamed away without him, Captain Blake only able to find one ton of cargo in his absence. They try to make Grey explain what happened, and he declares that maybe someday he will.

The highlight of this episode was seeing Celia Lovsky as Grandma Jo.

That said, the question begs: what do you get when you throw together an American, a Greek and an Austrian? Answer: Cajuns.

Odd casting, indeed. That said, the acting was fine, although Suzanne Pleshette had trouble maintaining the accent and Celia Lovsky didn't try, perhaps because she got to tell an Eastern European story about wolves. Nico Minardos frequently played the spurned Spanish/Mexican love interest and was right at home in New Orleans. At least none of them were cast as Scots...

"The Two Faces of Grey Holden" easily fell into a typical television format: a five-minute idea stretched thin over an hour episode. The telling and retelling of how everyone wanted to make Marie happy was old after the second time, became irritating by the third and outright maddening after that. Unfortunately, this was actually the crux (and sole) idea with which to fill sixty pages of dialogue.

This page, facing page: Before he tired of the game, Grey Holden romances Marie, little realizing that marriage was to be the ultimate outcome.

Two brief scenes between Blake and Carney served, yet again, to emphasize the contentious relationship between the two co-stars of Riverboat. *Blake was annoyed at Holden's absence (even if he was with a beautiful woman) and threatened to leave him behind if he didn't return by the time he filled the hold. Joshua was not in this episode and while there was no particular place for him, his absence was keenly felt.*

Writer Kathleen Hite (most recognized for working on Gunsmoke *in the early years) was habitually called upon to pen "women" scripts, of which this certainly quali-fied. Unfortunately, as in too many programs of the era, having a woman writer did not guarantee (and more often the contrary) strong female characters and her Marie was no exception.*

GUEST CAST

Suzanne Pleshette *(b. 1/31/1937, New York, NY; d. 1/19/2008, Los Angeles, CA, respiratory failure.)* One of the most distinctive and talented actresses of her age, an early credit was *The Birds* (1963), playing Annie Hayworth. Her greatest contribution, however, was in television where she co-starred on *The Bob Newhart Show* playing Emily Hartley. She made many guest star appearances on episodic television, one of the most memorable as Glory Bramley opposite Richard Kiley in the 1970 episode of *Gunsmoke* called "Stark." She was married to Tom Poston, her third husband, from 2001 until his 2007 death.

Thomas Gomez *(b. 7/10/1905, New York, NY; d. 6/18/1971, Santa Monica, CA, car accident.)* Born Sabino Tomas Gomez, he gained early fame as a Broadway actor (starring in such productions as *A Man for all Seasons*). A heavy-set man and a gourmet, he served on the Board of Directors of the Screen Actor's Guild for more than 40 years. Besides numerous film credits, he appeared with McGavin in an episode of *The Outsider* called "Behind God's Back" (1969) and in two episodes of *Twilight Zone*: "Dust" and "Escape Clause."

Celia Lovsky *(b. 2/21/1897, Vienna, Austria; d. 10/12/1979, Los Angeles, CA, natural causes.)* Born Caecilie Lvovsky, the daughter of a Czech composer, she studied at the Royal Academy of Arts and Music in Vienna. In 1928, she met future husband Peter Lorre in Berlin where she was already a star. They left for France in 1933 and were married a year later. They eventually made it to Hollywood, where, after their divorce in 1945, Celia went back to acting. While appearing in over 100 films and TV series, including *Soylent Green* (1973, playing the Exchange Leader), she will always be revered as T'Pau the Vulcan in the *Star Trek* episode, "Amok Time" (1967).

Lillian Buyeff. She has a short credit list, including *Dragnet, M Squad,* and *My Favorite Martian*, which is listed as her last role (1964). She also appeared in *Lad: A Dog* (1962), playing Miss Woodward.

Nico Minardos *(b. 2/15/1930.)* Born of Greek parents in the U.S., he was another character actor typically cast as a foreigner, usually a handsome hunk sort. He played a doctor on the *Twilight Zone* episode "The Gift" (1962) and played Andre Malif in the first season episode of *Mission: Impossible* called "Odds on Evil" (1966). On Sept. 28, 1966, he was in Peru filming a TV anthology with actor Eric Fleming when a canoeing mishap resulted in Fleming drowning at age 41; Minardos safely swam to shore. His last credit came in 1983 from an episode of *The A-Team*.

Herb Ellis *(b. 1921, Cleveland, OH.)* Born Herbert Siegel, he worked primarily in the 1950's and 60's, playing Officer Frank Smith on *Dragnet* (1951) for several episodes. He appeared in several episodes of *Bewitched* and *My Favorite Martian*.

Lomax Study. Usually had small roles, probably the most remembered of which was playing the part of Leveque in the classic *Twilight Zone* episode, "To Serve Man."

2.4 "River Champion"............................ *October 10, 1960*
Directed by William Witney
Teleplay by Rik Vollaerts
Story by William Fay
Produced by John Larkin

The scene: Glen City (above Natchez). A sparring match is going on, featuring prize fighter Dennis Fogerty (the Dublin Boy). His promoter, Gentleman Dan Muldoon watches with obvious pride. All seems set for a bout, but the local sheriff objects. He wants his cut and if he doesn't get it, no fight. Muldoon refuses and the Dublin Boy flattens the law officer, meaning they are both thrown out of town. Now, where can they hold the fight?

Captain Holden is all dressed up, anticipating a good time in the city. He tells Bill Blake he is off to secure cargo. Blake objects — Holden has told him there is no cargo in Glen City. But Grey has sparking on his mind and happily trots away.

In the local watering hole, Grey meets old friend, Danny Muldoon. Muldoon is the retired River Champion and now spends his time training fighters to take his place and promoting bouts. Unfortunately, he is flat broke and needs this latest pugilistic endeavor to make money.

While they are talking, Sarah Prentiss appears (in yet another instance of a lady entering a saloon). She, too, is old friends with Danny. More than that, she is in love with him and has determined to follow him around until he accepts her proposal of marriage. He can't marry her for reasons yet unexplained and hopes to make a big killing with his newest protégée, the Dublin Boy.

While Grey gets stuck paying the bar tab Danny offered to cover, two "kids" come up, bragging they have a system which will garner them "all the money" from the upcoming fight. The captain dismisses them as harmless drunks. They are anything but that: they are actually bank robbers, planning on stealing money from ticket sales and bets connected with the coming "10 knock-downs."

Muldoon talks Grey into holding the prize fight aboard the *Enterprise* by promising him 50% of the take. To encourage compliance, he says Holden can charge $20 a ticket and $30 for suites on the boat. Added to the winning purse, he should recover a tidy sum. The terms are agreed to and Grey intends to go

A glass jaw, an irony and the desire to help an old friend conspire to get Grey Holden into the prize fight ring.

off with a bevy of lovelies — until tall, handsome, blond Dennis steals them away from him.

Grey and Muldoon meet the Stagle brothers — Gunnar, the fighter and his brother, the promoter. They agree to meet the Dublin Boy aboard the *Enterprise* if Muldoon makes a large enough wager that Gunnar can break him.

Back on the boat, Bill Blake is angry that Grey has agreed to hold the bout aboard the *Enterprise*. He doesn't want to turn the steamer into a gambling boat

Bets and fists fly as Grey Holden volunteers to be a living punching bag in the Great Prize Fight held aboard the Enterprise. *Norma Crane gives advice from "above," but a positive outcome appears bleak.*

and threatens that if anything goes wrong, Holden will have to pay for it out of his share of the profits. Joshua, however, is intrigued by the idea, even more so when they see Dennis take a "wallop" at a punching bag. He misses but strikes a support, bringing the roof down on their heads.

Betting is hot and furious, bringing in at least $10,000. This is stored in a huge floor safe in Holden's cabin. The "kids" are also aboard, waiting their chance to steal the money.

Miss Prentiss needs help persuading Dan to marry her. She doesn't want Blake's assistance, however, determining Grey is a better bet. He mistakes her intention for a talk, presuming she wants to romance him and is sorely disappointed to find out otherwise. When she confesses her love for Muldoon, he reluctantly agrees to help. The answer, he decides, is to make Danny jealous. The pair are in the middle of a passionate kiss when Dan finds them — and promptly slugs Grey.

The plot thickens when it is revealed the reason Dan won't marry Sarah and run her livery business: he has bad eyes. One punch to the head while he's training fighters and he may suffer permanent blindness. He protests that a penniless man who may lose his sight is a bad bargain and that's why he's been running from her.

Gunnar and his brother wage $5,000 that he can beat the Dublin Boy, and Muldoon accepts, knowing beforehand that if Dennis loses he cannot meet the bet, so there is much riding on a successful outcome. Dennis goes up to Grey's quarters to rest before the bout and the two kids sneak in to case the safe. Fogerty finds them and a fight ensues. One of the robbers hits the fighter on the chin and he drops like a sack. Grey and Muldoon find him out cold and come to the startling realization that the Dublin Boy has a glass jaw. This means he cannot fight Gunnar because he would be killed in the ring.

Danny cannot call off the fight because that would mean losing the $5,000 bet so he determines to take the Dublin Boy's place. This horrifies Sarah, who finally confesses to Grey the reason Muldoon's career as a river champion was cut short — the trouble with his eyes. Holden cannot permit Danny to go in the ring: but what to do?

Meanwhile, the two robbers come back to blow the safe. They set the fuse (apparently using a very slow-burning one) as Grey and Muldoon come into the cabin. They find the kids and fight, Grey displaying tremendous fighting prowess in the fisticuffs. This convinces him to take on the Gunnar himself. In an amusing aside, Joshua declares that Gunnar will kill Grey and that he "liked him better alive."

The odds against Grey quickly go from 100 to 1 to 200 to 1. In order to establish his credentials, Grey decks the Dublin Boy by hitting him in the chin. This proves him a worthy opponent and the fight is set.

In order to keep Danny from interfering, he is tied up in Grey's quarters. The captain changes into Dennis' fight pants and shoes and prepares to meet his fate. First punch: Grey knocked out of the ring. Second punch: Grey dropped to the mat. It looks bad.

With Dennis running back and forth between Grey's cabin and the ring, he relays advice from Muldoon: jab and move; pop and weave. Go for the stomach. Nothing works. The odds go to 300:1.

Sarah finally agrees to untie Danny if he gives his word to marry her and abandon the fight game. He does and rushes down to the ring where Grey is bloody and battered. The Gunnar is in hardly better shape, but he still packs a wallop. Boom! Bang! Jabs to the stomach and Gunnar is down. Grey wins and becomes

No one in their right mind — and certainly no one who ever watched episodic TV in the 1960's — would bet against a series star in a Great Prize Fight. Here, Dick Wessel raises an exhausted, but victorious Grey Holden's arm as proof he is the new "River Champion."

River Champion! Unfortunately for Captain Blake, he bet on the wrong man. He should have known, he says. "Captain Holden always lands on his own feet."

In the end, Grey marries Danny and Sarah, refuses his share of the prize money but compensates by kissing the bride — and kissing her and kissing her...

John Larkin returned from Season One to produce and brought director William Witney with him. Their influence worked magic because "River Champion" was a light,

Winning had more perks than money, as evidenced by the group of lovelies surrounding Grey Holden in the saloon interior.

entertaining episode. If Bill Blake had not been in the show, it might have been taken for an unaired episode from the previous year. Despite the stereotypical characters and the casting (George Kennedy was going through his dumb-but-loveable phase, Denny Miller was playing his dumb Irish strong-boy and Dennis O'Keefe was the tough but soft-inside Irishman), this added to the predictable but easy-going air. Gerald Fried used lilting music throughout so nothing was taken too seriously and the tone meshed together for an enjoyable hour.

The fight scenes between Grey and Gunnar Stagle were effectively directed and the makeup by Leo Lotito, Jr., was first rate. Adding to the amusement was seeing McGavin (5'8" or thereabouts) in skin-tight fighting pants (he fit into Denny Miller's clothes?) bobbing and weaving around the 6'5" (or thereabouts) George Kennedy. Unlike Captain Blake, who bet on Gunnar, everyone in the audience would have gladly taken the 300:1 odds on McGavin and gone home happy.

GUEST CAST

Dennis O'Keefe *(b. 3/29/1908, Fort Madison, IA; d. 8/31/1968, Santa Monica, CA, lung cancer.)* Changing his name from Bud Flanagan in 1937, he was an extra in over 200 films. He also had some substantial credits, including the role of Jerry Manning in Val Lewton's *The Leopard Man* (1943). He also headlined the TV series *The Dennis O'Keefe Show* (1959) playing Hal Towne.

George Kennedy *(b. 2/18/1925, New York, NY.)* At 6'4½", he was a giant of a man in Hollywood and was often cast as a tough or an intellectually challenged character early in his career. He won an Oscar for his role in *Cool Hand Luke* (1967), appeared in all the *Airport* films and then bowled over audiences with his portrayal of Ed Hocken in the *Naked Gun* film series. He also played Carter McKay (1988-91) on *Dallas*, and had his own series called *Sarge* (1971), in which he played a priest.

Slim Pickens *(b. 6/29/1919, Kingsburg, CA; d. 12/8/1983, Modesto, CA, brain tumor.)* Born Louis Bert Lindley, Jr., Slim began riding broncos at the age of 12 and spent two decades touring the rodeo circuit, where he became a highly paid and respected rodeo clown. In 1950, he earned a small role in *Rocky Mountain*, and went on to have a prodigious film and TV career. He was Stanley Kubrick's first choice to play the role of Dick Hollaran in *The Shining* (1980) but after working with the director on *Dr. Strangelove*, he had no desire to relive the agonizing process of numerous re-takes.

Norma Crane *(b. 11/10/1928, New York, NY; d. 9/28/1973, cancer.)* Probably best recognized for playing Ellie Martin in *Tea and Sympathy* (1956), she played a feisty Jewish prostitute in the original *Night Gallery* pilot opposite Richard Kiley's escaped Nazi war criminal (1970). She also made an episode of *Thriller*, called "Dialogues with Death" (1960).

Ralph Reed *(b. 8/12/1931; d. 1/21/1997, Orange County, CA.)* A familiar character actor specializing in Westerns, he appeared in most of the major TV series of the 1950's such as *Rawhide, Wyatt Earp, The Rebel, Tales of Wells Fargo* and *Wagon Train*. His first role was the film *Since You Went Away* (1944); uncredited was his last role in *Destry*, in 1964.

Jack Hogan *(b. 11/25/1929, Chapel Hill, NC.)* He signed to play the character Pvt. Kirby on *Combat* (1962) and remained on that series until it was cancelled in 1967. He played recurring characters on *Adam 12* (1968) and *Sierra* (1974). Living in Hawaii running a building business, he played a recurring character on *Jake and the Fat Man* (1987) and also assumed a non-acting role by working as a casting director for *Magnum P.I.* (1980). His real name is Richard Roland Benson, Jr.

Denny Miller *(b. 4/25/1934, Bloomington, IN; also billed as Scott Miller.)* Cast by a Hollywood agent while attending UCLA on a basketball scholarship, his first role was *Some Came Running* (1958). He followed with *Tarzan, the Ape Man* (1959). He played Duke Shannon on *Wagon Train*, (1961-64) and worked fairly steadily through the 70's and 80's. His last credit was *Hell to Pay* in 2005. Aside from his stint as Tarzan, he is probably best known for playing the "Gorton Fisherman," wearing a bright yellow rainslicker, in the frozen seafood TV commercials. He was not replaced until 2005.

2.5 **"No Bridge on the River"** . . . . *October 24, 1960*
Directed by Lamont Johnson
Written by Raphael Hayes
Produced by Boris D. Kaplan

A train speeds across the land. Aboard the *Enterprise,* Grey sees it and shakes a fist, hoping that it falls into the river.

That sentiment established, the riverboat steams into St. Louis, where the co-captains observe a man named Jim Bledsoe trying to recruit workers for the railroad. The Iron Horse is constructing a bridge across the river and needs men. He offers $1.00 a day plus tobacco and whisky for anyone willing to sign up. He is met with resistance from the river folk who fear a bridge and the subsequent intrusion of the railroad across the water, which will ruin river cities like theirs. Grey and Blake are only too eager to agree.

Mrs. Moray, speaking in a heavily accented French dialect, comes back aboard the *Enterprise* after a day of shopping. She complains to Grey that her (elderly) husband of several weeks is spoiling her. She wants to be useful to him and "look married," but fears she cannot.

Anger on the docks turns violent and the locals pummel Bledsoe. Grey is forced to put a stop to it and the railroad man comes aboard as a paying passenger — if Holden will permit. Bill Blake objects, but Holden remarks, "I'd let the devil aboard if he had the money," and the "devil" thanks him.

Later, the boat steams up the river. Blake complains that he doesn't like navigating at night but Grey reminds him that with the new competition of the railroad, they have to speed up their schedule. A commotion on deck draws their attention and Grey has to break up a fight between Bledsoe and the crew after the former tries to recruit them for the railroad.

A small boat comes alongside. Drunken river men want to borrow tallow to use in burning the bridge. While Grey sympathizes with their plight, he cannot

Pat Michon plays the French wife of an elderly lawyer taking passage aboard the Enterprise. *Here she poses with Darren McGavin on the deck interior by the companionway leading to the pilothouse.*

condone their intended action and sends them away. Bledsoe wants to get a look at the miscreants so he can charge them, but Grey prevents him and they get in a fight.

Later, Holden is playing cards in the parlor. He wins $300 from Mr. Moray, a lawyer, who must pay with an IOU because he has spent all his ready cash trying to please his bride.

Bill's fears about nighttime navigation come to fruition when the boat is caught up in the current and driven into the pilings of the new bridge at Rock Island, sustaining $400 worth of damage to the Texas deck. Holden and Blake do not have the money to pay for damages, so Grey determines to get it from the railroad. A representative for the railroad comes aboard when they dock but refuses their demand, explaining that it is his position the *Enterprise* purposely rammed the bridge in a willful act of destruction. Grey protests the bridge is a menace to navigation, but gets nowhere.

If they wish to recover damages, they must take the issue to court. But neither he nor Bill has any legal experience. Since Ferdinand Moray owes Holden money, Grey decides to use the IOU's as payment to procure his services. They

Sandy Kenyon portrays railroad lawyer Abraham Lincoln in the episode "No Bridge on the River." While no scenes of Lincoln took place on the Enterprise, *his presence was a good excuse to show off the boat in these publicity photos.*

will not only sue for damages, but will contest the railroad's right to construct any bridge over the river.

Abraham Lincoln represents the railroad when the case goes to trial. Moray calls Bill Blake as his first witness and launches into a long, flowery speech before making a total muddle of the examination, raising the ire of his clients. Lincoln cross-examines, admitting his belief the river men did not intentionally damage the bridge, but professing the railroad's right to construct such a structure. He

Noah Beery, Jr., Pat Michon and Darren McGavin pose aboard the Enterprise, *figuratively showing off the boys mettle and their (sometimes) gentlemanly behavior.*

gets Blake to admit he was navigating at night, a dangerous time for steamboats to be on the water.

During a recess, Lincoln goes to the bridge and hires a boy to help him determine the speed of the current. In court, Grey is called to the stand and states his belief no one has the right to block the right-of-way. Lincoln concedes the bridge was constructed at the wrong angle, then goes on to demonstrate how the *Enterprise* was caught in a cross-current and dragged into the pilings. This,

Carpetbag in hand, Sandy Kenyon's Abraham Lincoln appears aboard the boat after booking passage in another publicity still.

he agrees, was an error that must be corrected, but no one has the right to say the bridge shouldn't be built.

He continues his argument that the river men have a monopoly — to date, all produce going from east to west must be transported by steamboats. The river men resent the railroad because it represents progress. Despite the fact those making their living on the river resent competition, it's coming, and they have no right to block it. Grey yells at his lawyer, demanding he protest, but Moray is unable to come up with any reason to object. The courtroom spectators howl in indignation with only one dissenting voice: Marie Moray. She has finally found a weakness in her otherwise perfect husband and now feels she can relate to him on a personal level, leading Grey to comment that while they may lose, at least something good has come out of the trial.

During summation, Moray finally finds his voice and pleads eloquently against the bridge, to the cheers from the audience. Not to be outdone, Lincoln reminds the court it cannot hold back progress, even if that means some people suffer.

At the local saloon, Grey and Carney are drinking together when Bledsoe comes in and tries to recruit men. They get in a fight, only broken off when the jury comes in with its decision.

The jury finds for the defendant: the railroad has the right to build a bridge. But they also find for the plaintiffs, determining they are due their $400 in damages.

In the end, Mr. Lincoln books passage aboard the *Enterprise,* lamenting the fact someone always gets hurt by progress.

Using historical people in a fictitious script is always dangerous ground, but writer Raphael Hayes handled the character of Abraham Lincoln with considerable skill, giving him clever, often humorous dialogue. Lincoln's dissertation of how the river-boat got caught in the crosscurrent was extremely well explained and his lament about people being hurt by progress was sensitive and true to the man. Sandy Kenyon was cast as the Illinois lawyer and played him with consummate prowess. Considering the entire episode hinged on his ability to pull off the difficult role, he rose to the occasion, making "No Bridge on the River" both memorable and entertaining.

The contest between the river men and the railroad was adeptly handled, and broached a subject of paramount importance to the river cities. Well explained in the dialogue, the conflict was one perfectly suited to Riverboat, *and took full advantage of the setting and the times. In fact, the advent of Western railroads eventually put an end to the era of steamboats and, after the Civil War, steam-powered vessels never again regained their dominance in the transportation of passengers and cargo.*

If there was a flaw in this episode it was the performances of both Pat Michon and Hayden Rorke. Both were incapable of pulling off French accents and by trying too hard, each made their dialogue nearly incomprehensible. Since there was no particular script necessity for the characters to be French, one review of the dailies might have convinced the production staff to re-shoot what they had done, doing away with the dialects.

Boris Kaplan returned as producer and this was, by far, his best effort. The direction by Lamont Johnson was fine and Gerald Fried's score well done. Joshua was again missing in action, making his significance to Season Two problematic.

GUEST CAST

Sandy Kenyon *(b. 8/5/1922, New York.)* He is the archetypical actor from the Golden Age of television — you know you have seen him a million times and can't remember his name. He could play anyone from Abraham Lincoln (as on *Riverboat*) to a gas station attendant on *Twilight Zone* in the episode "Valley of the Shadow" (1963). He also made two other *Twilight Zone* episodes, playing Hatch in "The Odyssey of Flight 33" (1959) and Frank in "The Shelter" (1961). He played a memorable shopkeeper in "The Hollow Watcher," an episode of *Thriller* (1962), and in later years did the voice of Jon Arbuckle in *Here Comes Garfield* (1982) as well as playing Rev. Kathrun on the series *Knots Landing* (1984-85).

Hayden Rorke *(b. 10/23/1910, Brooklyn, NY; d. 8/19/1987, Toluca Lake, CA, multiple myeloma.)* For better or worse, he will always be best known as Dr. Alfred Bellows in the TV series, *I Dream of Jeannie*. (Interestingly, Darren McGavin was originally offered the lead role in the series, which eventually went to Larry Hagman after McGavin turned it down.) Educated at the American Academy of Dramatic Arts, he began a stage career in the 1930's as a character actor, appeared in a brief recurring role on *Dr. Kildare*, and made his first appearance in an episode of *I Love Lucy* in 1952. His final appearance was in *I Dream of Jeannie – 15 Years Later* in 1985.

Pat Michon (see episode 1.19, "Forbidden Island," page 127.)

Denver Pyle *(b. 5/11/1920, Bethume, CO; d. 12/25/1997, Burbank, CA, lung cancer.)* A very familiar character actor, he had recurring roles in *The Life and Times of Wyatt Earp* (1955-56), *The Andy Griffith Show* (1963-67), *The Doris Day Show* (1968-70), *The Life and Times of Grizzly Adams* (1977), and *The Dukes of Hazzard* (1979). He appeared on almost every Western being filmed in the 50's and 60's, and was especially well-known for his appearances on *Gunsmoke*, where he occasionally showed up as Matt's old friend Caleb, and also played a relative of Festus. His most sensitive role as Dr. Henry S. Rand on the episode "Mad Dog" (1967) was probably his best. He also directed numerous episodes of *The Dukes of Hazzard* and *Death Valley Days*.

Bartlett Robinson (see episode 1.31, "The Sellout," page 174.)

Tyler McVey *(b. 2/14/1912, Bay City, MI; d. 7/4/2003, Rancho Mirage, CA, leukemia.)* His first credit was playing Brady, a government agent in the 1951 film *The Day the Earth Stood Still*. He made numerous episodes of *Gunsmoke*, including two during its first season. His final credit was an episode of *Highway to Heaven*, playing a pastor in the episode "Close Encounters of the Heavenly Kind," in 1986.

2.6 "Trunk Full of Dreams" . . . . *October 31, 1960*
   Directed by Hollingsworth Morse
   Written by Irwin and Gwen Gielgud
   Produced by Boris D. Kaplan

Grey Holden sees a mermaid! Yelling at pilot Bill Blake to reverse engines, he identified the sea creature, he explains, because he has "an eye for women."

Two castaways are on a small makeshift boat and require help. Grabbing a tackle, Grey is lowered down to rescue the young lady. He gets her half-way up when she complains that their trunk must be saved first. Holden reluctantly exchanges her for the heavy box and brings it aboard.

The trunk is full of costumes and the elderly gentleman accompanying the erstwhile mermaid identifies himself as Sir Oliver Garret of the Royal Repertory Company and his wife, Juliet. The boat they were traveling on sank. While other passengers and crew made it safely to shore, they remained afloat because they refused to give up their trunk.

Sir Oliver orders two of the best staterooms and Carney scurries to make them comfortable. Blake is not as enthralled as Holden over the new arrivals. While Grey complains they are better than the cargo of pigs the boat currently hauls, Bill wants his 3 cents per mile passenger money and has his sights set on picking up a cargo of cotton in Natchez.

While Carney plays footman to "His Lordship," a rumor circulates throughout the *Enterprise* that Garret wants to buy the boat and turn it into a floating theatre. This leads Grey and Bill to argue, each threatening to buy out the other and making private deals with the actor. They finally realize Garret has already taken over the boat without benefit of purchase and have a good laugh over the incident.

In the stateroom, Carney, who has become stage-struck, puts His Lordship's posters over the walls. Annoyed that his engineer is neglecting his duties, Grey goes down to repossess the crewman. Juliet serves tea, and the two develop a bond of affection. Romance aside, the captain explains his partner wants their passage fare in advance. No problem: Garret will pay with a check drawn on the Bank of England. He confirms the rumors he intends to buy the boat, stating he and his wife intend to become permanent guests aboard.

He is less forthcoming about the circumstances that found them in the river. After being grilled, he finally reveals they were on the *Floating Hippodrome,* Captain Smiley's showboat. It is no great loss, however, as that vessel was hardly worthy of his status. He wishes to be taken to Louisville, where he will open to rave reviews. Bad news, however: the *Enterprise* is five days out of Louisville. Her first stop is Natchez.

Juliet goes to Grey's cabin and makes a not-very-surprising confession: the pair are actually broke and she is not Garret's wife, but his daughter. He only tells people that to keep men away from her. She has never minded before now, but her attraction to Grey has changed that. She is worried about going to Natchez, implying that it isn't a good show town. Grey is already enamored with the idea of making the *Enterprise* a showboat by night and a riverboat by day, however, and promises all will be well.

In Natchez, he has posters prepared announcing the new theatre. While out soliciting patrons, he takes Juliet with them to meet his clients on "Natchez Over the Hill" — the area of the city where the wealthy live. He arrives with great fanfare, being well known to the daughters of his cotton shipper. The gentlemen are less than thrilled about the new turn of events and when they discover who the headline act is, they openly scoff. While never meeting Garret or his daughter, they heard that the pair had been in Natchez last week and were a total flop. This causes them to question Holden's judgment and they refuse him the consignment.

Back in "Natchez Under the Hill" — where the lower classes live — Grey meets Captain Smiley, who laughs at his endeavor. No one will come to the floating theatre because "Lord Hambone" has stage fright and can no longer act. Grey disregards the warning and commandeers the load of hogs for (a fast turnaround into) ham to be served at tonight's performance.

True to Smiley's prediction, no one comes to the theatre and Captain Blake is furious. He complains Holden has squandered their cargo of hogs (which he must now pay for out of his own pocket) and remarks Grey doesn't have enough money left to pay the crew. Grey tries to borrow funds from Blake but the price is steep: he must turn over his 50% share in the *Enterprise*. But, Bill not kindly remarks, he will keep Holden on as captain.

Distraught that he has lost everything he has in the world, Grey goes to the transformed parlor where Garret is taking down the stage props. Bitter that he has been betrayed by a washed up actor, he demands to know what happened to him. Sir Oliver confesses that he has never been the same since his wife died. She was his partner, his audience, his faith. Without the dream she instilled, every stage is a nightmare and now he's afraid to act.

Grey can sympathize with the loss of a dream, but only for himself. He worked all his life for the *Enterprise* and now lost it. He sits in the empty theatre and demands to be entertained. Juliet protests he is only torturing her father but Grey is adamant. The man ruined him and he must act. Not just to him but to those in Natchez.

In an act of desperation, he takes Carney and Bill and goes out in a rowboat, wrapping ropes around a dockside saloon. He then goes inside and makes a bet with Captain Smiley: if he can perform a magic feat by having the tavern fall into the river, Smiley must gather him a crowd for the theatre. Smiley goes one better and offers to pay the fare for everyone and the bartender, also skeptical, offers to pay for the refreshments. Grey then gives the signal and the ropes, attached to the paddlewheel, are pulled. The saloon starts to move toward the waterline. Just in time the bettors capitulate and the patrons swarm aboard the *Enterprise*.

"Sir Hambone" comes out and begins awkwardly. The patrons laugh, but as he gets into "Is this a dagger I see before me?" the old talent returns and he gives a brilliant performance. The patrons madly applaud and Grey remarks to Juliet, "He could play Natchez forever."

While the performance goes on, Grey and Juliet meet outside. They kiss, but he reminds her that she is only a "one night stand" for him. Juliet has figured this out for herself and skips away, leaving Grey to remark, "Great performance."

There are a few bones to pick with "Trunk Full of Dreams," but most are minor. It's easy to believe Grey would go along with the scheme to make the Enterprise *a floating theatre by night in the hope of making a double profit, but he bit hook, line and sinker too easily. And Natchez was just a small river town, hardly the type where patrons would be attracted by the boatload to pay $2.00 for a performance of Shakespeare. And even if they were, at $2.00 a head, that would hardly make up for the expense of sacrificing a cargo of hogs to supply food for the masses. The brief scene at the end about "one night stands" was also hard to believe, considering Holden was supposed to have a legitimate interest in Juliet, and seemed more a writer's plot to use stage vernacular than the summation of the episode.*

The one sore point that could not be glossed over was the grossly inappropriate score. Using what might be styled "circus music," loud, amusing and humorous, it completely destroyed whatever mood the director instilled. This was not a comedic episode: why Gerald Fried chose to inject lightheartedness into it is inexplicable.

That said, the camaraderie between McGavin and both Raymond Massey and particularly Bethel Leslie dominated the episode. The dialogue, some of it emotional and palpable, finally gave McGavin a chance to truly act and he shone throughout the hour. The scenes in particular where he felt he had lost his boat and subsequently his dream, were brilliant and stand out as being some of the best on Riverboat. *If he had been given more chances like this to emote, the entire series would have been truly special.*

Continuing the theme of tension between the two series regulars and Blake's established taste for profit and owning the Enterprise *outright, the dialogue between the two was appropriately antagonistic. It did not, however, make Captain Blake a more likeable character, a dangerous petition for "Family* Enterprise," *that added a constant undercurrent of unease. This is apparently what the producer wanted for Season Two, but series' without a cast tied by strong bonds of affection seldom succeeded.*

A solid script, great acting and a rapport between actors made "Trunk Full of Dreams" one of the most entertaining and memorable episodes.

GUEST CAST

Raymond Massey *(b. 8/30/1896, Toronto, Ontario, Canada; d. 7/29/1983, Los Angeles, CA, pneumonia.)* He received an Academy Award nomination for his portrayal in *Abe Lincoln in Illinois* (1940), which was written for him by Robert E. Sherwood. Better known, perhaps, for playing Boris Karloff's Broadway role of Jonathan Brewster in the film version of *Arsenic and Old Lace* (1944), he will always be remembered for playing opposite Richard Chamberlain as Dr. Gillespie in *Dr. Kildare* (1961-66). He was educated in Oxford and began his career on the British stage in the early 1920's.

Bethel Leslie (see episode 1.10, "The Faithless," page 86.)

Willard Waterman *(b. 8/29/1914, Madison, WI; d. 2/2/1995, Burlingame, CA, bone-marrow disease.)* Beginning his career on radio, he replaced Harold Peary in *The Great Gildersleeve*, and later went on to star in the TV series of the same name (1955). He also played Mr. Quigley on the TV series *Dennis the Menace* in 1959, Mac Maginnis on *The Real McCoys* (1957) and Carl Foster on *The Eve Arden Show* (1957).

Mary Tyler Moore *(b. 12/29/1936, Brooklyn, NY.)* Her career began as a dancing appliance (Happy Hotpoint) in 1955, and professionally, she never looked back. Another incredibly talented actress finding an early role on *Riverboat*, she achieved her first fame more-or-less as a pair of legs as secretary Sam on *Richard Diamond* (1957). She later rose to stardom as Laura Petrie, Dick Van Dyke's wife, on *The Dick Van Dyke Show* (1961) and later as Mary Richards on *The Mary Tyler Moore Show* (1970). Her personal life was troubled, however, as her sister died of a drug overdose in 1978, and her brother of cancer after a failed suicide attempt (with Mary tragically being the assistant). Her only child, son Richie, shot and killed himself in what was ruled an accident in 1980. In 1984, she entered the Betty Ford clinic for "social drinking habit." An insulin-dependent diabetic, she has long supported animal rights and stem cell research and has been a vegetarian for many years.

Hugh Sanders *(b. 3/13/1911, Illinois; d. 1/9/1966, Los Angeles, CA.)* A familiar guest actor, an image of his face is most likely conjured with a reference to Bosley Swain, art critic, in *The Addams Family* TV series. Among his film credits are *The Pride of St. Louis* (1952), *Jailhouse Rock* (1957) as the prison warden, and *To Kill A Mockingbird* (1962).

Jody Fair. A short career dating from the late 1950's to the early 60's, she appeared as Helen Weeks in "Late Date," a first-season episode of *Thriller*. Film titles include *Hot Rod Gang* (1958) and *Ghost of Dragstrip Hollow* (1959).

2.7 "The Water of Gorgeous Springs" . . . . *November 7, 1960*
Directed by Richard H. Bartlett
Teleplay by Montgomery Pittman and Raphael Hayes
Story by Montgomery Pittman
Produced by Boris D. Kaplan

A clan of hillbillies arrive at the dock. While one of the men carries a box marked "Danger, Explosives," the others board the boat. Seeing the marking, the crew scatter, leaving it to Bill Blake to address the situation (since he was the one who booked them as passengers). With Grey in attendance, he nervously introduces the Jennings: Rush and Lovie (the newlyweds), Charity and Gould and brother Barry. They have reserved for them the Deluxe Cabin and several other suites.

Convincing Gould to put the box down, he willingly shows the captains what he has inside. Not explosives, but a prize watermelon they are taking to the Fletcherville Fair. This relieves the river men of one problem but creates another: Grey has already pledged the Deluxe Cabin to another clan of hillbillies. They hope one or the other clan will give up their rights to the Deluxe suite but that turns out to be the least of their worries.

Gunshots ring out and Grey and Bill run to the deck. It seems the Cox clan, to whom Grey sold passage, hate the Jennings clan. Each side has vowed to kill the other and a tremendous battle breaks out with numerous holes being drilled into the *Enterprise.*

Mr. Cox sends for reinforcements, determining he has the Jennings trapped on the boat. Meanwhile, brother Barry, who has been seeing to the horses, is spotted. In order not to have his brains blown out, he leaps into the river.

Grey realizes he cannot permit the Cox clan from being reinforced but they cannot pull away because the boat is still docked. He dives into the river, cuts the mooring lines (the only time he ever used the knife he wears at his back since he changed costumes back in the middle of Season One), and gives the signal. The *Enterprise* steams away and both families are now stranded together.

During all this, Grey makes the acquaintance of Inez, one of the Cox clan. Raised like a boy, her one goal in life is to kill a Jennings. Holden flirts with her, first as a way of hiding young Barry Jennings in a closet, and then God knows why. He will more or less keep this up the whole episode.

With Joshua and Carney safely tucked away in the engine room, the clans stalk one another, taking pot shots whenever the director thought the action lagged. This goes on without much else happening for most of the episode until Grey has the brilliant idea to end the feud. He makes both sides agree to give up their guns (Inez steals hers back) and then launches into Cause and Effect.

It turns out the feud dates back fifty years, to a drought. The only water left in the country was at Gorgeous Springs (and you were wondering how the title would be worked in!). The spring was on Jennings land, but some of the Cox boys claimed it and tried to fence it off. Someone shot someone and they've been fighting ever since. In case anyone is concerned, they did not fight on Sundays and both families attended the same church. Preachers have tried to settle things between them but never succeeded. Fortunately, Grey's silver tongue had better luck.

Meanwhile, Inez Cox catches Barry Jennings sneaking out of the closet. In the one shining moment of the entire episode, she plugs him in the back.

Fortunately (or unfortunately depending on your point of view), she immediately regrets her action and bursts into tears. In a 1) desperate 2) foolish 3) manipulation of plot to stretch out the episode, she leaps into the water to 1) attempt suicide 2) practice swimming 3) reach land and practice her shooting because she didn't manage to kill Barry although she shot him at point blank range.

Once on land she 1) twists her ankle 2) plunges into a swamp 3) sinks into quicksand (all of the above). United in a common cause, the Cox and Jennings boys, plus Grey (shirtless), give chase. They find Inez, form a human chain and hoist her out.

Back aboard the *Enterprise,* Grey toasts to 50 years of (future) friendship and cuts the prize fruit, giving half to each side, so, you might say, instead of splitting hairs, the Jennings and Cox clans split melons.

All that was missing from this episode was Granny and it could have been mistaken for The Beverly Hillbillies. *In fact, Buddy Ebsen could have used footage from "The Water at Gorgeous Springs" as an audition for Jed Clampett.*

If you like episodes that feature hillbillies, this is your baby.

There is absolutely nothing positive to say about this show except that Barry Atwater did a good job as the clean-shaven, monster-hat-toting head of the Jennings clan and Jocelyn Brando did her level best to deliver lines with a straight face. Other than that, it was pure embarrassment. Grey's flirtation with Inez made you wish they were wearing bags over their heads and both actors looked as though they felt appropriately silly. The bulk of the hour was taken up by the clans running around the boat shooting one another (notoriously bad shots!) and Holden's Sudden Inspiration on how to end the feud (where preachers fear to tread) was worthy of a guffaw if you happened to be awake at the end.

The unexpected violence when Inez shot Barry in the back came as a shock, but seemed entirely out of keeping with the light, almost laughable tone set by the preceding 45 minutes.

Joshua had several small, inconsequential scenes, but Jack Lambert looked lost, as though he had no idea why he was brought back for so small a part and had quite forgotten how to play his character.

Raphael Hayes, who wrote "No Bridge on the River," (2.5) disappointed with this turkey, which had all the earmarks of being lifted directly from Mark Twain's Life on the River. *Richard H. Barnett makes his first appearance in Season Two.*

GUEST CAST

Buddy Ebsen *(b. 4/2/1908, Belleville, IL; d. 7/6/2003, Torrance, CA, pneumonia.)* Two words will always conjure his face: Jed Clampett, from *The Beverly Hillbillies.* He also played *Barnaby Jones* in the series of the same name (1973), achieving considerable success with the new character. He began his career on Vaudeville and also appeared on Broadway before uprooting to Hollywood with his sister Vilma. He won the role of the Scarecrow for *The Wizard of Oz* (1939) but then changed roles with Ray Bolger, who had been cast as the Tin Woodsman. After becoming ill from the make-up, he bowed out and the part went to Jack Haley. An outspoken Republican, he helped defeat co-star Nancy Kulp in her 1962 Congressional bid, describing her as "too liberal." They were estranged thereafter and never spoke.

Sherry Jackson *(b. 2/15/1942, Wendell, ID.)* A child actress who found it difficult to maintain a career as an adult, she made her mark in films early. She is fondly remembered as the Portuguese child who witnesses a vision in *The Miracle of Our Lady of Fatima* (1952), and as one of the children in the *Ma and Pa Kettle* series. She worked steadily on TV, playing Terry on *Make Room for Daddy* before her character "left for college." Predictably, she showed up on "What Are Little Girls Made Of?", the regrettable 1966 episode of *Star Trek*, and played Comfort in "The Last Rites of Jeff Myrtlebank" on *Twilight Zone* (1962). Later in her career she made innumerable low-budget cult films, usually playing the semi-clad "babe."

Barry Atwater *(b. 5/16/1918, Denver, CO; d. 5/24/1978, Los Angeles, stroke.)* A very familiar face who, like so many, achieved a sort of immortality by appearing on *Star Trek* ("The Savage Curtain," 1969). He achieved another sort of fame by playing Janos Skorzney in the first *Night Stalker* film (1972). Midway between *Riverboat* and his more famous roles, Barry starred on *General Hospital*, playing Dr. John Prentice. Always distinguished, he frequently played foreign characters or those requiring quiet dignity.

Jocelyn Brando (see episode 1.28, "The Night of the Faceless Men," page 164.)

Gregory Walcott *(b. 1/13/1928, Wendell, NC.)* Starred in the 1961-62 TV series *The 87th Precinct* with Robert Lansing, and probably earned his greatest claim to fame by playing opposite Clint Eastwood in four major Eastwood films, usually getting the stuffing beaten out of him by the hero.

Dody Heath. She had a few credits in the late 50's and 60's, including the film *The Diary of Anne Frank* (1959) as Miep, and playing Susanna in the *Twilight Zone* episode "Long Live Walter Jameson" (1960).

2.8 **"Devil in Skirts"** . . . . *November 21, 1960*
Directed by David Lowell Rich
Written by Irwin and Gwen Gielgud and Bob and Wanda Duncan
Produced by Boris D. Kaplan

Outside Vicksburg, Grey and Bill Blake are dressed up — but only one of them is going ashore. They have come to pick up a cargo of cotton, but Holden is worried that Colonel Ashley will see the *Enterprise* riding high on the water (meaning the boat is empty) and take advantage of them. He proposes that Bill let him off, and then that he take the boat around a bend in the river, hiding the fact they are desperate for cargo. That will give Grey the edge when determining the price for transport. Blake doesn't like the idea but agrees to go along.

Captain Holden attends a party given by Colonel Ashley, but the colonel is not prepared to talk business once he finds his son Tony dallying with a woman named Lucinda Lee on the couch. He chases both young people away with the comment that Tony likes to play the field and will never ask the schoolteacher to marry him. Ashley, himself, wouldn't mind making time with her, but he's "not offering the formalities." Offended, Lucinda retorts that she will be Mrs. Anthony Ashley or nothing.

Ashley changes his mind about talking business and reports that he has been spying on Holden. The river man hasn't had a cargo since Cairo and he's sitting high on the water. He may or may not give Holden his business: that depends on whether the captain will go along with his scheme.

Grey Holden was all "fuss and feathers" in Season Two, with an eye for the ladies and a willing participant in any fight which might come his way. Too often he found himself ashore, as in this publicity still, as the action went further and further astray from the Enterprise *and the river.*

The plan is simple. He offers Grey $4,000 for shipping the cotton and another $1,000 to romance Lucinda in an effort to prove to his son the woman is not worth his effort. This is an all or nothing deal. Grey either accepts, or he won't get the consignment and Ashley will see to it he is never again able to get credit on the river.

Grey refuses.

Grey goes out to take the air and Lucinda joins him. She overheard the colonel's offer, but rather than be offended she has her own proposal. Grey should accept the money and do his best to make Tony jealous. That way, the heir will be inspired to offer marriage — something she doubts he would otherwise do.

Grey agrees.

The colonel gives him $5,000 and the stage is set with both Ashley and Lucinda thinking they will get what they want, although for different ends.

A crewman who jumped ship off the *Enterprise* turns up in Lucinda's bedroom. He turns out to be her brother, Matt Jennings (no relation, presumably, to the feuding hillbillies from "The Water at Gorgeous Springs.) He has come to make the colonel pay for some past transgression; she, too, is working toward that end. Her plan is to make Tony marry her and make him and his father regret it "every day of their lives." She'd "marry the devil" (and thus the convoluted title) if it meant hurting the Ashleys.

In the morning, Grey and Lucinda go for a ride. Tony is jealous and follows them after his father remarks, "Holden is quite a lady's man." Later that day, as a shirtless Grey washes, the colonel tells him he is pleased with his progress. When it is all over, he would be obliged if Holden took Miss Lee away with him to the *Enterprise.* Grey agrees — if Ashley pays her passage money, proving he can be as cheap as the colonel.

The following day, Grey takes Lucinda to the wharf where he counts 20 bales of cotton ready to be loaded. She says he must lead an exciting life but he laments there are too many boats and too little cargoes, but he likes the life even if it means feast or famine.

Wandering away, he is attacked by Matt and knocked unconscious. Lucinda finds him and demands to know what happened. He can only say he knew the assailant as a former crewman who wanted him to relay a message to Colonel Ashley that he is "here to stay," and that he has as much right to the land as the Ashleys. While this makes no sense to Holden, the assertion frightens Lucinda.

Grey relays the message and the colonel is visibly upset. He admits Matt has an old grudge against him and takes out a gun. Before the explanation goes further, Tony breaks in and accuses his father of putting Holden up to romancing his girl. The colonel doesn't want to address that, being too worried about the appearance of an old enemy. The name "Jennings" doesn't mean anything to Tony, so his father gives the details. Matt's father had land the colonel wanted and everyone knew old man Jennings had both a drinking and a gambling problem. One night when he was drunk, the colonel played cards with him and won his land. The son has sworn vengeance on him.

He knows something else, as well. Lucinda is not what she seems and her surname isn't Lee — it's Jennings. She is Matt's sister and together they have plotted revenge. He only permitted her to stay in the house hoping to turn the tables. Tony does not believe him.

Just then, Lucinda enters and makes a full confession. She wanted to get back at the colonel through Tony but after seeing how hatred destroyed her brother, she has determined to abandon her evil plan and leave. Before she can do that, Matt enters with a gun, planning on shooting the Ashleys.

He tells their side of the story. After "paw" lost his land, he put a gun to his head and killed himself, leaving his two small children to fend for themselves. In the hungry, sleepless nights they spent, the pair plotted a way to get even. Lucinda meant to reclaim the land by marriage but now that she backed off, he will simply murder them.

Grey tries to talk him out of the deed, and then gets in a fight. The gun goes off, wounding Tony. This puts an end to the struggle and the colonel calls for the marshal. But Tony won't have it. He stands up to his father and says from now on, he's giving orders and the law won't be called.

The colonel finally gets to see his son "grow up before his eyes," Tony discovers he's really in love with Lucinda and Grey determines that the injured youth needs someone to care for him, thus setting the stage for a happy ending. Matt asks for his old job back aboard the *Enterprise* and Grey obliges.

Back on the boat, Bill Blake laments that he didn't go with Grey to spend a few days of leisure sipping mint juleps.

Writers Bob and Wanda Duncan, who wrote several scripts in Season One, united with Irwin and Gwen Gielgud for "The Devil in Skirts," and may have proved the old adage, "Too many cooks spoil the broth." Although well acted, the script was flat, predictable and rather uninspired.

For the eighth time in as many episodes, we are subjected to the tenet that Grey Holden is a lady's man and for the second time in two episodes he is shirtless. If the producer intended to capitalize on McGavin's sex appeal, this fell far short of convincing, the first idea becoming stale in repetition and, with all respect to Darren, the second flashy, but hardly enough to carry the episode.

The idea of the colonel shipping his own cotton is curious. (And why are Southern men always colonels, particularly before the Civil War?) Historically, Southern planters worked through a cotton factorage system, where men, primarily Northerners, handled all aspects of the cotton crop from harvest to sale. No planter ever saw to such details himself — and this certainly applies to every other Riverboat *episode where cotton was mentioned.*

Additionally, a bale of cotton weighed 200 pounds. If there were 20 bales on the wharf, that equaled 4,000 pounds, or two tons — the established weight to fill the Enterprise. *But cotton prices were extremely depressed in the 1840's. Middling New Orleans cotton sold for 16 cents a pound in New York as late as 1857 and it sold for 4-6 cents a pound in 1842. Any way you do the arithmetic, Colonel Ashley wouldn't be paying $4,000 just to ship his produce.*

The only scene worth singling out is the one where Grey talks about his life on the river and how difficult it is. This was poignant and if the writers had spent more time on that rather than the jealousy angle, it would have made a far better story.

The resolution with all parties living happily ever after came with lightning speed, more than a dash of plot convenience and seemed preordained. Perhaps the one eye-raiser came not from the script but the casting — for the first time, we actually saw two slaves (?) serving, one as a maid and the other, a groom. That said, it's a little harder to explain the "traditional" black jockey statue planted out in a field, miles away from the manse. Historical — possibly. Ridiculous — certainly.

GUEST CAST

Gloria Talbott (see episode 1.17, "Landlubbers," page 119.)

Frank Silvera *(b. 7/24/1914, Kingston, Jamaica, British West Indies; d. 6/11/1970, Pasadena, CA, accidental electrocution.)* Frequently cast as a Mexican or Latin character, his most easily recognizable role has to be as Don Sebastian Montoya, father of Victoria and Manolito Montoya on *The High Chaparral* in the 1960's. His last role was as a guest star on an episode of *Hawaii Five-O* in 1970.

Brad Weston. Primarily a TV actor, he appeared with McGavin on *The Outsider* episode "Love is Under L," and also had a small role in the McGavin film, *Hot Lead and Cold Feet* (1978). He played Ed Appel in the *Star Trek* episode "The Devil in the Dark."

Arthur Batanides (see episode 1.17, "Landlubbers," page 120)

2.9 "The Quota". . . . .*November 28, 1960*
Directed by Hollingsworth Morse
Teleplay by Bob and Wanda Duncan and Raphael Hayes
Story by Bob and Wanda Duncan
Produced by Boris D. Kaplan

The script opens in River Point where General Winfield Scott is arriving. His presence makes Sergeant Danny Phillips' task of recruiting men into the Army all the more imperative. He and Corporal Sam have only a short time left and they need three more to fill their quota. The pair meet a young dock worker and try to talk him into joining. He refuses, so they knock him on the head. When he wakes up, he finds himself enlisted.

The *Enterprise* steams into port with Captain Holden and a young crewman named Fallon preparing to go ashore. Dressed in formal wear, Grey explains this is to present an appearance of respectability and confidence to potential clients. Captain Blake gives the pair four days to obtain cargo. He'll have the boat back by then and expects a full consignment of produce waiting.

Grey has a scheme that he explains to Fallon but before they can implement it, the boy accidentally bumps into Sgt. Phillips. Grumbling to Sam to "put him on the list," they bide their time as the pair go about their business. Grey goes into the General Store of Mr. Latimer, casually asking which boat the merchant has chosen. He replies the Arkansas Belle, and Grey mumbles something about "bad boilers." This makes Latimer nervous. Before he can send his wife to check out the distressing news, Holden leaves and Fallon arrives. He states that he just signed up George Reynolds' cargo and hopes his captain hasn't agreed to take Latimer's because they don't have any room. This convinces Latimer his competition knows more than he does and he determines to ship his cargo with Holden.

Without knowing the successful outcome of his plan, Grey waits for his crewman in the hotel. Fallon never arrives, having been "shanghaied" by the two Army recruiters. Mr. Latimer appears with the news he wants Holden's services, and remarks the last he saw of Fallon was in the company of the soldiers. Grey leaves and confronts the men on the street. They profess not to have seen the boy but Grey disbelieves them and threatens to report the disappearance to their superior.

Placed in the position of having his seventeen-year career blemished, Danny determines he must prevent Holden from talking. The best way to do that is by "recruiting" him, as well. They lure him to the barn where the other men are kept prisoner behind a grate. Grey easily deduces how they have been signed up and remarks that he had been a soldier in the Blackhawk War but never saw anyone as despicable as the sergeant. Phillips pleads his case, wishing to exonerate himself and asserting his desire to be friends. If only Grey would join of his own free will, they could be good companions.

This is the last thing on the captain's mind, however, and realizing that if they let him go he will ruin their careers, the recruiters knock him out. When he wakes, Phillips tells him he has papers with Holden's name on it. If he tries to leave, he will be shot for desertion.

Danny and Sam lead a wagon train out of River Point with all the men they have bullied into the army. When Grey wakes from his beating, he promises to do everything in his power to escape and blow the whistle. This prompts Phillips to discipline him by having Holden's shirt torn off and staking him in the hot sun. Two days later, sunburned and dehydrated, Holden still refuses to capitulate.

A soldier rides up with news that there is trouble in the Seminole Territory and that the sergeant is to hurry his men to Florida. In the ensuing preparations, Grey escapes and runs through the woods, cleverly covering himself with brush as the soldiers search for him. When they are gone, he swims through a pond and finally makes it to a plantation and steals a horse. Riding full speed ahead, he returns to River Point to inform General Scott of the misdeeds perpetrated in his name.

The hotel clerk promises to take Grey to the general but betrays him by turning him over to Phillips. The sergeant wants to shoot him but Grey tells him the *Enterprise* is due back at any minute. He is a well-known man and no one would ever believe he joined the army, so even his dead body is a palpable threat. When they hear the boat whistle announcing its arrival, Grey breaks free and races for the dock, screaming all the way. Bill Blake hears him and gets a rifle. A gun battle ensues and Grey is winged but manages to get safely back aboard where Joshua and the captain protect him.

Phillips continues his one-man assault on the boat and is eventually shot and killed. The three river men decide Danny wanted to be shot. Grey remarks, "He was finished and he knew it. Poor man."

The recruits are freed and General Scott offers restitution for their ordeal. He then determines to mark this black incident in Dan Phillips' service record, marring an otherwise unblemished career. Holden prevents this by remarking that the first seventeen years of the sergeant's career ought to be allowed to stand without adding the last sad chapter. Scott agrees and the *Enterprise* steams away, presumably with Fallon and the cargo in tow.

There was a lot to like in "The Quota." Gene Evans gave a stand-up performance as Sergeant Danny Evans and his acting greatly supplemented the dialogue, giving a persuasive argument that he really was a good soldier placed in the untenable position of recruiting men for the army. James Griffith was equally effective as Sam, the hesitant but eventually willing co-conspirator.

The scenes where Phillips had Holden tortured were convincing and effectively played by McGavin. He was utterly convincing as a man dying of heat stroke and these scenes stand out as some of the best done on Riverboat. *The makeup and direction were first rate, conveying the heat of the sun and the agonies endured. They weren't rushed through, as too many promising scenes tended to be, and the overall effect was chilling.*

Although it was easy to guess that Holden and Fallon would be the last to make up "the quota," the writers and director managed to move the plot along and it never became bogged down with extraneous subplots. All the minor characters were well cast and the scene where the clerk betrays Grey by luring him into a side room where Phillips waited was as unexpected as it was exciting. Mr. Wilkie, played by James Nusser (billed as Jim Nusser for the only time we ever saw) was especially effective, proving the adage that a part is what you make it.

It was good to see Jack Lambert, even in a limited role. Dick Wessel was listed in the credits over him, but he didn't make it to the copy we reviewed.

There is not much to complain of in this writing collaboration of the Duncans and Raphael Hayes. The idea of a defeated man committing virtual suicide was already used in Season One ("Fort Epitaph") but it came across as credible. For the third episode in a row, McGavin raced around the set shirtless and his escape through the woods and pond gave rise to speculation the episode might have been called "The Night of the Shirtless Man," or "Grey's Olympic Adventure." It's difficult to believe anyone, even a riverboat captain, tortured for days in the hot sun, starved and dehydrated as he was, could have been so physically active immediately after escaping, but this was somewhat mitigated by director Hollingsworth Morse having him stuff food in his mouth at the plantation before riding off on a stolen horse.

On a less acceptable note concerning how the set was dressed, the same black jockey statue used the episode before in "Devil in Skirts" resurfaced outside the manse. But at least it wasn't stuck out in a field.

It is also a bit hard to swallow that Grey magnanimously granted Phillips an unblemished record in death after the man tortured him. But then, he's a nice guy and Gene Evans' acting might have influenced him, too.

The slim bit of characterization that Grey fought in the Blackhawk War seemed odd and if true, one can only wonder if he met Abraham Lincoln there and lament the fact those two veterans didn't have a conversation about it in "No Bridge on the River."

GUEST CAST

Gene Evans *(b. 7/11/1922, Holbrook, AZ; d. 4/1/1998, Jackson, TN, natural causes.)* A red-haired, gruff-voiced, burly character actor, he stands out in memory from his role as the father in the TV series *My Friend Flicka*. After performing with a troupe of GI's during WWII, he went to Hollywood. Early films include *The Steel Helmet* (1951), *Park Row* (1952), *Hell and High Water* (1954), and *Shock Corridor* with Peter Breck in 1963.

James Griffith *(b. 2/13/1916, Los Angeles, CA; d. 9/17/1993, Avila Beach, CA, cancer.)* He appeared in several episodes of *Rocky Jones, Space Ranger* (1954) and as one of the octet in *Eight Iron Men* with Richard Kiley (1952). Closer to home, he played Schwartz in *The Night Stalker* episode, "Bad Medicine" (1974). He made two *Thriller* episodes: "Paradise Mansion" (1961) and "The Storm" (1962). He played Aaron Adams on *Trackdown* (1957) and also worked on *Range Rider* (1951). Once a musician with Spike Jones' Band, he usually played Southerners or hillbillies. He also wrote individual episodes for *Mission: Impossible* and *The Fugitive*.

Ron Hagerthy *(b. 3/9/1932).* Prolific character actor, he is probably best recognized from *Sky King*, where he played Clipper from 1952-55. He made an episode of *Twilight Zone* ("Dead Man's Shoes," 1962). His last credit was an episode of *Lassie* (1968).

Tom Gilleran. His credits include three episodes of *Alfred Hitchcock Presents* from 1955 and *Riverboat*.

Stuart Randall (see episode 1.25, "Fort Epitaph," page 152.)

James Nusser *(b. 5/3/1905, Ohio; d. 6/6/1979, Los Angeles, CA.)* Billed as Jim Nusser on *Riverboat*, this beloved actor earned eternal fame playing Louie Pheeters on *Gunsmoke* (1961-69), giving the performance of a lifetime on the two-part episode "Nitro" (4/8-15/1967). His first TV credit was *Space Patrol* (1951) and his last was on an episode of *Cannon* (1976) called "The Reformer." He also appeared in a 1968 episode of *The Outsider* with McGavin entitled "I Can't Hear You Scream."

2.10 "Chicota Landing" . . . . *December 5, 1960*
Directed by David Lowell Rich
Teleplay by Raphael Hayes
Story by Herman Groves
Produced by Boris D. Kaplan

A gang of banditos on horseback hold a white man captive. They bring him to the river, stand him up on shore and execute him, firing-squad style. The *Enterprise* just happens to be steaming by. Grey's romancing of a young woman is interrupted by the noise and excitement on the riverbank and he gets out his spyglass to have a better look. Yup, they shot the poor guy. The captain chivalrously decides to retrieve the corpse for his nearest and dearest. Too bad, too, because he had just promised Miss Lucy Bridges (whose father is an army colonel) to please her by joining the army and becoming tame.

That might have salvaged this episode. Then again, it might not have. He might have been lying, since only the week before he refused to join up, even to please his would-be pal, Sergeant Phillips.

If the above doesn't scare you off, you're in for a doozie.

The *Enterprise* steams into Taylorsville and brings out the body. He is identified as Deputy Sam Bates (there was a "Sam" in the last episode, too). Sheriff Dave Madson takes Grey and Bill and an army lieutenant, Dave Winslow, to his office where he has a Mexican general locked up. He is the commander of the band of banditos seen in the Teaser. Careless of him to be captured; no explanation was forthcoming about how he found himself in such unfortunate circumstances.

The townsmen determine to form a lynching party and hang General Cortilla (whom McGavin & Co. persisted in calling General "Tortilla"). Sheriff Madson deputizes Grey and Bill and orders them to go outside and hold off the mob while he and the lieutenant sneak out the back with the prisoner. Things look grim as the mob push our heroes aside and enter. Finding the object of their desire gone, they decide to get even by burning the jail.

Back aboard the boat, the co-captains find Dave, Dave and *el generalissimo* waiting for them. Madson decides that Holden ought to take the captive with him upriver, deliver twenty kegs of gunpowder Winslow has been ordered to transport, and then come back. By that time, he reckons he'll have things under control and Cortilla can get a fair trial.

With that hope springing eternal, Grey accepts the commission, but Bill misses the opportunity to demand Cortilla's passage fare "in advance." They presumably take aboard the gunpowder (stored in kegs the size of watermelons) and steam off.

Chained to a bed, the general unloads his life story on Grey. He started out as a peon and rose in the ranks to sergeant, winning a score of medals in the process. Considering the fact his father was only a peon, he could rise no farther, so he set out on his own, eventually raising an army to loot, pillage and murder. Grey sympathizes.

Having nothing better to do, Lieutenant Winslow begins courting Miss Lucy. Gray announces that if anyone is going to marry her, it will be he and then predicts a peaceful trip. Just at that pithy moment, the gang of Mexicans appear on shore and, like the Injuns from "Fort Epitaph," they follow the boat, boding ill. Holden determines it is too unsafe to dock for the night. Bill protests. There are snags in the river. (This is great for continuity, but unfortunately the last time we heard this dialogue it was between Grey and Ben.) Joshua and Carney made an appearance just in time to (almost) fall overboard when the *Enterprise* hits a sandbar and gets stuck.

While the crew successfully free the boat, *el general* escapes. It seems a support from the cabin roof fell down and Cortilla wiggled out of his chains.

The *Enterprise* pulls into the landing where soldiers from the fort (actually a shabby outbuilding) help unload the gunpowder. Unfortunately, no one noted any resemblance between soldiers and banditos for it is soon revealed that the Mexicans have murdered all the troops and taken their uniforms. If you didn't see this coming, you weren't watching "Jessie Quinn."

Cortilla/Tortilla takes over the boat. He orders the powder back aboard and reveals his plan. He will have Holden bring the boat back to Taylorsville then blow it up, incidentally blowing up the entire town, as well. No doubt he saw how fast the jail went up and it inspired him.

They start the return journey. One of the banditos steals Grey's watch and Grey takes exception, although he has never once been seen to tell the time from it. He fights for it in one of the worst fight scenes yet staged on *Riverboat* and gets it back. He does wind it, but doesn't check the time. Considering McGavin's dislike of the costume, it's a wonder he didn't simply offer the knife riding up his back and be done with it.

The general decides he will marry Miss Lucy because when he returns to Mexico he plans on becoming a king. (See "Guns for Empire" for more "continuity.") Grey refuses to perform the ceremony. No problem. There are two captains aboard. Cortilla will shoot Grey and have Blake do the honors.

The general wants the boat to travel at night because he is eager for his conflagration. Grey protests that with all the powder on board, they may hit the same sandbar they did on the upward journey and blow themselves up too soon. Cortilla reminds him they didn't explode the first time but Grey is ready with his answer. He says that's because they didn't have gunpowder aboard on that trip. No doubt he figures the general has a short memory.

Lucy jumps overboard (see "The Water of Gorgeous Springs") and now they have to stop for the night to look for her. The crew is herded into the engine room while Grey is taken out to be shot. In a moment of Television Inspiration, he tosses a handful of dirt on the Bad Guys and every one of them drops like deflated balloons. Grey escapes.

There is another fight scene between Grey and a bandito. Fortunately for the audience, Holden is wearing a white shirt because otherwise it would have been impossible to tell the stunt doubles apart. He wins and in a true classic, goes to deliver the fatal blow when the thug drops at his feet. Grey gives his fist a quizzical look, and then sneaks back onto the *Enterprise* by climbing up the paddlewheel (a technique first demonstrated by Chip in "The Blowup"). He makes it to the pilothouse and communicates to the boys via the tube system. The filtering over the intercom on Season Two was tinny to make it sound "realistic" (as opposed to Season One where it sounded more natural), but in this instance the voices sounded exactly as though Grey and the boys were speaking over a telephone. Even in this episode, the effect was unnerving.

Holden has a plan. When he gives the signal, the crew is to rush the door and escape. He has a pistol and will shoot the general in the melee. An overlong fight scene ensues (known in the parlance as "filler") and Grey draws a bead on the general. Just as he's about to plug him a shot rings out (from somewhere, never explained) and Cortilla drops down. They grapple and Grey wins, adding, "Tie this dog up."

Back at town, Sheriff Dave proudly announces the jail has been rebuilt, the same size as the last one. Too bad, Grey laments. "Now you have a housing problem."

The lieutenant and the girl go off into the sunset together.

Television in the 1950's and '60's was notoriously poor when it came to presenting "Mexican" episodes and this was the cream of that bad crop. Aside from Joe DeSantis' rather decent portrayal of el general (he even managed to make his lines articulate), there was not much good to say about it.

A very green Richard Chamberlain played the lieutenant, but was more decorative than useful. Chamberlain's part was superfluous and so was that of Miss Lucy. Her role seemed to be written merely for Grey to romance (See episodes 1-9 of Season Two.)

Aside from all the other horrors in this episode (writing, directing), the one issue that sticks out was the mysterious shot fired at the end. An initial impression was that Lucy had come back, somehow managed to get a gun and was taking her revenge for almost being married to the general. Unlike "Night of the Faceless Men," however, that was too honorable for Season Two and so the writers or the director or the editor simply opted to have the Hand of God intervene.

God, in this case, being uncredited.

GUEST CAST

Joe DeSantis *(b. 6/15/1909, New York, NY; d. 8/30/1989, Provo, UT, COPD.)* A character actor who usually played Italian mobsters or Western heavies, he often wore a beard in later years and had over one hundred credits to his name. He co-guest starred with Simon Oakland in the classic first season episode of *Mission: Impossible* ("The Frame"), also appeared on *Gunsmoke* ("Lyle's Kid," and "The Jackals" both in 1968) as well as films such as *Tension at Table Rock* (1956).

Connie Hines *(b. 6/5/1936, Dedham, MA.)* As any early TV buff can identify, she played Carol Post, wife of Wilbur, on *Mister Ed* (1961-66). Her first credit was an episode of *Whirlybirds*. She made all the usual Revue series before being cast in *Riverboat*. Her last credit was an episode of *The Mod Squad* in 1971.

John McLiam *(b. 1/24/1918, Alberta, Canada; d. 4/16/1994, Los Angeles, CA, Parkinson's Disease.)* Usually cast as an Irishman, he frequently played policemen, doing so several times on *Twilight Zone*: "Uncle Simon," "Miniature," "The Midnight Sun" and as "a man" in the episode "The Shelter." He played several law officers on *The Fugitive* and in 1966 played the part of Anton Usakos in the third season *Mission: Impossible* episode "The Play" (1968).

Richard Chamberlain *(b. 3/31/1934, Beverly Hills, CA.)* Born George Richard Chamberlain, he attended Pomona College before being drafted and served in Korea for 16 months. His acting career began in a 1959 episode of *Alfred Hitchcock Presents* called "Road Hog"; *Riverboat* is one of his earliest credits. He achieved stardom in the series *Dr. Kildare* (1961) before pursuing a dramatic career in theatre. He went to England in 1968 for a role in Richard Lester's *Petulia*, and then earned serious acclaim for *Hamlet* (1969) and *Richard II* (1972). He shone in two related pieces, *The Count of Monte Cristo* (1975) and *The Man in the Iron Mask* (1977) before going on to mega TV hits such as *Shogun* (1980) and *The Thorn Birds* (1983) with Richard Kiley and Barbara Stanwyck. In 2003, he wrote an autobiography entitled *Shattered Love*.

2.11 "Duel on the River" . . . . *December 12, 1960*
Directed by Tay Garnett
Written by Milton S. Gelman
Produced by Boris D. Kaplan

Grey, Bill and Carney are in a gentleman's bar in Vicksburg. Carney is drunk (reference "The Quick Noose"). They expect to be thrown out because of the disturbance he's making but instead a gentleman comes up and introduces himself as Brian Cloud. While affecting friendship, he warns the river men to leave the Yazoo River to him. He controls what produce is shipped, particularly King Cotton, and avows the planters belong to him.

This need not necessarily be a problem, as the co-captains have sworn off cotton because the market is shaky. The planters don't have any money to pay shipping and it is the boys' policy to exact payment before any service is rendered. They are spending their time making short trips up and down the river carrying merchandise and local produce.

Grey receives a perfumed note from a woman professing to be an old friend. Leaving Bill and Carney at the bar he goes over to meet her at a side table. It turns out he does not know her; she only used that as a ploy to get his attention. Being attractive, she succeeds.

Laurie wants to talk "cotton." She has a shipment that needs to be taken to Memphis. The hitch is, she can pay him only after the cotton is sold in Memphis. He regretfully refuses. Mr. Cloud intervenes and reminds her Mr. Rollins, her husband, is waiting for her at Shadow Dance, their plantation.

Later that day she has returns home. Bodrey Rollins is angry. He tells her their cotton is going to be shipped by Mr. Cloud. She retorts, saying he is cheating them, and then launches into a tirade about how the cotton crop has ruined the soil. If only Bodrey had planted some other cash crop they wouldn't be strapped for cash and she wouldn't be in danger of losing her beloved plantation. He protests that Cloud is the only one who extended the planters credit; shipping with him is not only a matter of business, but honor. If Mr. Rollins is anything, he is an honorable man. This becomes the central theme of the script.

Mr. Cloud and his very tall thug Job meet Grey on the boat. No crew is present, having all gone ashore. Ostensibly there to warn Holden off compromising a lady again, Cloud sets his henchman on Grey with a whip. After a rough and tumble fight, Grey wins and throws them both off.

Laurie invites Grey to Shadow Dance and drives him there in her buggy. Along the way they stop for a picnic. While they finish up the fried chicken, Mrs. Rollins explains that she and her husband also had a "Shadow Dance" in Mississippi but the land wore out there, too, from the detestable cotton, and they moved to Vicksburg. Bodrey swore off cotton but when he needed money, he went back to his old ways. Now they are nearly penniless.

Before they can move out, unseen assailants begin firing on them. Without his pistols Grey is helpless and it looks bad. The attackers tire of the game and come out of hiding. It turns out it was a case of mistaken identity. The primary shooter, Wingate Pritchart Pardee, is Laurie's blood relation. He likes her, but not Mr. Cloud, and he's not overly fond of Bodrey, either. He invites them up to his something-less-than-a-plantation and explains how Cloud has taken advantage of the planters because the land is poor and they don't have any money to meet their obligations to him.

Saying good-bye, the pair go to Shadow Dance. Laurie shows Grey into the parlor, remarking that the room and all its possessions are more important to her than anything in the world. He protests they can be replaced, and she counters by saying, "Not the memories."

Grey exchanges literary quotes with Cloud (see "Path of the Eagle" and "Three Graves") and restates his position: his honor is predicated on the axiom, "Pay as you go," meaning he won't ship their cotton on credit. This doesn't prevent Bodrey from getting jealous of his wife's interest in Grey.

A commotion outside brings the party to the lawn where Job has caught and is whipping a trespasser who turns out to be Wingate Pritchert Pardee. Grey attacks Job, placing a burning faggot against the other's whip. Grey wins, Wingate leaves and the party goes back inside.

Cloud states he will have a boat on the dock in the morning to carry away Bodrey's cotton. Grey says if the planter can pay him, he will offer his services. Bodrey writes Grey a check payable on the Bank of Memphis, using his word as a gentleman as his bond, and they strike an agreement.

Sometime in the next few hours Grey leaves Vicksburg and goes to Memphis and returns. He has discovered Rollins' account there has been closed for insufficient funds. Very angry at being cheated, he returns to Shadow Dance and demands his money. (It is unclear whether Holden took the cotton with him or not and even more unclear how he traveled that distance and back overnight.)

Bodrey challenges Grey to a duel for some convoluted slight of honor (he is an honorable man even though he writes bad checks) and they meet at dawn. Wingate, who is acting as Grey's second, remembers it is the right of the challenged to choose weapons, so he makes the two combatants exchange dueling pistols. They pace ten steps away and face one another, opposing eyelids closed in concentration. Bodrey will not shoot and it turns out that by exchanging guns, his plan was spoiled. The pistol Rollins meant to use had a blank in it; the one Grey was given had a fully loaded charge.

You guessed it. Bodrey meant for Holden to kill him because he (Bodrey) is an honorable man.

In the flick of an eye, the furniture in Shadow Dance is "beamed away" (and DeForest Kelley won't even be on *Riverboat* for two more episodes!) Laurie laments the lost belongings that her husband sold to pay his debts — being an honorable man. It appears she has lost everything. Grey reads her a chapter from the *TV Bible*, reminding her she can't be on two sides at once: hers and her husband's. She must be on his side to save the marriage. He is, after all, an honorable man.

The script ends with an extremely long (read: boring) scene with Wingate, Rollins, Laurie and Grey discussing land and cotton. When all is said and done, Wingate and all his money will save the Rollins and help them preserve Shadow Dance. Somehow, it all ends in a good laugh.

Writer Milton S. Gelman ("The Long Trail") had good ideas but absolutely no clue how to make them entertaining. He touched on how cotton depleted the soil, which was a very real concern to Southern planters in the antebellum period, but neglected to offer the viable solution: scientific farming. Instead of crop rotation and fertilizer, which were commonly practiced in the North and widely publicized in scientific journals of the day, the only suggestion he offered was not to plant cotton (an economic disaster) or to move.

As with his previous script, none of his characters were likeable and they garnered no sympathy for their plight. The idea of "honor" was beaten to death and the "duel" where husband Bodrey set the scene for his suicide was too often used on Riverboat *(see "Fort Epitaph" and "The Quota"). Three times and you're out.*

In a curious recurring theme, the writer has a lady enter a saloon without raising eyebrows: this was something that was simply not done, particularly in the South. The "mistaken identity" leading to a shootout between Wingate (a name also used, coincidentally, in "The Quick Noose") and Grey at the picnic site was an extremely weak ploy to introduce the character and all Wingate's subsequent scenes were muddled as though too many re-writes lost him in the pink pages.

The time frame was imaginary (Grey goes to Memphis and back in a night) and the furniture disappearing truly predated phasers on Star Trek. *Too many subplots (the husband's out-of-nowhere jealousy, Laurie's fixation on material goods, Wingate's wealth, bad soil, depressed markets, honor, Cloud's "owning the Yazoo," Job and his whip, dueling and Bill's desire to own the* Enterprise, *but-not-at-the-expense-of-Grey's-life) were all too much.*

Perhaps the shining moment of glory came when Wingate took Grey and Laurie to his "plantation." Up the winding path they went — right to the door of Norman

Bates' house! Of course TV viewers in 1960 didn't know it yet, but the release of Alfred Hitchcock's Psycho *(filmed at Universal the same year) gave the set immediate identification — almost as fast as faithful viewers of* Riverboat *identified the Southern mansion exterior of Shadow Dance as that used in countless previous episodes — replete with the black jockey.*

Scary, indeed.

On an unrelated note, the film score was better than usual, abandoning the overuse of the theme and the lilting music too often used by Gerald Fried. The credits revealed why. For the first time in Season Two, Fried was listed under the heading "Riverboat Song by" and music score was credited to R. Dale Buts. Fried's credit was dissembling, in that the "song" was, in effect, the theme for Season Two. It was actually a weak re-write of Elmer Bernstein's brilliant original theme, but Bernstein was given no acknowledgment. Calling it a "song" apparently mitigated a charge of plagiarism and probably earned Fried less money for the effort.

GUEST CAST

Fay Spain *(b. 10/6/1932, Phoenix, AR; d. 5/8/1983, Los Angeles, CA, cancer.)* One of her earliest TV appearances was as a contestant on the game show *You Bet Your Life*. She quickly earned roles as a starlet, changing hair color as often as character names, as required by the role. Her career faded in the mid-1960's and her last role was a bit part in *The Godfather: Part II*.

Claude Akins (see episode 1.7, "Escape to Memphis," page 78.)

Robert Emhardt (see episode 1.11, "The Boy from Pittsburgh," page 92.)

Edgar Buchanan *(b. 3/20/1903, Humansville, MO; d. 4/4/1979, Palm Desert, CA, stroke.)* A dentist by trade, he moved to Altadena, CA, and eventually joined the Pasadena Playhouse. At the age of 36, he gave up his dentistry to become a full-time actor. A familiar face, easily recognizable by everyone in the 1950's and 60's, he co-starred on the TV shows *Judge Roy Bean*, *Petticoat Junction*, playing Uncle Joe Carson (he was one of only three stars to remain with the series for its entire seven-year run), *Cade's County* and a recurring role on *Green Acres*.

2.12 **"Zigzag"** . . . . *December 26, 1960*
Directed by Sidney Lanfield
Written by David Lang
Produced by Boris D. Kaplan

A man is seen working his way through brush. In the clearing is a cabin. He knocks. No one is home. He signals his partners — two men emerge, carrying a gravely wounded man between them. They get him situated on a bed, then urge him to divulge where he buried the $100,000 stolen from a long-ago robbery. The group has just escaped from Hillsboro Prison and their only reason for bringing the blind convict is to extract this information. The dying Lear promises to tell, but only after they bring his son to see him one last time before he dies.

At Killian's Station below Memphis, the *Enterprise* pulls into the wharf. Carney has a bad tooth and his moaning and groaning over the past three weeks have driven Grey and Bill nearly mad. Holden determines his engineer will have the tooth pulled so he can get some sleep. Toward that end, he sends Blake and Carney into town to find the doctor while he delivers a cargo. The boat will be back the next day. By that time, he expects to have the situation resolved.

Bill and Carney opt to have a drink to stiffen their nerves before the extraction. They go into the local saloon for "just one" and end up finishing the bottle. Now, both are drunk, and stagger into Stephen Lear's medical office. The physician isn't there so Bill, in his tipsy state, determines to pull the tooth himself after Carney passes out on the exam table. He is in the process of doing this when the escaped convicts enter. Mistaking him for the doctor, they take him away.

Master Pilot Blake regains sobriety quickly when he realizes the case of mistaken identity. He tries to explain the error but Eagan doesn't want to believe him. Back at the cabin (an 8 - 10 mile hike), the truth will out as farmer Pinty and his daughter Lisa do not recognize Blake. Fortunately, the dying man is blind and hasn't seen his son in fifteen years so Crowley asks a favor of Bill. Just go in, hold Lear's hand and listen to him talk. Blake is made to understand Lear knows where $100,000 is buried. Get that information and they will let him go.

Bill goes in and the pathetic old man gladly welcomes the son he abandoned in childhood. If he has done nothing else right in his life, at least he has given the world a physician. He has held on this long just to hold his boy's hand. There is no loot, he confesses. That was just a story he had been telling for the past fifteen years so the other convicts would respect him. He used it again to advantage to entice Crowley and the others to include him in their escape plans.

He makes this extraordinary deathbed statement to Bill. There is no one else in the room because Lear wanted to be alone with his boy and can sense the presence of others. He promises to tell the gang he lied but before he can, he dies. It doesn't take long for the river man to realize his dire predicament. Clearly the outlaws won't believe him and will think he is holding out to keep the treasure for himself.

That's exactly how it plays out. In order to make him talk, Crowley has him tied to a rafter and intends to torture him by putting hot coals under his bare feet. It might have worked but farmer Walters grabs a rifle, holds off the convicts and escapes with Blake and his daughter.

They race through the swamp. Not to worry, he says. He knows the back-country and the gang doesn't. They can lose them in the swamp and then hide out in an abandoned mine until the coast is clear. In the meantime, he suggests Lisa and Bill get to know one another better. She's a pretty woman and will make a respectable fellow a good wife. And besides, he wouldn't mind a cut of the $100,000.

Lisa would like to hitch up with a nice man like Bill and they have several long conversations about what ladies wear in New Orleans and St. Louis before, during and after they reach the mine. Bill is vaguely interested and gets his chance to kiss the girl.

Back at Killian's Landing, Holden has returned. Carney staggers aboard without any clear memory of what happened. He expected to find Blake there but he's missing. He and Grey have to go look for him, the latter suspecting Blake went off into the sunset with two lovelies on either arm. At the sheriff's office he describes his partner as a "dapper, stocky fella wearing a mustache, a pilot's cap and a pea coat." The lawman found the coat at the doc's office, but assures Grey he could not have found the doc because he's gone to a medical convention.

Blake, with only one lovely on his arm, and farmer Pinty make a raft, presumably so they can use it to sail downriver and find buried treasure. Unfortunately, during the interim the outlaws discover their whereabouts and recapture them. In order to delay the inevitable, Blake guides the party back to the abandoned mine where he says the loot was buried. In a highly imaginative ploy learned from watching *Riverboat*, he tosses sand in their eyes, attacks the men and defeats them.

Back on the *Enterprise*, Bill waves good-bye to Lisa and her father. Too bad he wasn't younger, he says, because Lisa is a mighty pretty girl. But with the reward money she got for helping capture the convicts, she can get an education and find herself a decent husband.

Carney begins groaning again and this time the boys have to take things into their own hands. Grey pops him on the jaw, the bad tooth comes out and the day is saved.

This was the first (and last) "Bill Blake episode" and Noah Beery handled it well. Finally given a chance to carry an episode, he came off as likeable and credible, making an otherwise unremarkable story credible.

Although Charles Bronson was given "Guest Star" recognition in both the opening titles and the end credits, he was largely wasted in "Zigzag." There was nothing special about the character of Crowley, his screen time was limited and the main theme of escaped prisoners looking for $100,000 actually turned into a subplot amid Pinty's romantic manipulations for his daughter. This was too bad, for even at a young age Bronson was a formidable presence and cast alongside John Milton, a stalwart of 1950's and '60's TV, they were a powerful combination. It would have been a far superior hour if writer David Lang had concentrated on the escapees, particularly because he gave the character of Crowley a soft, almost sympathetic air — or at least he came across that way under Bronson's skillful touch.

William Fawcett and Stella Stevens were both fine as the father-daughter combination although it might be argued Fawcett could have played the character in his sleep. Both took pains not to fall into the stereotypical trap and largely succeeded. The idea of a farmer seeking a husband for his child was already shopworn by 1960, however, and there wasn't much anyone could do to enliven those scenes.

Wessel was good as usual but in this episode in particular he abandoned all attempts at a dialect, merely deepening his voice when speaking in character. He never seemed sure which accent to use and by Season Two, seemed resigned to try none more often than not.

Gerald Fried was back as music director and again, the background music was too light and fluffy. The sets, too, were nothing special. The "swamp" was dry and brittle, the backdrops seemingly no more than a sheet draped across boards (a technique made famous at Universal Studios; see Frankenstein *for a classic example) and the "swamp noises" filtered in by sound man John W. Rixey were more appropriate to a jungle adventure than Tennessee.*

GUEST CAST

Charles Bronson *(b. 11/3/1921, Ehrenfeld, PA; d. 8/30/2003, Los Angeles, CA, pneumonia.)* A long way from being a superstar when he made his *Riverboat* appearance, he already had a list of impressive credits. Probably best known for the *Death Wish* series of films, he was a scene-stealer as Danny, the Tunnel King in *The Great Escape* (1963). One of his earliest roles was in *You're in the Navy, Now* (1951) where he was billed as Charles Buchinski.

Stella Stevens *(b. 10/1/1936, Yazoo City, MI.)* She was the Playboy Playmate of the Month for January 1960, and was discovered modeling in Goldsmith's Department Store in Memphis, TN. Her real name was Estelle Caro Eggleston. She worked in many films during her early years including *Girls! Girls! Girls!* and *The Poseidon Adventure* (1972). She later became a regular feature on made-for-TV movies and worked on *General Hospital* as Jake.

William Fawcett *(b. 9/8/1894, High Forest, MN; d. 1/25/1974, Sherman Oaks, CA, natural causes.)* Born William Fawcett Thomas, he earned a Ph.D. in theatre arts and taught at Michigan State before WWII. After the war, he went to Hollywood and thereafter was never out of work. It seems he appeared in every TV Western but is probably best known for the irascible character Pete Wilkey that he played on *Fury* (1955).

Don O'Kelly *(b. 3/17/1924, New York, NY; d. 10/2/1966, Culver City, CA, cirrhosis of the liver and esophageal varices.)* Occasionally billed as "Donald Kelly," he worked primarily in the 1950's and 60's, probably best remembered as playing Monk in the *Twilight Zone* episode "The Mighty Casey" (1960).

John Milford *(b. 9/7/1929, Johnstown, NY; d. 8/14/2000, Santa Monica, CA, skin cancer.)* John obtained a bachelor's degree in civil engineering and has been credited with creating the original design for the Hollywood Walk of Fame. He appeared in many series in the late 1950's and 60's, including *Gunsmoke* ("Snow Train," 1970), *The Big Valley* ("Run of the Cat," 1968) and *Columbo* ("Double Exposure," 1973). His last credit was *Chicken Soup for the Soul* (1999).

Ray Teal *(b. 1/12/1902, Grand Rapids, MI; d. 4/2/1976, Santa Monica, CA.)* Most of his roles were bit parts, uncredited. He appeared in *Judgment at Nuremberg* (1961) as Judge Curtiss Ives and along with countless TV appearances, appeared in a *Thriller* episode entitled "The Purple Room" and a *Twilight Zone* episode, "Printer's Devil." His last credit is *The Hanged Man* (1974).

Tom Fadden *(b. 1/6/1895, Bayard, IA; d. 4/14/1980, Vero Beach, FL.)* After hundreds of credits, perhaps his most famous role was an uncredited one: the tollhouse keeper in *It's A Wonderful Life* (1947). He also played Ben Miller (1964-66) in *Petticoat Junction*.

Phil Tully. An actor/stuntman who played a recurring character on *The Deputy* (1960). His last part was on *Tales of Wells Fargo* in 1962.

2.13 **"Listen to the Nightingale"** . . . .*January 2, 1961*
Directed by Sidney Lanfield
Written by Fred Freiberger
Produced by Boris D. Kaplan

A lady and gentleman attempt to cross a muddy Memphis street by balancing on a board across the rather formidable puddle. Grey and Bill observe the proceedings, Holden caustically observing that he "bets" the dandy doesn't make it but the woman does," to which Blake retorts, "You can't afford a bet."

Two locals, also amused by the scene, accost the pair, one of them pushing Jeffers into the mud. Grey gallantly rescues the woman by ignobly tossing her over his shoulder and depositing her down in the relative safety of the sidewalk, for which she is unduly grateful. Grey departs and Jeffers observes she ought to give him a reward. No, she won't do that because she suspects the "uncomplicated, basic" fellow is not the type who accepts gifts of money.

Back aboard the *Enterprise,* Bill complains that the hold is half empty and two-thirds of the cabins are unoccupied. If they're lucky, they will only lose $500 this trip. It seems, he adds, that "Gabriel's horn is sounding for the *Enterprise.*"

As his words of doom and gloom fade, a flashy promoter shows up, asking the co-captains to transport his troupe to New Orleans. By the looks of the assembled parade behind him, that is a considerable and lucrative request. But the boys are naturally suspicious and demand payment in advance. The promoter regretfully admits he hasn't a penny to his name but offers to pay them upon arrival. He expects a hefty sum in New Orleans where his star attraction has a staggering contract to sing.

Blake rejects the proposition but Grey is more enthused. He goes among the performers and discovers the singer is none other than the woman he saved from the mud puddle. She is Miss Julie Lang, the "English Nightingale." He immediately senses a profitable and exhilarating trip and agrees to take them on board for the promise of future reward. Bill quashes his enthusiasm by identifying the promoter as one Sampson J. Binton, a notorious huckster who "taught P.T. Barnum all he knows."

Grey remains obstinate and the troupe come aboard, taking all the best cabins, with the Deluxe reserved for Miss Lang. He tries to impress her by dressing up, replete with a boutonniere, but she is uninterested in finery, saying she is tired of being sweet-talked. What she really wants is to be a "simple woman," with "simple needs." He tosses the flower away and it is picked up by Gabe, an

Darren McGavin poses on the waterfront set, with the Enterprise *in the background, in this early First Season publicity photo. For a series that started with so much promise, nothing seemed to go right. As "Gabriel's horn" sounded the end of* Riverboat's *year and a half voyage, there was a lot to regret.*

escape artist. He, in turn, is sweet-talking the tattooed lady (who has no obvious tattoos).

The saloon is all decked out and the troupe band plays while the passengers dance. Grey takes Julie around the room then maneuvers her outside where she confesses a desire to get out of her gilded cage. She is tired of the grand life and seeks only peace, quiet and the simple life. If only she didn't have a contract to perform in New Orleans she would drop all pretenses and go among the common folk.

Soon afterward she discovers a necklace, given her by the King of Norway, has been stolen. They have a thief aboard and she wants him caught. Miss Lang is less concerned about retrieving her property, for, as she explains, Mr. Binton has the $10,000 piece of jewelry fully insured. Binton must then admit he has let the policy lapse and she flies into a rage. Grey is terribly concerned but Bill less so, declaring the entire episode nothing but a stunt for publicity.

Julie assures him the matter is not only real but extremely serious and if the necklace is not recovered she will refuse to perform in New Orleans. This is bad news. If she doesn't sing, Binton won't be paid. If he's not paid, he will not be able to cover the travel expenses. Someone must convince her to change her mind.

Explaining Grey is "irresistible," Bill assigns him the task of working on Miss Lang's sensibilities. He tries, but unfortunately cannot live up to his partner's good opinion as Julie is thrilled at the prospect of finally being free to live a normal life. Not even a passionate kiss will do, forcing Holden and Blake to try to recover the necklace.

While Grey is crawling along the corridor, "playing detective," someone takes a pot shot at him. This makes Bill realize they really have a thief aboard and the two determine to search the passengers' cabins. In the room of the tattooed lady they find pay dirt and bring the woman in for questioning. She is confounded by the discovery, then quickly asserts she stole the necklace. Gabe, her boyfriend, steps forward, saying she need not protect him. In fact, he bought it and it has no value — the item is made of paste, designed to appear valuable but is, in fact, worthless.

Ashamed by their mistake, the river men hurry away. Bill is especially embarrassed and Grey says he will gladly buy Blake out but as neither of them have any money, the offer is moot.

Outside on the deck, Julie observes a poor family on a raft. She wishes she had that kind of life and turns a deaf ear on Grey's pleas to honor her contract. When he explains that he planned on using the fee garnered from transporting the troupe to pay a note coming due on the boat, and that if he doesn't meet his obligation he will lose the *Enterprise,* Julie decides that would be for the best. As he has never been overly successful as a riverboat captain, he ought to try some other occupation.

Clearly, Miss Lang is both callous and naive and a different approach must be taken. Grey has an instinct that is like "money in the bank." He will give Julie the simple life she desires. At the next stop he takes her ashore. They go off together to rough it in the wilderness (but with separate bedrooms). He takes her into the wood, then leaves her to cook while he goes out to hunt. Returning with a dead muskrat, he demands she skin it and offers his knife. That's enough of the simple life and Miss Lang hurries back aboard. But even though her fantasy has been rudely destroyed, she still won't sing until her necklace is recovered.

Bill and Grey decide they have been going about their detective work all wrong. Instead of trying to find the necklace, they will try to discover the thief. Once again searching the cabins, they discover a beeswax mould and a key made out of a musician's reed. The key opens the door to Miss Lang's cabin. This, then, is how the thief got in.

While Miss Lang sings (but not opera, her specialty), the boys confront Jeffers, the clarinet player. They beat the truth out of him and he confesses — but hardly with shame. He has talent, he says, and stole it because he wanted money to go to Europe, take lessons and advance his career. If he really were a thief, he would have stolen all the jewels, not just the necklace.

Miss Lang is given back her property but refuses to press charges. If Mr. Jeffers really has talent, then he ought to have the right to develop it. She gives him the prize and finally agrees to resume her interrupted career.

At the end, after the captains have been paid and all is well, Julie rewards Grey. He expects something substantial, but receives no more than a pass to the show.

There were a number of eerie coincidences in "Listen to the Nightingale," not the least of which was Bill Blake's comment that it seemed Gabriel's horn was blowing for the Enterprise. *In that he was right, for this was the final episode of* Riverboat. *It is also ironic that Fred Freiberger wrote the script. As* Star Trek *fans know, not so many years later Freiberger earned the reputation as being a series killer. In his capacity of producer, he oversaw the last seasons of both* Star Trek *and* The Wild Wild West. *It is also interesting to note that DeForest Kelley and Jeanne Bal co-starred in the premiere of* Star Trek, *called "The Man Trap." (And for those keeping track, yes, Kelley was wearing his ring.)*

There was not much to like about this final installment. The opening scene where Miss Lang was crossing a muddy street was reminiscent of "The Barrier" (1.2) and Riverboat *had already overused the actor theme. The fact Grey pursued her reeked of Carney's stage-struck attitude (see "Trunk Full of Dreams, 2.6) and never came off. It seemed the writer could not decide whether to make this a comedy or a drama and the combination made it entirely uneven and awkward, leaving the actors to overplay the humor and underplay the more serious aspects.*

The naïveté of the English Nightingale was beaten to death and repeated so often it became almost a joke in itself. The Jack Albertson character was stereotypical and the other characters under-developed and overlooked. Jeffers, himself, the villain of the piece, made only two appearances — in the Teaser and at the conclusion, and his brassy assertion he wasn't really a thief — and Julie's subsequent reward of the necklace — was simply flat and unrewarding.

The extended scene where Grey took Julie out into the wilderness was filler of the worst sort, with both McGavin and Bal looking as though they would rather be doing something else. Even Carney forgot how to speak (another example of Dick Wessel abandoning his "voice"). Even the final scene where Holden expects a monetary reward went against the opening where his "uncomplicated, basic" nature belied such a gift, as though Freiberger had forgotten what he wrote.

"Listen to the Nightingale" was a sad end to a series which could have been something special but never found a way to distinguish itself or to present characters worthy of a sustained viewership.

GUEST CAST

Jeanne Bal *(b. 5/3/1928, Santa Monica, CA; d. 4/30/1996, Sherman Oaks, CA, metastasized breast cancer.)* Yet another *Star Trek* alumnus, she starred in the very first episode aired, "The Man Trap," playing Nancy Crater, the salt monster. She also had a memorable role in *Thriller*, the episode "Papa Benjamin," based on a Cornel Wilde short story. Interestingly, she co-starred with DeForest Kelley on both her *Riverboat* episode and on *Star Trek*.

DeForest Kelley *(b. 1/20/1920, Atlanta, GA; d. 6/11/1999, Sherman Oaks, CA, stomach cancer.)* Full name: Jackson DeForest Kelley. Probably the greatest loved and most revered actor of any of *Riverboat*'s guest stars, De Kelley made his first voyage aboard the *Enterprise*, not on a sleek starship but on a riverboat. At the time of this casting, he had innumerable credits to his name, including *Apache Uprising* (1966), *Where Love Has Gone* (1964), *Raintree County* (1957) and *Gunfight at the O.K. Corral* where he played Wyatt Earp. His earliest credit was also one of his best film roles: playing Vince Grayson in *Fear in the Night* (1946). He is, of course, immortal for his role of Leonard "Bones" McCoy on *Star Trek* (1966-69).

Jack Albertson *(b. 6/16/1907, Malden, MA; d. 11/25/1981, Beverly Hills, CA, cancer.)* An old hoofer of vaudeville, he left his legacy (and collected an Emmy) for his role on *Chico and the Man*. Among his other awards were an Oscar for Best Supporting Actor in the film *The Subject Was Roses* (1965) as well as a Tony for the Broadway production of the same play.

Paul Stader *(b. 2/13/1911, Missouri; d. 4/10/1991, Los Angeles, CA.)* Primarily a stuntman, he doubled for Johnny Weismuller, Gregory Peck, Cary Grant and John Wayne in his career.

Hal Needham *(b. 3/6/1931, Memphis, TN.)* After serving as a paratrooper in the Korean War (and doing some work as a model for Viceroy cigarettes), he went to Hollywood and began working as a stunt double. He did the stunt work for Richard Boone on *Have Gun, Will Travel*, and then went on to work in many other series, including *Gunsmoke* and *Rawhide*. He became a stunt coordinator and worked extensively with Burt Reynolds on *White Lightning* (1973), *The Longest Yard* (1974) and *Gator* (1976). He wrote and directed the Reynolds headliner

Smokey and the Bandit (1977) and went on to direct such films as *Cannonball Run* (1981).

Claire Carleton *(b. 9/28/1913, New York, NY; d. 12/11/1979, Northridge, CA, cancer.)* Active in the 1940's and 50's, she played Nell Mulligan on *The Mickey Rooney Show* (1954) and Unis Appleby in the episode "The Watcher" of *Thriller* (1960). In an uncredited part, she played a thieving waitress in *Mildred Pierce* (1945).

John Warburton *(b. 10/20/1887, Huddersfield, Yorkshire, England; d. 10/27/1981, Sherman Oaks, CA, cancer.)* A frequent guest star on the 1950's TV series *Judge Roy Bean*, his role on *Star Trek* as a Centurion in the episode "Balance of Terror" immediately puts a face to him for most fans.

PART XIV.

CREDITS

(The designation "Guest Star," "Starring," *or* "Co-Starring" *indicates the actor's name was listed in the front titles as well as the end credits unless otherwise stated.)*

2.1 "End of a Dream" ....

    Guest Star   Cliff Robertson

    With   Dick Wessel
              Robert Wilkie
              June Vincent
              Ben Wright
              George Mitchell
              Adrienne Marden
              Theodore Newton
              Alice Backes
              Harry Swoger
              Anthony Jochim
    With   Susan Cummings as Tekla Kronen

2.2 "That Taylor Affair" ....

    Guest Star   Arlene Dahl

    (Separate credit)   Jack Lambert
                      Dick Wessel

                      Robert Ellenstein
                      Stanley Adams
                      Milton Frome
                      Bill Giorgio
                      Peter Hornsby
    With   Paul Fix as President Zachary Taylor

2.3 "The Two Faces of Grey Holden" . . . .
    Co-Starring   Suzanne Pleshette

                 Thomas Gomez
                 Nico Minardos
                 Dick Wessel
                 Lillian Buyeff
                 Herb Ellis
                 Celia Lovsky
                 Lomax Study

2.4 "River Champion" . . . .
    Guest Star   Dennis O'Keefe

                 Norma Crane

    Separate credit   Dick Wessel
                 Jack Lambert

                 George Kennedy
                 Denny Miller
                 Slim Pickens
                 Jack Hogan
                 Ralph Reed

    Uncredited   Barbara Raymond
                 Coca Morriss
                 Joan Swift
                 Marcia Myles

2.5 "No Bridge on the River" . . . .
    With   Dick Wessel
                 Hayden Rorke
                 Pat Michon
                 Denver Pyle
                 Bartlett Robinson
                 Tyler McVey
                 Mike Ragan
                 Charles Fredericks
                 Dal McKennon
                 Gil Rogers
    And   Sandy Kenyon as Abraham Lincoln

2.6 "Trunk Full of Dreams" . . . .
    Guest Star   Raymond Massey

    Separate credit   Bethel Leslie

        Dick Wessel
        Willard Waterman
        Huge Sanders
        Mary Tyler Moore
        Jody Fair
        Robert Foulk

2.7 "The Water of Gorgeous Springs". . . . .
    Also Starring   Buddy Ebsen *(at end only)*

        Sherry Jackson

    Separate credit   Dick Wessel
        Jack Lambert

        Jocelyn Brando
        Gregory Walcott
        Lance Fuller
        Dody Heath
        John C. Strong

2.8 "Devil in Skirts" . . . .
    Co-Starring   Gloria Talbott *(at end only)*

        Frank Silvera

    With   Arthur Batanides
        Brad Weston

2.9 "The Quota" . . . .
    Co-Starring   Gene Evans *(at end only)*

    Separate credit   Dick Wessel
        Jack Lambert

        James Griffith
        Ron Haggerthy
        Tom Gilleran
        Stuart Randall
        Jack Mather

Jack Searl
Jim Nusser
Vince Williams
Robin Blake
Edward G. Robinson, Jr.
Steven D. McAdam
Nan Adams

2.10 "Chicota Landing" ....

Separate credit   Dick Wessel
Jack Lambert

Joe DeSantis
Connie Hines
(indented)   John McLiam
Ted deCorsia

With   Richard Chamberlain as Lt. Dave Winslow

2.11 "Duel on the River" ....

Co-Starring   Fay Spain
Claude Akins

Robert Emhardt
Edgar Buchanan

Dick Wessel
Michael Green
Jack Halliday

2.12 "Zigzag" ....

Guest Star   Charles Bronson

Stella Stevens

Dick Wessel
William Fawcett
John Milford
Don O'Kelly
Tom Fadden
Ray Teal
Phil Tully

2.13 "Listen to the Nightingale".................................
    Co-Starring   Jeanne Bal
                Dick Wessel

                Jack Albertson
                DeForest Kelley
                John Warburton
                Claire Carleton
                Paul Stader
                Hal Needham

PART XIII.
PRODUCTION CREDITS

(Bold indicates the person's name appears in conjunction with other artists elsewhere.)

DIRECTORS

Richard H. Bartlett 2.6 "The Water of Gorgeous Springs"

Tay Garnett 2.11 "Duel on the River"

Lamont Johnson 2.5 "No Bridge on the River"

Sidney Lanfield 2.12 "Zigzag"
2.13 "Listen to the Nightingale"

Allen H. Minor 2.2 "That Taylor Affair" *(also wrote)*

Hollingsworth Morse 2.6 "Trunk Full of Dreams"
2.9 "The Quota"

David Lowell Rich 2.1 "End of a Dream"
2.8 "Devil in Skirts"
2.10 "Chicota Landing"

R.G. Springsteen 2.3 "The Two Faces of Grey Holden"

William Witney 2.4 "River Champion"

WRITERS

Bob and Wanda Duncan 2.9 "The Quota"
And **Raphael Hayes** *(teleplay)*
Bob and Wanda Duncan *(story)*

Fred Freiberger 2.12 "Listen to the Nightingale"

Milton S. Gelman 2.1 "End of a Dream"
                  2.11 "Duel on the River"

Irwin and Gwen Gielgud 2.6 "Trunk Full of Dreams"

Irwin and Gwen Gielgud and 2.8 "Devil in Skirts"
Bob and Wanda Duncan

Raphael Hayes 2.5 "No Bridge on the River"

Raphael Hayes *(teleplay)* 2.10 "Chicota Landing"
Herman Groves *(story)*

Kathleen Hite 2.3 "The Two Faces of Grey Holden"

David Lang 2.12 "Zigzag"

Allen H. Minor 2.2 "That Taylor Affair" *(also directed)*

Montgomery Pittman 2.7 "The Water of Gorgeous Springs"
(teleplay and story)
Raphael Hayes *(teleplay)*

Rik Vollaerts *(teleplay)* 2.4 "River Champion"
William Fay *(story)*

PRODUCERS

Boris D. Kaplan 2.1 "End of a Dream"
                 2.2 "That Taylor Affair"
                 2.3 "The Two Faces of Grey Holden"
                 2.5 "No Bridge on the River"
                 2.6 "Trunk Full of Dreams"
                 2.7 "The Water of Gorgeous Springs"
                 2.8 "Devil in Skirts"
                 2.9 "The Quota"
                 2.10 "Chicota Landing"
                 2.11 "Duel on the River"
                 2.12 "Zigzag"
                 2.13 "Listen to the Nightingale"

John Larkin 2.4 "River Champion"

MUSIC

Gerald Fried 2.1 "End of a Dream"
2.2 "That Taylor Affair"
2.3 "The Two Faces of Grey Holden"
2.4 "River Champion"
2.5 "No Bridge on the River"
2.6 "Trunk Full of Dreams"
2.7 "The Water of Gorgeous Springs"
2.8 "Devil in Skirts"
2.9 "The Quota"
2.10 "Chicota Landing"
2.12 "Zigzag"
2.13 "Listen to the Nightingale"

RIVERBOAT SONG BY

Gerald Fried 2.11 "Duel on the River"

MUSIC SCORE

R. Dale Buts 2.11 "Duel on the River"

DIRECTOR OF PHOTOGRAPHY

Neal Beckner 2.11 "Duel on the River"
2.12 "Zigzag"

Buddy Harris 2.1 "End of a Dream"
2.2 "That Taylor Affair"
2.3 "The Two Faces of Grey Holden"
2.4 "River Champion"
2.6 "Trunk Full of Dreams"
2.8 "Devil in Skirts"
2.13 "Listen to the Nightingale"

Jack MacKenzie 2.7 "The Water of Goegeous Springs"

Ray Rennahan 2.5 "No Bridge on the River"

Bud Thackery 2.8 "Devil in Skirts"
2.9 "The Quota"
2.10 "Chicota Landing"

ART DIRECTOR

George Patrick   *All episodes*

EDITORIAL SUPERVISOR

David J. O'Connell   *All episodes*

FILM EDITOR

Howard Epstein   2.3   "The Two Faces of Grey Holden"
2.4   "River Champion"
2.6   "Trunk Full of Dreams"
2.8   "Devil in Skirts"
2.10 "Chicota Landing"
2.11 "Duel on the River"
2.13 "Listen to the Nightingale"

Lee Huntington   2.9   "The Quota"

George Nicholson   2.12 "Zigzag"

Stanley E. Rabjohn   2.1   "End of a Dream"
2.2   "That Taylor Affair"
2.5   "No Bridge on the River"
2.7   "The Water of Gorgeous Springs"

MUSIC SUPERVISON

Stanley Wilson   *All episodes*

SOUND

Victor B. Appel   2.4   "River Champion"
2.8   "Devil in Skirts"

Lyle Cain   2.13 "Listen to the Nightingale"

Earl Crain, Sr.   2.5   "No Bridge on the River"
2.6   "Trunk Full of Dreams"
2.7   "The Water of Gorgeous Springs"

Melvin M Metcalfe, Sr.   2.9   "The Quota"
2.10 "Chicota Landing"

John W. Rixey 2.11 "Duel on the River"
                          2.12 "Zigzag"

William Russell 2.1 "End of a Dream"
                         2.2 "That Taylor Affair"
                         2.3 "The Two Faces of Grey Holden"

ASSISTANT DIRECTOR

Ben Bishop 2.1 "End of a Dream"
                    2.12 "Zigzag"

George Bisk 2.6 "Trunk Full of Dreams"
                    2.13 "Listen to the Nightingale"

Edward K. Dodds 2.5 "No Bridge on the River"

Jack Doran 2.2 "That Taylor Affair"
                   2.8 "Devil in Skirts"

William Dorfman 2.3 "The Two Faces of Grey Holden"
                         2.4 "River Champion"
                         2.9 "The Quota"
                         2.11 "Duel on the River"

Charles S. Gould 2.7 "The Water of Gorgeous Springs"

Wallace Worsley 2.10 "Chicota Landing"

SET DIRECTOR

John McCarthy and 2.6 "Trunk Full of Dreams"
James M. Walters 2.7 "The Water of Gorgeous Springs"
                    2.8 "Devil in Skirts"
                    2.9 "The Quota"
                    2.10 "Chicota Landing"
                    2.11 "Duel on the River"
                    2.12 "Zigzag"
                    2.13 "Listen to the Nightingale"

James M. Walters 2.1 "End of a Dream"
                   2.2 "That Taylor Affair"
                   2.3 "The Two Faces of Grey Holden"
                   2.4 "River Champion"
                     2.5 "No Bridge on the River"

COSTUME SUPERVISOR

Vincent Dee   *All episodes*

MAKEUP

Leo Lotito, Jr.   *All episodes*

HAIR STYLIST

Florence Bush   *All episodes*

PART XV.
BIOGRAPHIES

ACTOR

Noah Beery, Jr. (credited as Noah Beery; b. 8/10/1913, New York, NY; d. 11/1/1994, Tehachapi, CA, cerebral thrombosis.) Son of acting star Noah Beery, he attended Harvard Military Academy before breaking off into acting. Probably best known as playing James Garner's father in *The Rockford Files* (1974-80), his first credit (unlisted) was *The Mutiny of the Elsinore*. By 1960, he had accumulated 95 more, including playing Uncle Joey on *Circus Boy* (1956-57) and John Stebbins in *Inherit the Wind* (1960). He later played Buffalo Baker on *Hondo* (1967), which starred Kathie Browne, the future Mrs. Darren McGavin. He appeared with Darren and Kathie on *The Richard Petty Story*, in 1974, and was a regular on *The Yellow Rose* (1983-84) playing Luther Dillard. Noah's last credit was an episode of *The Love Boat* entitled "Hello Emily" in 1986.

DIRECTORS

David Lowell Rich *(b. 8/31/1923, New York, NY.)* His first credit was *Big Town* (1950). By 1958, he was at Revue, directing *M Squad* and *Tales of Wells Fargo* before moving over to *Riverboat*. He later directed *Zane Grey Theater* (1959-61), *Naked City* (1961-62), *Route 66* (1961-63), *The Borgia Stick* (1967), and *The Berlin Affair* (1970) with Darren McGavin. His last directing credit was *Infidelity* (1987). He also produced episodes of *The Alfred Hitchcock Hour* (1963-64) and *Choices* (1986), among others.

Bud Thackery *(b. 1/31/1903 in Oklahoma; d. 7/15/1990, Los Angeles, CA; also known as Ellis Thackery.)* Known exclusively as a Cinematographer, his first credit was *Darkest Africa* (1936) as a process photographer. His innumerable credits include 18 episodes of *Stories of the Century* (1954-55), seven episodes of *The Adventures of Dr. Fu Manchu* (1956) and *Coronado 9* (1959), before jumping onto *Riverboat*. He also worked on 6 episodes of *Thriller* (1960-62), *Wagon Train* (1963-64), and he did *The Outsider* (1967) with McGavin. He later did 87 episodes of *Ironside* (1968-72) and 51 episodes of *Emergency* (1972-77).

WRITERS

Raphael Hayes *(b. 3/2/1915.)* He began his professional career with an episode of *The Adventures of Ellery Queen* (1950) and had several other credits including two episodes of *Sugarfoot* (1958-59) before coming to *Riverboat*. He subsequently wrote for such varied series as *Voyage to the Bottom of the Sea* and *The Defenders*, and was a staff writer for *Daniel Boone* (1965-69). His last credit was an episode of *High Chaparral* in 1969. He was nominated for an Academy Award for co-writing *One Potato, Two Potato* (1964) with Orville H. Hampton.

Milton S. Gelman *(b. 9/11/1919; d. 5/2/1990, Sherman Oaks, CA.)* His first credit was *Robert Montgomery Presents* (1950) and he had several Western credits to his name, including *Tombstone Territory* (1958), *Mackenzie's Raiders* (1959), *The Rebel* (1960), and wrote an unsold pilot for Richard Kiley called *Indemnity* (1958), before coming to *Riverboat*. He later wrote for *The Loner* (1965-66), *The High Chaparral* (1969), *Bonanza* (1968-70) and *Banyon* (1972-73). His last credit was *One Man's Hero* (1999). He also taught screenwriting at Loyola Marymount.

Gwen Gielgud. Her two listed credits are *Pursuit* (1958) and *Leave it to Beaver* (1962).

Irwin Gielgud *(b. 5/10/1919; d. 11/9/1961, Los Angeles, CA).* His first credit is *Amazon Quest* in 1950. He also wrote two episodes of *Alfred Hitchcock Presents* (1956), four episodes of *Climax!* (1956-8) and *Pursuit* (1958). *Riverboat* is his last listed credit.

PRODUCER

Boris D. Kaplan *(b. 8/29/1915, New York, NY; d. 7/18/1999, Westlake Village, CA.)* Graduating from Cornell in 1935, he worked as Film Supervisor for the TV series *Omnibus* (1952-56). Moving to the West Coast, *Riverboat* was his first job as producer. He is also credited with producing *Let No Man Write My Epitaph* (1960) for Columbia Studios and the TV series *87th Precinct* (1961). He later joined CBS as a Director of Development and was involved with the development of such series as *All in the Family* and *Mannix*. He later taught broadcasting history at Loyola Marymount.

MUSIC

Gerald Fried *(b. 2/13/1928, New York, NY.)* Educated at Juilliard, he was the first oboist for the Dallas Symphony before being signed by Revue, where he worked until 1960 (the end of *Riverboat*.). His first score was *Day of the Fight* (1951), followed by many others in the 1950's including low-grade horror films such as *Mark of the Vampire* (1957) and *The Return of Dracula* (1958). Becoming a freelancer, he worked at Desilu/Paramount on such inspired series as *Star Trek*,

Mission: Impossible and *The Man From U.N.C.L.E.* He worked all the way into 2004, doing the music for an episode of *Star Trek: The New Voyages* (2004).

COSTUME SUPERVISOR

Vincent Dee. Another stalwart of Revue, he grew up in the ranks of television, working on the usual suspects: *M Squad, Suspicion, Coronado 9, Shotgun Slade, Johnny Staccato* and *Checkmate.* He also worked on *Alfred Hitchcock Presents, Leave it to Beaver,* and *The Alfred Hitchcock Hour,* as well as *Thriller, McHale's Navy, Wagon Train,* and Alfred Hitchcock's film *Marnie* (1964). He did costume supervision for *The Munsters* (1964-66) and *The Virginian,* as well as *Adam 12.* His last credit was on *The Kent Chronicles* (aka *The Bastard*) in 1978.

HAIR STYLIST

Florence Bush. Talented and prolific, the name Florence Bush appears on nearly every Revue/Universal series of the late 1950's and 1960's. Her first credit was *Soldiers of Fortune* (1956). Other Revue series which utilized her talents were *M Squad, Coronado 9, Shotgun Slade* and *Checkmate.* She also worked on the Alfred Hitchcock film, *Psycho* (the set of which was actually used on an episode of *Riverboat*). She worked on *Thriller,* and then went on to such notable series as *Alfred Hitchcock Presents* (1956-62), *Leave it to Beaver* (1957-63), *McHale's Navy* (1962-3), *Wagon Train* and *My Three Sons.* She worked on *Gunsmoke* (then shot at Paramount) and her last credit was *The Meanest Men in the West* (1967).

INDEX

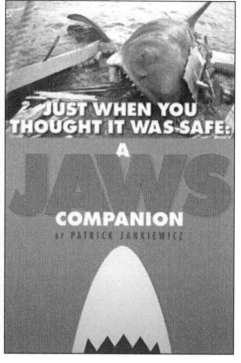

CPSIA information can be obtained at www.ICGtesting.com
Printed in the USA
BVOW08s1234040814

361596BV00034B/1270/P